East Asia and Food (In)Security

T0347294

This book presents a study of perceptions of food insecurity in East Asia, and explores how individual countries are developing strategies to deal with the situation. It also looks at how the perception of food insecurity has increasingly influenced the nature of international interactions, not just within East Asia, but also in the region's relations with major external actors.

Many of the challenges facing East Asia are generic food security issues that face people and governments across the world – for example, the implications of climate change and demographic changes on food supplies. This book places the East Asian context in the wider discussion of food (in)security in global politics. However, it also identifies potential regional 'differences' – for example, the significance of rice for the region, and the unavoidable impact of China as a major regional player. What the Chinese state, and Chinese companies, decide to do in response to concerns about food insecurity have an impact not just on the rest of the region, but on the rest of the world.

Taking too much of a Sinocentric focus, however, ignores other actors in East Asia, or merely relegates discussion to how they respond to Chinese policies or external strategies. This book considers the region as a whole, both when it comes to thinking about food security challenges and responses within the region itself, and also in the outward projection of regional food insecurity on the rest of the world.

This book was originally published as a special issue of *The Pacific Review*.

Shaun Breslin is a Professor of Politics and International Relations at the University of Warwick, UK. His is co-editor of *The Pacific Review*.

Christopher W. Hughes is a Professor of Politics and International Relations at the University of Warwick, UK. His is co-editor of *The Pacific Review*.

East Asia and Food (In)Security

Edited by
Shaun Breslin and
Christopher W. Hughes

Routledge
Taylor & Francis Group

LONDON AND NEW YORK

First published 2016
by Routledge
2 Park Square, Milton Park, Abingdon, Oxon, OX14 4RN, UK

and by Routledge
711 Third Avenue, New York, NY 10017, USA

First issued in paperback 2017

Routledge is an imprint of the Taylor & Francis Group, an informa business

© 2016 Taylor & Francis

British Library Cataloguing in Publication Data
A catalogue record for this book is available from the British Library

ISBN 13: 978-1-138-29522-3 (pbk)
ISBN 13: 978-1-138-94669-9 (hbk)

Typeset in Times New Roman
by RefineCatch Limited, Bungay, Suffolk

Publisher's Note
The publisher accepts responsibility for any inconsistencies that may have arisen during the conversion of this book from journal articles to book chapters, namely the possible inclusion of journal terminology.

Disclaimer
Every effort has been made to contact copyright holders for their permission to reprint material in this book. The publishers would be grateful to hear from any copyright holder who is not here acknowledged and will undertake to rectify any errors or omissions in future editions of this book.

Contents

Citation Information

The chapters in this book were originally published in *The Pacific Review*, volume 26, issue 5 (December 2013). When citing this material, please use the original page numbering for each article, as follows:

Chapter 1: Foreword
East Asia and food (in)security
Shaun Breslin and Christopher W. Hughes
The Pacific Review, volume 26, issue 5 (December 2013) pp. 431–432

Chapter 2
Rice security in Southeast Asia: beggar thy neighbor or cooperation?
Amy Freedman
The Pacific Review, volume 26, issue 5 (December 2013) pp. 433–454

Chapter 3
Food in China's international relations
Daojiong Zha and Hongzhou Zhang
The Pacific Review, volume 26, issue 5 (December 2013) pp. 455–479

Chapter 4
Supermarkets, iron buffalos and agrarian myths: exploring the drivers and impediments to food systems modernisation in Southeast Asia
J. Jackson Ewing
The Pacific Review, volume 26, issue 5 (December 2013) pp. 481–503

Chapter 5
Food security, the palm oil–land conflict nexus, and sustainability: a governance role for a private multi-stakeholder regime like the RSPO?
Helen E.S. Nesadurai
The Pacific Review, volume 26, issue 5 (December 2013) pp. 505–529

Chapter 6

Going out: China's food security from Southeast Asia
Nicholas Thomas
The Pacific Review, volume 26, issue 5 (December 2013) pp. 531–562

Chapter 7

'Land grabbing' or harnessing of development potential in agriculture?
East Asia's land-based investments in Africa
Franklyn Lisk
The Pacific Review, volume 26, issue 5 (December 2013) pp. 563–587

Chapter 8

Food security: global trends and regional perspective with reference to
East Asia
Ching-Cheng Chang, Huey-Lin Lee and Shih-Hsun Hsu
The Pacific Review, volume 26, issue 5 (December 2013) pp. 589–613

For any permission-related enquiries please visit:
http://www.tandfonline.com/page/help/permissions

Notes on Contributors

Shaun Breslin is a Professor of Politics and International Relations at the University of Warwick, UK. His is co-editor of *The Pacific Review*.

Ching-Cheng Chang is a Research Fellow at the Institute of Economics, Academia Sinica, Taipei, Taiwan.

J. Jackson Ewing is a Research Fellow and Coordinator of the Environmental, Climate Change and Food Security Programme at the Centre for Non-Traditional Security Studies in the S. Rajaratnam School of International Studies (RSIS), Nanyang Technological University, Singapore.

Amy Freedman is Professor and Department Chair of Political Science and International Studies at LIU Post, Brookville, NY, USA. She has published widely on questions of democracy in Southeast Asia, as well as on political economy in the region. Her most recent book is *The Internationalization of Internal Conflicts* (Routledge, 2013).

Shih-Hsun Hsu is a Professor at the Department of Agricultural Economics, National Taiwan University, Taipei, Taiwan.

Christopher W. Hughes is a Professor of Politics and International Relations at the University of Warwick, UK. His is co-editor of *The Pacific Review*.

Huey-Lin Lee is an Associate Professor at the Department of Economics, National Chengchi University, Taipei, Taiwan.

Franklyn Lisk is a Professorial Research Fellow at the Centre for the Study of Globalisation and Regionalisation, University of Warwick, UK. He is currently engaged in research and provision of technical advisory services to international and regional organisations and governments on social and economic development policy issues, focusing on the political economy of African development. He is also a Senior Associate of the Center for Research on Political Economy, a regional think tank, in Dakar, Senegal.

Helen E. S. Nesadurai is an Associate Professor in the School of Arts and Social Sciences at Monash University, based at the Malaysia Campus, Kuala Lumpur, Malaysia.

Nicholas Thomas is an Associate Professor in the Department of Asian and International Studies at the City University of Hong Kong. His current research explores subnational ties between China, Japan and Taiwan.

Daojiong Zha is a Professor of International Political Economy at the School of International Studies, Peking University, Beijing, China, and an expert in Chinese energy policies and food and water security in Asia.

Hongzhou Zhang is an Associate Research Fellow with the China Programme at the S. Rajaratnam School of International Studies (RSIS), Nanyang Technological University, Singapore. His main research interests include China and regional resources security (food, water and energy), agricultural and rural development, China's fishing policies and maritime security.

INTRODUCTION
East Asia and food (in)security

This short foreword is not intended to act as an introduction as such, but merely to give some explanation to why this special issue has come about. It emerged as an offshoot from a project on different conceptions of human security being undertaken at the University of Warwick, and started from a very simple premise – food security is unlikely to become less important in the region in the future and it would be a good idea to pull together people working on the topic. This was not an attempt to provide a comprehensive overview of all the debates and all of the issues; this is simply not possible inside the covers of one journal issue. Rather, the aim was to provide a fla-vour of the type of research currently being undertaken in the sub-field. And of course if this helps establish the idea that *The Pacific Review* is a good place to carry forward this research and continue the debates in the future, then that would be no bad thing for us.

Having said that, there were a number of issues that we wanted to make sure the papers collectively covered to provide something of a basis for future debates. First, while there has been much concern in parts of East Asia about how safe it is to consume certain foodstuffs – mushrooms, dumplings and formula children's milk are just three examples – this is not a primary concern here. Rather, the focus is on the more generally accepted understanding of access to food – albeit access to the necessary nutritious (and therefore 'safe') food to maintain a healthy life. Second, there are a range of challenges facing the region today that are pretty much common across the globe. The implications of climate change and demographic changes are two example here. And so our objective here was simply to place the Asian context in the wider discussion of food (in) security in global politics. This task is largely fulfilled in the final paper in the collection by Chang, Lee and Hsu which provides a comparative statis-tical analysis of indicators of Asian food insecurity in a comparative per-spective. But thinking about how generic issues have become manifest in the region is found throughout the papers.

And this generates a third but related theme – the question of potential regional 'difference'. For example, the extent to which the significance of rice for the region and an inclination to strive for grain self-sufficiency cre-ates specific and special concerns and problems is an issue that recurs throughout this collection of paper. So too is question of whether the speed and size of both population growth and population movements – primarily through urbanisation – make generic global challenges more acute in Asia.

Building on this, a fourth objective was to ensure that we did not treat either individual countries or indeed the region as a whole as hermetically sealed entities. Individual country challenges and national policy responses are clearly important. But what happens in one country in the region is affected by other regional actors, and in turns impacts on the rest of the region as well. Moreover, the nature of food production, pricing and distribution is global in nature. And notably, while the region might have previously been largely a 'recipient' of global flows (in terms of importing key produce), it is now increasingly also a generator of transnational interactions.

Finally, we wanted to make sure that we were not constrained in the focus of analysis. China is clearly an important dimension of any study of food security in the region, and indeed beyond. As the articles in this special edition collectively demonstrate, what the Chinese state and Chinese companies decide to do in response to concerns about food insecurity have an impact not just on the rest of the region, but far beyond as well. For example, although we only provide an analysis of Africa in this collection, China looms large in discussions of food security in Latin America and the Caribbean as well. But it is all too easy to develop a Sinocentric focus that either ignores other regional actors or relegates them to a secondary status as merely responding to what is done in China or recipients of Chinese external strategies. So one aim for this collection was to ensure that we did not simply focus on China alone but considered the region as a whole – both when it comes to thinking about food security challenges and responses within the region itself, and also in the outward projection of regional food insecurity on the rest of the world.

The Editors

Rice security in Southeast Asia: beggar thy neighbor or cooperation?

Amy Freedman

Abstract   High commodity prices in 2007–2008 and again in 2011, particularly for crops such as rice and corn, have forced countries in Southeast Asia to look more closely at their agricultural and trade policies for rice and grains. While all countries in the region are heavily dependent on rice for food security, there is significant variation in countries' abilities to be self-sufficient in rice production. This paper examines the factors that contribute to food insecurity in SEA, which communities are hit hardest, and the diversity of responses to this situation. And, the paper asks what the prospects might be for greater cooperation in coordinating rice (and other crops more generally) policies so as to better ensure reliable access for more citizens in the region. Thailand, Vietnam, and Cambodia are all major exporters of rice; whereas Indonesia, Malaysia, Singapore, and the Philippines are all importers of rice. Since the sharp spike in prices in 2008, countries which import rice have developed more comprehensive plans to become self sufficient in rice production. Individual country's policies will have dramatic effects on regional trade relations and dynamics. There have been some regional attempts to create a more cooperative framework for addressing food security, but these efforts have not yet played a significant role in reshaping domestic policies. This paper will assess the chances of further cooperation and success (or the chance of failure and less engagement) in the future.

Introduction and thoughts about cooperation

While humanity has succeeded in creating mind-boggling technology, and life expectancy has sky-rocketed over the last half a century, we may again be faced with Malthusian-type problems of food insecurity. The World Health Organization (WHO) defines food security as existing 'when all people at all times have access to sufficient, safe, nutritious food to maintain a healthy and active life'. Food security is built on three pillars: food availability (sufficient quantities of food, consistently available), food access (having sufficient resources to obtain appropriate food for a nutritious diet; affordability), and food use (appropriate use based on knowledge of basic nutrition and care, adequate water and sanitation) (Butler 2009; World Health Organization 2012). In 2013, we are looking ahead to a future of possible widespread food insecurity, particularly in the developing world.

Southeast Asia in particular is facing escalating food challenges. This article will focus primarily on questions of rice security. Rice is a critical crop in Southeast Asia, and the discussion here over problems and possible cooperation over the rice trade demonstrates the larger questions and problems inherent to food security more generally. Thus, this work will use 'food security' and 'rice security' in interchangeable ways. Southeast Asia is a diverse region; it is home to some of the world's largest rice exporters, but also home to some of the largest importers and largest consumer populations in terms of rice consumption per capita. Southeast Asia continues to enjoy sustained economic growth (despite the European and American slow down), and poverty reduction. Yet, over 15% of Asia's undernourished population lives in Southeast Asia. The region has abundant natural resources, and is rich agriculturally, but environmental stresses, changing demographics, lifestyles, and eating habits, threaten many key ecosystems and thus pose a threat to future food production. Historically, food shortages have been a result of poor social, economic, and political policies; often combined with environmental problems of drought, floods, blight, etc., which can exacerbate unequal allocation of resources (also discussed by Chang and Hsu in this collection).

Today, the most probable cause of food insecurity for millions of people around the world will be changing demographics coupled with the effects of climate change. The ability of societies and governments to effectively cooperate to deal with the effects of climate change will pose a significant challenge for states in the near term and longer in to the future. Southeast Asia is faced with all of these challenges. There are some important actions being taken currently to address issues of food security, but adoption and implementation has been slow and uneven. This article will look at the creation of institutions in Southeast Asia to promote information sharing and policy coordination on rice cultivation and trade. It will also examine some individual national policies choices and challenges. Preliminary research shows that there have been some real and promising efforts to cooperate regionally on food security, however, these measures are far from being firmly instituted and operational. The paper also offers a theoretical lens with which to understand why efforts to cooperate on food security have gotten underway, but why such efforts may not be enough to fully address potential food crises.

In response to food challenges of the past, countries in Southeast Asia have implemented several measures to address the risks of food insecurity.

These include export restrictions, price controls, price subsidies, and import facilitation. Such approaches are understandable and at times seemingly the only option available to governments. However, there are both costs and benefits from these types of state intervention in food markets, as these strategies potentially involve competing objectives, that of protecting consumers, against that of assisting agricultural producers to benefit from rising prices. (RSIS Centre for Non-Traditional Security Studies 2011: 7)

These measures (undertaken by a number of countries in Southeast Asia at one point in time or another), constitute 'beggar they neighbor' policies, where countries enact measures to protect their own citizens. The larger effect of these policies can sometimes be a worsening of conditions (in this case food security conditions) across borders.

While these actions are at times necessary and are understandable, they illustrate a fundamental problem of international relations. What one country does (internally) then impacts other countries. When a food exporter decides to reduce or stop exporting that product, it can have dire consequences elsewhere from those who rely on importing that food commodity. Thus, states need to cooperate with each other, but often find it difficult to do so. Cooperation is hindered by a lack of leadership; imperfect information; a lack of regular mechanisms for designing agreements; and variation in the level of interest from states in cooperating on any given issues.

Hegemonic stability theory argues that large powers (leaders) help promote cooperation and stability in the international system by providing public goods. Key public goods include supplying liquidity, open markets for trade, and international organizations to promote cooperation. A hegemon, Kindleburger and others argue, can encourage cooperation on common problems by showing leadership and shouldering some or most of the cost involved in solving an international problem (Corden 1990; Hunt 1990; Kindleburger 1973; Milner 1998). Such action could be taken unilaterally through the leadership of the great power, or more indirectly, through international organization(s). An international organization (IO) can provide the information and transparency needed in order for countries to come to agreement and stick with it; an IO can also monitor if agreements are being kept. These benefits can help countries feel less insecure, and so increase the likelihood that they will cooperate on economic issues and be less likely to resort to the kinds of beggar thy neighbor polices listed above. International cooperation can also be explained by the role of interest groups, or domestic politics more generally, within countries. When powerful groups favor protectionist policies, or non-cooperative behavior, then it is more likely that cooperative efforts will fail. When interest groups stand to gain from international cooperation (on all kinds of issues such as trade policies, environmental agreements, research on new or emerging infectious diseases) then, we are more likely to see policies implemented which lead to cooperation. One of the best examples of these dynamics can be seen in the change in United States policy towards the use of CFC's (chlorofluorocarbons) and the global environmental issue of ozone depletion. In the 1980s there were only a handful of large producers of CFC-based products. US manufacturer DuPont was one of the largest of such producers. Once DuPont developed a cheap substitute for CFC's for many of its applications, it actively lobbied the US to regulate, and ultimately heavily restrict, the use of CFC's domestically. This paved the way for US leadership in negotiations leading up to the Montreal Protocol in 1987. The Montreal Protocol, which set targets for phasing out CFC's, halons, and other ozone-depleting substances, is widely held up as a model of international cooperation on an environmental problem. While US leadership was not the only positive ingredient that led to the signing and success of this sort of international cooperation, there is no question that it was a necessary element of it. Domestic political dynamics, the significant role of interest groups in shaping American policies, contributed to strong US leadership in the drafting, ratifying and complying with the international agreement that would significantly reduce global use of ozone-destroying substances. This example shows that cooperation on issues of human security is possible as long as there is leadership and when there are incentives for cooperation (Sooros 1997: 160–161).

This article will largely argue that poor cooperation on rice security in Southeast Asia can be best explained by a lack of leadership, rather than simply saying that states don't see it as in their interest. This article will show that states do seem to see cooperation as in everyone's interest, and steps have been taken to try to create institutions and organizations to foster such cooperation. However, powerful domestic interest groups, and a lack of a clear leader in the region on issues relating to the rice trade seem to provide a compelling explanation of why we don't see robust cooperation.

If we want to see greater cooperation in SEA on rice security, we need to ask who will play a leadership role? In Asia it isn't completely clear who the hegemon might be. Japan has the largest economy, but has not acted in ways to help influence and shape the cooperative efforts of other Asian neighbors. China has the largest population and will soon have the largest economy in the region. While China is playing more of a role in regional and international affairs, they are not yet in the position of wanting or trying to take on a leadership role. As Thomas' article in this volume explains, China too is preoccupied with its own food security. The United States, although geographically far away, has continued to exercise a significant role as a vital trade partner, and as a militarily presence in Asia. However, the United States is not a member of ASEAN, or ASEAN Plus Three (APT), and the US has largely been content to stay out of regional discussions about food security. This article will discuss the role that institutions like ASEAN and APT have been playing in facilitating cooperation on food security. Indonesia has traditionally been viewed as the hegemon within Southeast Asia. However, since the fall of Suharto in 1998, Indonesia has seemed to prefer to lead by example, rather than taking on a more vigorous leadership style pushing for policies and changes, they have practiced quieter diplomacy and multilateralism. More on Indonesia's role in promoting cooperation on food security in Southeast Asia will be discussed later in this work.

Food insecurity

Southeast Asia will need leadership and greater cooperation in the years to come if they are to address food needs in a changing global and regional context. There are many factors and trends emerging which threaten Asian and global food security. First, the number of people who are food *insecure* in Asia has been on the rise. While strong economic growth has bumped a number of states towards middle income status, a large number of the world's undernourished live in Asia (India accounts for 43% of the undernourished, and China for 24%). The region's population is projected to increase from 3.6 billion to 4.5 billion people. Most of that growth will occur in urban areas, as the urban population is set to surpass the rural population as early as 2028 (RSIS Centre for Non-Traditional Security Studies 2011: 8). At the same time, there has been a global decline in investment in agriculture, from 20% share of ODA for agriculture in 1979, to 5% in 2007 (OECD 2009). There is also a paradox, economic growth and prosperity are unquestioningly a good thing, however, as societies become wealthier, they also eat differently, consuming more animal products. Thus, there is increased pressure on agriculture to produce for livestock instead of for human consumption. This can result in increased prices for grains and stable commodities, further hurting poorer citizens and areas.

Another complicating factor making food security difficult to tackle is that there is tremendous variation both across borders in SEA, but also within countries as well. Not surprisingly, poorer countries in the region, such as Laos, Cambodia, Timor Leste, and Myanmar, have the highest levels of food insecurity (even while Cambodia, and to a lesser extent Myanmar, are rice exporters). However, within some of the better off countries in SEA, there are significant numbers of food insecure people. Pockets of food insecurity are found in specific provinces or states, and so it is important to map in-country food insecurity as well as national and regional trends. Particularly vulnerable are poor, land-less families or communities (often this means the urban poor), female-headed families, and rural landless households (Tyuen 2009). Also vulnerable are many ethnic minorities living throughout Southeast Asia. Some ethnic communities are being marginalized by changes in rural land use (for industrialization or biofuel production just to name two), and these communities are among the poorest and most food insecure in Southeast Asia.

Given levels of urbanization, changing dietary habits, socioeconomic variation across the region, the challenges of climate change, and increasing land diversion to biofuel production; Southeast Asia is already in a precarious position as far as food security is concerned. In 2007, we witnessed how what *should* have been a small shift in food trading circumstances escalated into a region-wide panic. This example, detailed below, illustrates the urgent need for greater cooperation on food security throughout Asia and it points to a critical need to focus more global attention on the importance of understanding food prices, not just as one economic factor, but as a larger socio-economic and political driver.

Skyrocketing rice prices in 2007

Although this paper started with the basic assumption that food insecurity is often driven by poor policies and poor growing conditions (natural disasters, or the effects of climate change), there is a recent, and critical, example of a food panic that was not triggered by either of these factors. In October of 2007, the Indian government decided to buy more rice for its own food distribution programs. This was a perfectly rational decision as the rice was intended to replace wheat, as commodity prices for wheat had escalated sharply in 2007. To make sure there was plenty of cheap rice available the Indian government made it illegal to export most Indian rice. Global response was almost instantaneous. The next day trading prices for rice in Bangkok shot up to $75 a ton.

The jump in price triggered a worldwide panic over rising prices and possible scarcities. Individuals and governments throughout the world started stocking up on rice. During the first four months of 2008 major exporters started to hold on to their rice crops. 'Egypt, Pakistan and Vietnam all started hording their rice crop. So, there was still plenty of rice in the world, but there was less for sale' (Siegel 2011). That put a tremendous pressure on importing countries like the Philippines. Rice is a large part of peoples' diet in the Philippines and the price spikes caused more than just anxiety, people in the Philippines were actually going hungry as rice became hard to find at any price. While the crisis might have been manifest by psychological factors, the impact was quite real. Estimates show that before the rice price spikes in 2007, there were 542 million people in the region whose caloric intake was below the minimum dietary requirement of 1800 calories a day. As a result of the rice crisis, that number rose to 582 million people (Tyuen 2009: 493–497). Another effect of the crisis was to increase the incentives for corruption. Peter Timmer explains that the high prices amplified the opportunities for corrupt officials to line their pockets. The

Philippine government used state funds to buy rice from a state-owned company in Vietnam, Vinafood, at sky-high prices. Vinafood was able to use some of that money to buy the actual rice from Vietnamese farmers, but there is still a huge profit margin from the transaction which can then be split with officials from the Philippines government engineering the transaction (Siegel 2011).

Timmer, an economist, and Tom Slayton, a rice trader, realized that the price hikes and panic were more about psychology than actually about scarcity. They knew that there was one and half million tons of high quality rice in Japan, WTO rice.

> To settle a trade dispute with the US, Japan had agreed to take in a lot of American rice that it didn't really want. That rice just sits in warehouses. Japan is not allowed to export it, unless the US says it can. Timmer and Slayton started a lobbying campaign. They said to the US, let the Japanese sell this rice just this once. (Siegel 2011)

By mid May 2008, the US had agreed. Just the public announcement that this rice would be coming on to world markets was enough to start bringing the price down. By the end of the year, the price of rice had been cut in half. Ultimately, none of the rice in Japan ever got on to the market. The cause of the crisis was psychological, and once the FEAR of too little rice being available on rice markets was put to rest, then prices could stabilize.

What this episode clearly illustrates is that actual food supplies are just one part of the issue. Consumers, importers, exporters (whether private companies or state agencies), and governments will act in rational ways. But this rational behavior is driven by available information, which may be imperfect, and by perception, which may not be 'rational'. So, if a decision is made to stop exporting, because there is a belief that supplies may be low, then that decision triggers other decisions by importers, other governments, and consumers. And, the results as we saw in 2007–2008 can be quite troubling. There are several solutions to this, as Timmer and other have proposed, first, countries (either individually or cooperatively) can enhance their reserves of rice and other staple crops. Secondly, more transparent mechanisms can be created to provide more accurate information on supply levels. The rice market in particular is not terribly transparent. If more precise information was available on supplies and prices, then decision-making could also be more rational and less given to panic behavior. While these remedies may seem fairly simple, in practice they are not.

National concerns and actions on food security

Asian countries are some of the world's largest importers and exporters of rice. On the import side Asian countries import about 41% of rice traded on global markets: the Philippines imports about 3.6% of world rice imports; Bangladesh 3.4%; China 3.2% (but growing sharply); North Korea 2.4%; Japan 2.3%; Malaysia 1.8%; Indonesia 1.3% (but declining steadily); and Singapore 1.2%. On the export side Asia farms more than 91% of the global rice harvest (International Rice Research Institute 2008; Workman 2008). The largest rice exporters are Vietnam, Thailand, India, and Cambodia. I will discuss key countries in turn.

Malaysia

Malaysia is a rice importer. From 1996–2003 Malaysia on average needed to import 29% of its domestic consumption (Dawe 2006). For Malaysia, rice security is a matter of national security. A July 2011 conference in Malaysia on rice intensification system looked at how to bolster domestic rice production (Butler 2009). In reaction to global price hikes in 2007–2008 the government of Malaysia passed the Food Security Policy (FSP). Under this policy, RM 506bn was allocated for agricultural development, particularly rice cultivation and production. In the spring of 2011, the government extended this policy. Malaysia's NAP (National Agricultural Policy) for 2011–2020 will determine whether Malaysia will be able to achieve food security through self-sufficiency, or whether Malaysia will continue to be dependent on imports. The NAP involves both input and output subsidies in agriculture, guaranteeing a minimum price for paddy output, fertilizer subsidies, and subsidies for paddy cultivation, seeds, and rice price supports. The coordinating agency for this is FAMA, the Federal Agricultural Marketing Authority (which is like Indonesia's Bulog) (Adnan 2011). These policies may produce short-term self-sufficiency, but if the experiences of other countries are any guide, these policies are expensive to maintain and may not be environmentally sustainable.

Indonesia

In the 1970s and 1980s Indonesia followed policies similar to those mentioned above and found that the cost of food self-sufficiency was extremely high. Input subsidies to help farmers, such as fuel, fertilizers, pesticides and irrigation were quite costly. For example, in 1986–1987 the total cost of these subsidies equaled US$725 billion. The government also was heavily involved in building infrastructure and trans-migration programs, again to bolster agricultural production. Although genuinely increasing food production, these programs also resulted in costly externalities. Too much fertilizer and pesticides were used because they were cheap to the farmers, so not only was there a huge government outlay to increase crop yields, but there was environmental damage done as well in trying to achieve self-sufficiency (soil erosion, contamination of surface water and a decrease in fishing stocks were all consequences of policy choices made in the 1980s). These policies were unsustainable then both because of their costly and damaging nature (Barbier 1989).

Since rice is a critical commodity for Indonesia, there has been a lot of attention paid to agricultural policies and trade policies that affect rice supplies and prices. After Suharto consolidated power in the 1960s, his new order regime embarked on attempts to stimulate rice production and to improve the country's over all food security. Highly interventionist policies were pursued, with goals of bolstering food production and stabilizing prices. When there was an excess supply of rice, the state subsidized the farmers by buying the surplus. When there was excess demand for rice, the state subsidized imports of rice from foreign sources. This was a successful strategy on two fronts: it provided price stability to farmers which gave them confidence to make necessary investments to raise productivity; and with increased productivity, prices decreased. However, like other interventionist policies, this approach became quite expensive in the longer run. Additionally, these policies created a bias towards rice farmers which caused difficulties in diversifying Indonesia's other agricultural sector (Timmer 2004). Since 2011 there has been a ban on rice imports by private traders. Only bulog is allowed to import rice (*Asiaone* 2004).

Over the last few years the government agency has imported a significant amount of rice. This is true even while domestic harvests have been quite good. Some of the reasons for importing foreign rice are to keep the prices low for consumers and to combat or counter act smuggling. When it comes to food security, particularly the issue of rice cultivation and trade, Indonesia has not acted in a concerted way to change the way trade and reserves are structured. This may in part stem from Indonesia's position of being mostly self-sufficient in rice production, and thus they neither import huge quantities of rice, nor are they economically reliant on exporting rice to their neighbors. In 2010 Indonesia had a sufficient supply of rice from domestic production and only allowed imports of specific types of rice in the amount of 250,000 tons (USDA 2010). Then, in 2011 Indonesia bought considerable amounts of rice, 1.9 million tons. In 2012, Indonesia also imported rice, although the amounts were down to between 500,000–770,000. Bulog officials expressed desire to purchase this rice from India and Vietnam citing cost concerns and annoyance over Thailand's domestic price supports to Thai rice farmers. (*Jakarta Globe* 2012) Stockpiles of rice supplies are high throughout the region and government officials and traders welcomed the news from Indonesia about their rice purchases (Reuters 2012).

One of the other problems that Indonesia faces (they are not the only ones facing this issue) is that farmers are aging. The younger generation in rural areas is more likely to move to urban areas to seek a different lifestyle than that of a small farmer or peasant. These problems are also detailed by Chang and Hsu in their article.

Indonesia is building in West Papua the Merauke Integrated Food and Energy Estate. This is a 480,000 hectare agricultural estate. It is scheduled to be completed in 2014. When it is finished it will be able to produce two million tons of rice, two million tons of corn, 167,000 tons of soybeans, 2.5 tons of sugar, 937,000 tons of palm oil and grazing space for 64,000 cattle (*Jakarta Globe* 2011).

Singapore

Singapore has traditionally been a passive consumer of food, importing virtually all manner of food stuffs. It is now repositioning itself to create a more stable global food system. There are four parts to Singapore's strategy:

1. As a well-respected center of higher education, Singapore can focus resources on research and development in the areas of agriculture, aquaculture, and adaptation to climate change.
2. Singapore can reposition itself as a hub for agribusiness. Singapore's economic Development Board is supporting the set up of operational headquarters and trading operations and research facilities for companies on the cutting edge of developing new crop varieties for the region.
3. Even densely-populated Singapore sees potential in urbanized solutions to food security. Thus, they are experimenting in urban farming, rooftop farming, vertical farming, hydroponic farming and the like.
4. Last, is the goal of achieving more local production of three key food items: eggs, leafy vegetables, and fish. A $20 million food fund, launched in December 2009 is in place to provide incentives to explore new farming technologies and to increase Singaporean production capacity (Kassim 2011a).

Both government and private resources are being mobilized towards these goals. Singapore is also partnering with foreign companies abroad to explore other ways of ensuring access to food. Plans are in development for the China–Singapore Jilin food zone. Jilin Province in China has fertile soil, water resources, and good growing conditions for a wide variety of crops. Planning in the early phases for a 1450 square kilometers (more than twice the size of Singapore) super farm which could produce: staples like corn, soybeans and rice; grains like wheat, barley, oat and rye; sugar beets, poultry, pork, beef, dairy products, fruits, vegetables, flowers, and roots/herbs (Lee 2010: A13). In some ways Singapore's investment in China is ironic. China's arable land holdings are shrinking and China itself is looking elsewhere in SEA (The Philippines and Indonesia) to expand its agricultural security (Thomas, this volume). Singaporean citizens and firms have also been buying land in Thailand for rice cultivation. Singapore is clearly looking for a multitude of different options for dealing with food supplies in the future.

Philippines

The Philippines too is seeking to increase their own food security. Rice is an integral part of the history, culture, and especially the diet, of the Philippines. There is a great deal of anxiety in the Philippines that the country is not self-sufficient in rice production. Some of the reasons for this include urbanization, conversion of rice land to other uses, deteriorating irrigation systems, lack of access to credit for farmers, and poor government policies (Dawe 2006). They are launching a site for production of 'golden rice' (rice with vitamin A in it). Production is proceeding with this and this rice is scheduled to come on to the market by 2013. The Philippines is pioneering the use of this genetically modified strain of rice, as well as moving ahead with the use of Bt (genetically modified) corn in Asia as early as 2002. Golden rice promises higher yield and Bt corn is suppose to be hardier and higher yielding (Aguiba 2011). This initiative is in keeping with broader efforts to bolster agriculture. The government has initiated a campaign: Agri-Pinoy, to guide various services and government programs relating to: Food security and self-sufficiency, sustainable agriculture and fisheries, natural resource management, and local development.

   While these domestic policies may improve an individual country's food security posture, by themselves, these policies may not be enough. Only through cooperation between food exporters and food importers will longer-term prospects and mechanisms for dealing with food insecurity and periodic crises be improved.

Rice exporters
Thailand

Thailand is the world's largest exporters of rice, particularly of high-quality, fragrant rice (Jasmine rice). Thailand aims to produce about 30 million metric tons (MMT) of rice a year, of which it was projected to export about 9 MMT in 2012 (*Business Recorder* 2012; Korves 2012). Making good on an election promise, Pue Thai Party Prime Minister, Yingluck Shinawatra reinstated a previous rice support program. The government pays farmers 15,000 baht ($490) per ton for paddy which is well above market prices of around 9,000 baht. This has allowed the government to build up nearly a seven million ton stockpile, and it has improved prices for farmers. However, it has hurt Thai rice exports dramatically. Thai rice exports have halved from a year ago because of the high prices, Thailand may now only export between 6–7MMT, the lowest levels exported since 1999–2000 (Korves 2012: 1). Domestic Thai politics has been chaotic and sometimes even violent over the last five years. The Pue Thai party's victory in 2011 was viewed as a return to power of politicians who tended to favor rural interests over Bangkok elites. The rice supports may in the short term help Thai rice farmers, but will hurt exporters and may over the long term damage Thailand's global position in rice markets (Indonesia's decisions this year to buy from India and Vietnam is an illustration of this). There has been a push back in Thailand against these price supports from business groups, and exporters, and Yingluck may have a hard time renewing these policies once they expire (Pratruangkrai and Pongvutitham 2011).

Vietnam

Vietnam has been the second largest exporter at an average of 6.1MMT. This year's projections place Vietnamese exports at close to 7.0MMT. Unlike Thailand, Vietnam's exports are going in an upward direction. With surging demand and contracts from China and the Philippines, Vietnam's exports climbed to 2.87 MMT tons in the first half of the year (*Bloomberg News* 2012). The government of Vietnam plays a significant role in controlling the rice trade in Vietnam. The government ministry – the Vietnam Food Association oversees rice cultivation and trade. The government is promoting efforts to raise the quality of Vietnam's rice, increase the crop yields, and promote exports (Government of Vietnam 2012). Vietnam is also contemplating greater cooperation with Thailand on creating a rice cartel under the umbrella of a regional federation for rice among ASEAN producing nations. The hope is that rice exporters will be able to command higher prices for their farmers if they work together as a group to set prices and control supply (Angimex 2012). There are significant obstacles to this, however. Rice producing countries vary in their approaches to cultivation, storage, and logistics capabilities. The partnership could mean sharing of storage facilities and higher prices for Vietnamese rice. This could weaken Vietnam's competitiveness, but could bring higher prices to their producers and/or the middlemen in the rice trade.

Cambodia

Cambodia is trying to break into the ranks of large exporting countries like Thailand and Vietnam. As of 2012, Cambodia's rice is much cheaper than Thailand's and Vietnam's, but much of the rice that Cambodia exports first goes to Vietnam for processing (as Cambodia doesn't have enough good quality mills and because of weak trade networks between producers, millers, and traders in Cambodia (Radio Free Asia 2012). Cambodia is looking to join forces with Myanmar to cooperate on rice production and export. Cambodia would like to see the establishment of a rice cartel of Southeast Asian exporters as it would help offset fluctuating international market prices. Cambodia is interested in bringing in Myanmar, as Myanmar is in a relatively similar position to Cambodia, both faced financial difficulty in the spring of 2012 as abundant harvests, and shrinking demand have pushed prices quite low. Since Cambodia and Myanmar are lower on the production chain, they have fewer opportunities for making money on the processing side of the rice trade and thus are even more vulnerable to market variability. Cambodia plans to buy a rice-polishing machine from China and will also look into building a rice storage facility in Kandal province, both measures aim to improve Cambodia's position in the rice trade (Kunmakara 2012). Cambodia has reached out to China and the Philippines to sign trade contracts for rice with these two growing importers (*Manila Times* 2012).

Areas of cooperation

While regional discussions about food security predate the rice crisis in 2007, it was partly in response to the sharp increase in international food prices in 2007–2008 that leaders in Southeast Asia pledged to embrace food security as a matter of permanent and high priority. They adopted a 'Statement on Food Security in the ASEAN Region', which commits, among others actions, to the implementation of the ASEAN Integrated Food Security (AIFS) Framework and the Strategic Plan of Action on Food Security in the ASEAN Region (SPA–FS) (2009–2013). This is a five-year strategic plan to assure long-term food security in the region through increased cooperation and mutual help.

The (Senior Officials Meeting) SOM–AMAF is the main ASEAN body that oversees ASEAN cooperation in food and agriculture, with the guidance of the ASEAN Ministers on Agriculture and Forestry (AMAF). Sectoral working groups/joint committees/boards, and experts groups have been established to implement the respective cooperation sectors of food, and the various sub-sectors of agriculture and forestry. The ASEAN Secretariat is charged with overall coordination of programs. ASEAN has implemented numerous cooperative projects relating to food, agriculture and forestry sectors, which cover a wide spectrum of activities ranging from exchange of information, crop production, post-harvest and handling, training and extension, research and development as well as trade promotion in the areas of crops, livestock, fisheries, and forestry.

In order to respond to trade globalization, ASEAN cooperation in food, agriculture and forestry is now more focused on the enhancement of food, agricultural and forestry products' competitiveness in international markets, while sustaining agricultural production. Harmonization of quality and standards, assurance of food safety, and standardization of trade certification are among the priorities being addressed. This attempts to build upon the experience of some member states and existing international standards.

At ASEAN meetings in 2010, Ministers welcomed and reaffirmed the ASEAN Plus Three Cooperation Strategy on Food, Agriculture and Forestry with the goal to ensure long-term food security and to improve the livelihoods of farmers in the ASEAN and Plus Three Countries. The Cooperation Strategy provides a comprehensive framework to foster cooperation among the ASEAN Plus Three countries in the areas of Strengthening Food Security, Biomass Energy Development, Sustainable Forest Management, Climate Change Mitigation and Adaptation, Animal Health and Disease Control, and Cross-Cutting Issues (i.e., enhancement of capacity-building and human resource development; strengthening of information and knowledge networking and exchange; enhancement of productivity, quality and marketability of agriculture and agricultural products; and strengthening collaboration on research and development). The Ministers agreed to formalize the ASEAN Plus Three Emergency Rice Reserve (APTERR) as a permanent scheme for meeting emergency requirements and achieving humanitarian purposes. The Ministers urged all ASEAN Plus Three Countries to sign the agreement and signal their support through early implementation. By 2010 some progress had been made in creating the ASEAN Food Security Information System (AFSIS), including early warning systems and information on agricultural commodities. These were created to provide information hopefully instituting an early warning mechanism to signal information on food supplies before a crisis was full-blown (AMAF Plus Three: 2010).

At the 2011 ASEAN meetings, food security was again on the agenda. There was a renewed sense of importance and urgency at these meetings. Commodity prices were again climbing, and heavy rains in Thailand were threatening to affect the rice harvests.

Additionally, the events of the Arab spring heightened government concerns over volatility of food prices because of the clear relationship between food security and political stability. The protests throughout the Middle East and North Africa clearly showed the world that the combination of high food costs, few economic opportunities for advancement, and authoritarian regimes which denied citizens meaningful participation and accountability, coupled with state-capitalist regimes that reward regime-insiders with economic benefits while most citizens were locked out of both greater economic and political opportunities is a recipe for psychological feelings of relative deprivation and ultimately protest movements (Gurr 1970)!

The November 2011 ASEAN Summit took place against the backdrop of widespread floods in Thailand, and questions about yields of rice from the region's largest exporter. The unusually heavy floods may have provided the needed push to jump start (previously somewhat slow) efforts to address issues of food scarcity. The ASEAN-related meetings had a full agenda of issues to address: negotiations on conduct in the South China Sea, political changes in Myanmar, the on-going dispute between Cambodia and Thailand, as well as the usual discussions over reducing trade barriers and community-building efforts. With the intense rains, food security moved up the priority list of things to address.

On 12 October 2011, Indonesia, as ASEAN Chair for the year, issued a special statement concerning the floods.

> Jakarta expressed concern over the rising waters deluging some member states. But it also 'emphasized the importance of strong cooperation and coordination' among states and the 'need for full implementation' of two key mechanisms to deal with food emergencies. (Kassim 2011b)

The two mechanisms discussed are: the ASEAN Agreement on Disaster and Emergency Response or AADMER, and the second is the ASEAN Coordinating Centre for Humanitarian Assistance on Disaster Management (AMA Centre). While these institutional structures exist, they have not yet been tested to see if they are ready to play their designated roles in addressing challenges to human security.

Also at the fall 2011 meeting, the ten members of ASEAN signed an emergency rice reserve agreement with their three Northeast Asian dialogue partners (China, Japan and Korea), the ASEAN Plus Three (APT). Based on earlier cooperation, the APT signaled their support for the ASEAN Plus Three Emergency Rice Reserve (APTERR). Under the current plan, the 13 signatory states will stock up 787,000 tons of rice to be used in the event of a sudden instability in rice supplies. This reflects nervousness among regional leaders over environmental conditions and the close connection between food supplies, costs, and domestic stability (Kassim 2011a). Indonesia's President Yudhoyono (SBY) has consistently called on ASEAN to consider using APTERR not just for responding to natural disasters but also in the event of economic upheaval. This clearly reflects political considerations in light of the experience of shocks to the rice market as happened in 2008, and the uprisings in the Arab world, partly driven by economic malaise and rising food costs throughout the world.

Signaling that food security is a big issue outside of just Southeast Asia, the East Asia Summit (EAS) (which involves the APT and Australia, New Zealand, India, the United States and Russia has also taken up the concern. The EAS met at the end ASEAN meetings in November. While the US has signaled an interest and concern over food security issues, because the US is not a member of ASEAN, nor of APT, it is hard to see how the US could play a more significant role within the context of these institutions (since that is where most of the cooperative measures are being built) in addressing regional food cooperation.

Prospects for greater cooperation

Peter Timmer has pointed out a contradiction in the area of food security policy. International donors discourage countries from 'stabilizing' domestic food prices in the face of a crisis. This sort of intervention in the market is frowned upon by liberal economists pushing for market freedoms and less government distortion. Instead, donors encourage a policy of social safety nets, proscribing that governments should have in place safety nets to help the poor. Thus, when a crisis hits, the poor will be able to cope with price fluctuations. While these policies may make long terms sense, they are not useful for quick reactions when a food crisis looms (or hits). Longer term planning and the creation and maintenance of safety nets for the poor are certainly desirable, but they are costly, and take years to put into place. So, more active measures are needed to prevent food price spikes, both domestically and internationally. Timmer recommends strategically held stockpiles (held nationally, regionally, or internationally) which could be used to offset price jumps in certain situations. Reserves could serve two different, but both useful, purposes. First, the stockpiles could be used to offset periods of scarcity in limited situations. More strategically, the reserve could act as a stabilizing force in the event of instability in supply and/or price of a particular crop. In other words, such reserves could increase market stability for basic commodity crops such as rice, maize, soy, etc. (Timmer 2011).

The discussions at the November 2011 ASEAN Summit are promising. APTERR aims to do exactly what Timmer is calling for. However, if the past is any indication, it may be harder than it seems to get agreement on more structured cooperation, either on the logistics of the strategic stockpiles for rice reserves, greater transparency in the rice markets, or on greater liberalization of export controls over rice. WTO discussions and rules almost all focus on import barriers rather than export controls. However, there is widespread agreement that price instability occurs because of export manipulation as well. It is difficult to imagine countries being willing to give up policy control on the export side, especially when it is the export of a stable food crop which is up for discussion. States tend to view food supplies and control over food supplies as a question of national security. So, it is hard to imagine large food exporters wanting to be constrained in how they control the distribution of such resources. Of course, there is also the basic problem that the interests of food exporters and food importers are dramatically different. In Southeast Asia, Vietnam and Thailand are big exporters of rice, and the Philippines and Malaysia are significant importers of rice. Indonesia is in an interesting position; from year to year it varies whether they import significant supplies of rice, or whether they are actually exporting some tonnage of rice. Naturally, the interests of countries on both sides of the rice trade vary tremendously.

In theory, both importing and exporting countries would both benefit from greater transparency (discussed shortly), and greater liberalization of the rice trade. There could be large pay offs from greater efficiency and better allocation of resources. There would be greater stability of prices and supplies, and it would reduce the tendency of actors to hoard stocks, and reduce the likelihood of price panics. So, why don't countries liberalize trade in rice and increase their cooperative efforts? Peter Timmer views this cooperation challenge as a prisoners' dilemma. All countries would be better off if everyone cooperated. However, if a country defects (doesn't cooperate, implements import or export controls, etc.) while other countries cooperate, then the defecting country will come out ahead. This then generally produces the understandably rational decision of each individual country to forego cooperation in favor of beggar thy neighbor policies (even though cooperation by all would produce the best outcome). Timmer explains that the ways to resolve this dilemma are (1) to agree on a formal mechanism for cooperation (through ASEAN or a related organization) with binding commitments (like GATT/WTO trade agreements which have governed other areas of trade but in which rice is currently exempt); (2) alternatively, gradual learning by all actors can produce greater cooperative outcomes in prisoners' dilemmas. Through repeated rice price crises, countries may come to realize that cooperation is the best way forward. This of course, is a painful way to get to greater cooperation (Timmer 2011: 14).

There is another problem that relates to prospects for greater cooperation on rice in Southeast Asia; the nature of the market itself. The rice market is relatively small (in comparison with other commodity markets), and it is highly segmented and 'imperfect' as economists would say. Most import and export deals on rice are made behind closed doors by governments without very much transparency or accountability (Timmer 2011: 11).

Recommendations and conclusions

In order to envision greater cooperation on food security in Southeast Asia, it will take significant leadership. Indonesia is the largest power in Southeast Asia and they are showing renewed interest in acting like a regional great power. During Indonesia's time chairing ASEAN in 2011, they pushed hard to strengthen the capacities and role of the ASEAN Intergovernmental Commission on Human Rights (AICHR), and pursued the goal of establishing a network of peacekeeping centers in ASEAN member states, and they laid the groundwork for the SEANWFZ (Southeast Asia Nuclear Weapons Free Zone) Treaty to be signed by the US, UK, Russia, France and China. These efforts reflect Indonesia's growing desire to be seen as a leader on issues of human rights, peacemaking, and stability among great powers (Alexandra 2011). It would behoove

Indonesia to push for longer-term goals like policies to engage in better integration of the Asia rice market with more open trade policies, and much greater transparency. As countries in the region continue to see strong economic growth rates and increasing levels of prosperity, this may get easier. As populations get richer they will be better able to afford different diet options and demand for rice may shrink. As demand drops, states may then have greater flexibility in how they view their control and access to rice supplies.

Secondly, Indonesia could continue to push for larger and better coordinated rice reserves in member states of the ASEAN Plus Three. Realistically, reserves wouldn't be of a significant enough size to prevent a crisis, but it could increase confidence and thus act as a psychological buffer to a crisis (much as releasing the WTO rice stocks in Japan did in 2008). This kind of limited stockpiling of rice under the control of the regional organization has been under discussion for a number of years with little firm progress made. Timmer also suggests that having Australia serve as the coordinator and holder of a reserve supply of rice for the SEA region might also work. Australia is a relatively small market for rice and can serve as a trusted, neutral player in this role (Timmer 2011: 23–24). There are significant criticisms of this plan, however. While Australia might be 'neutral' in terms of the rice trade, Australia's foreign relations with countries in Southeast Asia more generally is marked by both cooperation *and disagreement or conflict*. So, it is not really a foregone conclusion (as Timmer might have thought) that countries in the region would see Australia as a good steward for a regional rice reserve.

Asia has to a large extent been able to manage keeping domestic food prices low, but this has a negative externality for world markets. The 2007–2008 rice panic illustrates important lessons regarding food security. The reactions to India's decision to curtail rice exports reflected how price expectations for basic food grains are formed by farmers, traders, governments and consumers. The crisis shows how critical it is to know what policy actions can be taken to stabilize food prices and keep consumers more food secure. To do this, Asia needs to find more efficient ways to stabilize domestic food prices, particularly for rice, without harmful spillover effects on domestic producers, on world markets, or on the environment.

Rice is increasingly a food consumed by the poor. As people climb out of poverty, their diets become less dependent on rice. To deal with food security based on adequate availability of low cost rice, is only to deal with part of the problem. Food security is very much part of larger questions. One of those questions relates to how countries deal with the wider problem of poverty. Policy-makers must implement long-term measures to stimulate pro-poor economic growth and sustain that growth for decades in order to have a measurable impact on poverty rates. At the same time, countries need short-term measures to address every day issues of food security, and policies in place to deal with possible crisis. These are the challenges that policies makers in much of Southeast Asia face, and at their core these are questions of human security.

Food security is also clearly linked to the larger challenges posed by climate change. Climate change will have profound effects on living conditions and human security, and will impact many diverse issues: water resources, agriculture, forestry, health, migration patterns, energy systems, and arguably larger economy itself. Stresses that arise from climate changes can exacerbate and trigger new conflicts among groups within states and across national borders. The Center for Strategic and International Studies stated in November 2007 that climate change 'could destabilize virtually every aspect of modern life' (Scheffron and Battaglini 2011: S27–S39). Food insecurity in this context is just one of a myriad of issues that will require long-term planning and regional cooperation. The German Advisory Council anticipates that a global warming of between two to four degrees Celsius would lead to a drop in agricultural productivity world-wide and that this decrease will substantially increase desertification, soil salinity, and water security. One of the reasons that human security issues are often hard to tackle is that we live in a world still defined by states and national security interests. Addressing human security (human security encompasses food security as well as economic security, environmental security, health security, personal security, community and political security) needs requires a shift in focus from being concerned about state-centered approaches to security, to focusing on people-centered approaches to security. This would require both a rethinking of notions of security, priorities, and actors, as well as necessitating vastly more cooperation across state boundaries. This is incredibly difficult, but not impossible.

In 2009, Indonesia and Malaysia initiated a series of bilateral discussions on cooperating on food security. The two countries stated their intention to jointly develop investment programs in agriculture. Indonesia has vast agricultural assets, and Malaysia is more technologically advanced. The goal would be that Malaysia would invest capital and technology into Indonesia's agricultural sector for mutual benefit. This would enhance regional cooperation and serve as a model for more multilateral efforts within ASEAN, and it would improve food security and help prevent food crises. As an example and a first step towards this larger goal, Indonesia and Malaysia agreed to cooperate on marketing of palm oil, this was viewed as a powerful indicator of what is a possible coming together of forces since together Malaysia and Indonesia control about 80% of the world's supply of palm oil (Scheffron and Battaglini 2011: S31).

Hegemonic stability theory finds that successfully solving cooperation problems often requires strong leadership. Since the largest rice exporters in SEA are NOT the region's most powerful actors, it is difficult to predict greater, more successful or robust cooperation in the near term. Indonesia should be in this position as regional leader, but as a frequent importer of rice, it is harder to view how they could take the lead on this particular issue. Price instability over the last few years and, prospects of more fluctu-ations in the future, may be a catalyst for greater action. As the region's largest exporter, Thailand could be the leader in promoting cooperation on the rice trade. However, domestic politics in Thailand are highly con-tentious and Prime Minister Yingluck's decision to reinstate rice subsidies for Thai farmers, and the blow back from exporters and business groups shows how policies there (like elsewhere) are driven by internal dynamics, not necessarily by regional concerns. What we saw in the ASEAN meetings of fall 2011 may be the beginning of an attempt to put regional cooperation more squarely on countries' agendas. But, it will take regional leadership for more to be accomplished. The attempts by Thailand, Vietnam, Cambo-dia (and Myanmar) to cooperate on exports and to move towards a more-cartel-like organization is an example of cooperation, but it isn't clear how this cooperation would benefit the region more generally.

More work needs to be done to increase transparency in rice markets (that is to build institutional cooperation and to provide information on rice supplies, prices, etc.); and more needs to be done to balance needs of producers and consumers. There is a need for more research to be done to understand domestic politics, and interest group dynamics behind rice poli-cies in rice exporters like Vietnam, Thailand, and Cambodia. And, there needs to be greater regional leadership from these exporters. This is an important piece of the puzzle of trying foster greater cooperation between importers and exporters. The cooperative efforts that have happened through APT are an important step, but these efforts have not yet played a significant role in reshaping domestic agricultural policies.

Acknowledgements

Much thanks go to my research assistants for this project: William Lind-berg and Alexis Banschbach. Also, I appreciate comments and suggestions from my fellow panelists at the Association of Asian Studies Conference in Toronto, Canada in March 2012 and especially the constructive feedback from Nick Thomas. All errors and omissions are my responsibility.

References

Adnan, H. (2011) 'Food security policy may be extended', *The Star (Malaysia)*, April 10, p. 2.
Alexandra, L. (2011) 'Indonesia is emerging', *The Diplomat*, August 11; accessed at http://thediplomat.com/asean-beat, 8 December 2011.
Aguiba, M. (2011) 'Philippines to play a critical role in global food security with 2012 Golden Rice launch', *Jakarta Globe*, March 19, p. 1.
AMAF (ASEAN Ministers on Agriculture and Forestry) Plus Three. (2010) 'Joint press statement of the tenth meeting of the ASEAN Ministers on Agriculture and Forestry and the Ministers of Agriculture of the People's Republic of

China, Japan and the Republic of Korea', 10th AMAF Plus Three, Phnom Penh, October 24.

Angimex. (2012) 'Vietnam to cooperate with Thailand on ASEAN rice cartel', *Angimex*, June 26; accessed at http://oryza.com/Rice-News/, 28 June 2012).

Asiaone. (2011) 'Indonesian rice production and trade policy', March 3; accessed at www.asiaone.com.sg, 26 November 2011.

Barbier, E. B. (1989) 'Cash crops, food crops, and sustainability: the case of Indonesia', *World Development* 17(6): 879–895.

Bloomberg News. (2012) 'Rice shipments from Vietnam reach 2.87 MMT to June 14', June 18; accessed at www.bloomberg.com, 10 August 2012.

Business Recorder. (2012) 'Thai Rice exports slump on intervention: Vietnamese exports surge, April 22; accessed at www.brecorder.com, 1 December 2012.

Butler, C. (2009) 'Food security in the Asian-Pacific: climate change, phosphorus, ozone and other environmental challenges', *Asia Pacific Journal of Clinical Nutrition* 18(4): 590–597.

Corden, M. W. (1990) 'American decline and the end of hegemony', *SAIS Review* 10(2): 13–26.

Dawe, D. C. (2006) 'The Philippines imports rice because it is an Island Nation', *ATI@Ilocos Region.*

Government of Vietnam. (2012) Vietfood rice information; accessed at http://www.vietfood.org.vn/en/default.aspx?c=111, 30 June 2012.

Gurr, T. (1970) *Why Men Rebel?*, Princeton, NJ: Princeton University Press.

Hunt, M. H. (1990) 'American decline and the great debate: a historical perspective,' *SAIS Review* 10(2): 24–40.

International Rice Research Institute, Data on Rice Importers and Exporters, various years; accessed at http://www.irri.org/worldricestatistics, 20 November 2011.

Jakarta Globe. (2011) 'Indonesia can not afford to ignore food security', *Jakarta Globe*, January 8, p. 1.

Jakarta Globe. (2012) 'Indonesia's Bulog estimates 2012 rice imports could reach 770,000 tons', *Jakarta Globe*, October 16, p. 1.

Kassim, Y. R. (2011a) 'ASEAN's role in Asian food security', *The Business Times*, September 14, p. 21.

Kassim, Y. R. (2011b) 'The 19th ASEAN Summit: tackling floods, food and stability – analysis', *Eurasiareview*, November 17; accessed at http//www.eurasiareview.com, 17 February 2012.

Kindleberger, C. (1973) 'An explanation of the 1929 depression', in *The World in Depression, 1929–39*, Berkeley, CA: University of California Press, pp. 291–308.

Korves, R. (2012) 'Thailand's domestic rice policies upset trade patterns', February 9; accessed at http://*Truthabouttrade.org*, 10 August 2012.

Kunmakara, M. (2012) 'Phnom Penh autonomous port to push rice exports', *The Phnom Penh Post*, June 8; accessed at www.phnompenhpost.com, 25 June 2012.

Lee, Y. N. (2010) 'S'pore eyes huge China farm project', *The Straits Times*, May 22, p. A13.

Manila Times. (2012) 'Philippines, Cambodia to sign rice trade deal', *Manila Times*, May 3; accessed at www.manilatimes.net, 22 June 2012.

Milner, H. (1998) 'International political economy: beyond hegemonic stability', *Foreign Policy,* Vol. 2, No. 110 (Spring).

OECD. (2009) 'Share of ODA for Agriculture (percent)', in *Conflict and Fragility Do No Harm International Support for State Building,* OECD Creditor Reporting System.

Pratruangkrai, P. and Pongvutitham, A. (2011) 'Rice scheme will hurt Thais and help Vietnam', *The Nation*, September 5; accessed at www.nationmultimedia.com, 1 December 2011.

Radio Free Asia. (2012) 'Rice cartel plan resurfaces', *Radio Free Asia*, March 21; accessed at www.rfa.org/english/news/cambodia, 26 June 2012.

Reuters. (2012) 'Update: 2-Indonesia to import up to 2 mln T rice in 2012', *Reuters*, February 22, p. 1.

RSIS Centre for Non-traditional Security (NTS) Studies. (2011) International Conference on Asian Food Security 2011: Feeding Asia in the 21st Century: Building Urban–Rural Alliances, 10–12 August, Report, Singapore, p. 7.

Scheffron, J. and Battaglini, A. (2011) 'Climate and conflicts', *Environmental Change* 11, Supplement 1: S27–S39.

Siegel, R. (2011) 'How fear drove world rice markets insane', *National Public Radio*, November 2; accessed at www.npr.org/templates, February 2012.

Sooros, M. (1997) *The Endangered Atmosphere*, South Carolina: University of South Caroline Press.

Timmer, P. (2004) 'Food security in Indonesia: current challenges and the long-run outlook', Working Paper 48, Center for Global Development, Washington, DC; accessed at http://www.cgdev.org/content/publications/detail/2740/, 10 July 2012.

Timmer, P. (2011) 'Managing price volatility: approaches at the global, national and household levels', Stanford University Symposium Series on Global Food Policy and Food Security in the Twenty-first Century, May 26.

Tyuen, L. D. (2009) 'Food and health security in Southeast Asia', *Asia Pacific Journal of Clinical Nutrition* 18(4): 493–497.

United States Department of Agriculture (USDA). (2010) Foreign Agricultural Service Grain Report, 'Indonesia rice and corn update', April 23.

Workman, D. (2008) 'Rice import dependent countries Nigeria, Saudi Arabia and Philippines among biggest rice buyers', April 16; accessed at http://suite101. com/article/rice-import-dependent-countries, 8 December 2011.

World Health Organization. (2012) Accessed at http://www.who.int/trade/glossary, 10 October 2012.

Food in China's international relations

Daojiong Zha and Hongzhou Zhang

Abstract Food is a tireless referent in international relations studies about China and its ties with the rest of the world. This paper addresses two contemporary issues. First, why is China so sensitive about grain self-sufficiency? Second, why does there seem to be a lack of effective dialogue between epistemic communities in China and outside over China's overseas agricultural activities? The first part of the paper reviews the development of China's agricultural sector and underlines the importance of China's contribution in stabilizing the world food markets. Next, it explores the ideational sources of Chinese food insecurity, in spite of its success in attaining high levels of self-sufficiency in grain. The third part of the paper reviews the evolution of China's overseas agricultural activities and analyzes the factors that contribute to a mismatch of understanding about the political implications therein. The paper concludes by proposing a couple of conceptual road maps for securitizing food as a referent in debates about China's security environment and Chinese international relations.

Introduction

Food is a constant concern in deliberations about world security and China is constant as a reference point. The centrality of China to the global supply and demand margin in food, along with fluctuations in price of the world's trade food, is an issue for agricultural and more generally macroeconomists to debate. In international relations studies, Chinese performance in feeding its own population now and in the future is worthy of constant attention, at least in the realm of 'non-traditional security' or international political economy.

This article addresses two questions. First, why is China so sensitive about grain self-sufficiency? Second, why does there seem to be a lack of effective dialogue between epistemic communities both within and outside of China over China's overseas agricultural activities in recent years?

In assessing China's standing in terms of world food security, there is across-the-board agreement on the overall state of affairs. Home to over 20% of the world's population, China only boasts 9% of the world's arable land and 6% of the world's surface fresh water supply (China State Council 2011a). This makes food issue the top priority for the Chinese government. Ensuring self-sufficiency of food, cereal in particular, is the fundamental policy of China's food security strategy and it is highly prioritized in the central government's work. In the past three decades, though constrained by water and land resources, China has been more or less sufficient in food, particularly cereal.

This record of achievement aside, there are also broadly accepted concerns about the future sustainability of agriculture in China. In terms of the country's factor endowments, China does not have a competitive advantage in producing the share of total world grain supply. In domestic governance, the pursuit of self-sufficiency in grain has meant enormous economic loss for Chinese farmers, as they have been deprived of the opportunity to grow economic crops which could otherwise offer them much higher economic returns from input (Cheng and Beghin 2000; Carter and Rozlle 2002; US International Trade Commission 2011). As has been noted, a key feature of grain production in China is a heavy reliance on intensive farming and excessive use of chemical fertilizer and pesticide, which has led to severe land degradation, threatening China's future grain production (Ye and Van Ranst 2009). Furthermore, due to a decline in arable land and water resources, shrinkage in the rural labour force, as well as pollution and climate change, it is increasingly difficult for China to maintain the high degree of grain self-sufficiency. On the other hand, as the Chinese become wealthier, their dietary patterns and food preferences have changed dramatically. Direct consumption of grain in China is in a pattern of decline, with a corresponding increase in demand for meat, milk, vegetables and fruits. This has resulted in the diminishing importance of grain in China's food security, which invites questions on the importance of grain self-sufficiency to China's overall food security.

However, in spite of the huge opportunity costs suffered by Chinese farmers, the increasing unsustainability of China's agricultural sectors, and continuous calls from scholars to relax this long-lasting food self-sufficiency policy (Mao and Zhao 2011; Xu and Li 2011; X. Li 2011), the Chinese government continues to claim that China must be self-sufficient in supplying farm produce, and that general self-sufficiency of grain and food security are of utmost importance to the nation. In the meantime, fully aware that the country is experiencing severe shortage of agricultural resources in per capita terms, especially in terms of land and fresh water supply, China is also increasingly expanding its agricultural presence overseas while upholding its long-standing policy of grain self-sufficiency.

As part of its grand 'Going-out' policy, China's agricultural industry is speeding up the pace of its engagement with international agricultural markets. This has attracted a string of negative headlines claiming that China aims to tackle the problem of feeding over 1.3 billion people – 20% of the world's population – by importing food from land purchased or leased abroad, particularly from poor countries in Africa where high poverty levels problematize the food export industry. Yet, despite international concerns and a backlash with regards to China's overseas agricultural expansion, China is stepping up efforts to expand its agricultural operations overseas.

This paper, then, aims at bridging the conceptual gaps that contribute to Chinese sensitivities over accessibility to external sources of food supply on the one hand and lack of effective dialogue and understanding between the Chinese and the international community on Chinese behaviour that affect food and food related concerns in the wider world on the other hand.

The paper is organized as follows. The first part of this paper reviews the development of China's agricultural sector and underlines the importance of China's agricultural sector in the world. Next, it explores the ideational sources of Chinese food insecurity. The third part of the paper reviews the evolution as well as analyzes the factors which contribute to the misunderstanding towards China's overseas agricultural activities. The paper concludes by proposing a couple of conceptual road maps for securitizing food as a reference in debates about China's security environment and Chinese international relations.

China's agricultural sector and its global significance

For big countries like China, agriculture plays a fundamental role in feeding and enriching its people, and the country's food security strategies are, to a large extent, determined by the development of its agricultural sector. In the past three decades, China's agricultural sector has experienced phenomenal growth. As shown in Table 1, the country's agricultural production has increased dramatically from 1978 to 2011. China's grain production increased by 87.4% between 1978 and 2011; during the same period, the increases of the production of fruits and fishery products were even more remarkable, being 33.6 times and 11 times respectively. Furthermore, China's meat

Table 1 Outputs of major agricultural products (10,000 tons)

	Grain	Cotton	Oil bearing crops	Fruits	Fishery products	Meats	Milk
1978	30476.5	216.7	521.8	657.0	465.4	NA	NA
1980	32055.5	270.7	769.1	679.3	449.7	NA	136.7
1985	37910.8	414.7	1578.4	1163.9	705.2	1926.5	289.4
1990	44624.3	450.8	1613.2	1874.4	1237.0	2857.0	475.1
1995	46661.8	476.8	2250.3	4214.6	2517.2	5260.1	672.8
2000	46217.5	441.7	2954.8	6225.1	3706.2	6013.9	919.1
2010	54647.7	596.1	3230.1	21401.4	5373.0	7925.8	3748.0
2011	57120.8	658.9	3306.8	22768.2	5603.2	7957.8	3810.7
Change	87.4%	204.1%	533.7%	3365.6%	1104.1%	313.1%	2687.6%

Source: China's Statistical Yearbook (2012).

production has also increased threefold from 1985 to 2011, and the country's milk production increased from 13.6 million tonnes in 1980 to 381 million tonnes in 2011. Relying on merely 9% of the world's cultivated land, China has not only managed to meet the demand of over 1.3 billion people for grain and other agro-products, but also been able to provide raw materials, labour and a huge consumer market for industries, services and other sectors. The remarkably development of the agricultural sector has enabled China to achieve food security through domestic production.

China's agricultural production is not only of great importance to China, but also plays a crucial role in global food security. In spite of its resource constraints, China is the biggest producer of food in the world (USITIC 2011). If one draws up a list of the top producers of agricultural products, China comes in first. For instance, in 2010 China accounted for close to 60% of global vegetable production, 47.3% of global pig-meat production, over one third of egg production, and over one fifth of global cereal (rice, wheat and maize) production, as shown in Table 2. In terms of agricultural trade, so far, China remains a marginal player in the international trade of cereal, including wheat, rice and maize, as shown in Table 3. China's total cereal imports only made up of 1% of the global cereal trade in 2010. However, it seems that China is on track to emerge as a major cereal importer. In 2012, China's cereal imports, including wheat, rice and corn, amounting to 12.96 million tonnes, increased over 300% when compared to the year before.[1] Looking into the future, China's grain import is set to increase. The latest projection by Fan Shenggen, the director general of the International Food Policy Research Institute, suggests that by 2020, China will need to import 100 million tonnes of grain each year (South China Morning Press nd).

In contrast to the cereal trade, China is a major player in international trade for other agricultural products. As shown in Table 4, close to 60% of grain, 40% of cotton, 40% of tropical fruits, and 17% of palm oil traded

Table 2 China's share of the world food production (2010, MT)

Food items	China	World	Share
Vegetables freshness	152987093	257065378	59.51%
Apples	33265186	69511975	47.86%
Indigenous pig meat	51673874	109100198	47.36%
Hen eggs, in shell	23827390	63782277	37.36%
Tomatoes	47116084	151699405	31.06%
Rice, paddy	197212010	696324394	28.32%
Cotton lint	5970000	23295107	25.63%
Potatoes	74799084	324420782	23.06%
Maize	177540788	840308214	21.13%
Wheat	115181303	653654525	17.62%
Indigenous chicken meat	11799394	85860953	13.74%

Source: FAO (2012).

28

Table 3 China's share of international cereal trade, 2010

Maize	Import quantity (tonnes)	5.794%
Maize	Import value (1000 $)	5.463%
Maize	Export value (1000 $)	0.147%
Maize	Export quantity (tonnes)	0.118%
Rice	Export value (1000 $)	2.149%
Rice	Export quantity (tonnes)	1.879%
Rice	Import value (1000 $)	1.740%
Rice	Import quantity (tonnes)	1.558%
Wheat	Import value (1000 $)	1.842%
Wheat	Import quantity (tonnes)	1.659%
Wheat	Export value (1000 $)	0.003%
Wheat	Export quantity (tonnes)	0.001%

Source: FAO (2012).

internationally went to China [went to?]; meanwhile, China supplies nearly half of the dehydrated vegetable trade and is also a top supplier of tea on the international market. Therefore, given the huge share of China in global food production and its important role in international food trade, any change in China's agricultural policy will have profound impacts on global food availability.

De-puzzling China's sensitiveness towards grain self-sufficiency

Ensuring national food security is a vital concern of all governments and before an international food regime first emerged in the late nineteenth century, food self-sufficiency had been the cornerstone for almost all

Table 4 China's share of global agricultural trade (excluding cereal), 2010

Soybeans	Import value (1000 $)	59.82%
Soybeans	Import quantity (tonnes)	59.59%
Palm oil	Import quantity (tonnes)	16.95%
Palm oil	Import value (1000 $)	16.52%
Cotton lint	Import value (1000 $)	40.48%
Cotton lint	Import quantity (tonnes)	39.56%
Fruit, tropical freshness	Import value (1000 $)	48.42%
Fruit, tropical freshness	Import quantity (tonnes)	39.41%
Vegetables dehydrated	Export value (1000 $)	48.69%
Vegetables dehydrated	Export quantity (tonnes)	47.91%
Tea	Export quantity (tonnes)	15.12%
Tea	Export value (1000 $)	12.61%
Vegetable frozen	Export quantity (tonnes)	18.73%
Vegetable frozen	Export value (1000 $)	17.95%

Source: FAO (2012).

countries food security strategy. However, with the emergence of international food regimes (rule-governed structures of production and consumption of food, Friedmann, 1993), and the rapid advancement of globalization and international trade liberalization, the importance of food self-sufficiency to a country's food security has diminished significantly. This has led to a worldwide redefinition of global food security. In 1996, the FAO defined food security as follows: 'Food security exists when all people, at all times, have physical, social and economic access to sufficient safe and nutritious food that meets their dietary needs and food preferences for an active and healthy life' (FA 1996).

Yet, in the Chinese context, the notion of food self-sufficiency is still paramount. It is understandable that big countries like China wish to achieve food security by following a policy of self-sufficiency, but China appears to be obsessed with the idea. Although, until now, no clear definition of food security has been given by the Chinese authorities, food security is equivalent to grain security, with a central focus on grain self-sufficiency (F. Lu 1998). Moreover, despite the fact that grain in China includes not only cereals such as rice, wheat and corn, but also soybeans and root tubers, the importance of soybeans and root tubers to China's grain security has declined notably in recent years. Hence, China's food self-sufficiency policy mainly aims to produce enough staple grains including rice, wheat and corn to feed its increasingly affluent population. In 1996, China set up a bottom line 95% of domestic grain supply (China State Council 1996) and in the country's first official national grain security plan which published in 2008, it stated that by 2020, China will maintain a grain self-sufficiency rate above 95%, and a cereal self-sufficiency rate of 100% (China State Council 2008). China's sensitiveness towards food self-sufficiency is rooted in its unique cultural, political and economic structures and shaped by China's interpretation of the outside world.

A domestic construct

China's sensitiveness towards grain self-sufficiency is a rooted in its unique cultural, political and economic structures.

Firstly, huger and famine is deeply ingrained in the cultural mindset of the Chinese. China has often been described as a land of famine (Mallory 1926). As stated by Lillian Li (2007), 'no other civilization has had such a continuous tradition of thinking about famine, and no other nation's modern history has been so influenced by hunger and famine'. It is estimated that from 108 BC to 1911 there was a drought or flood-induced famine in at least one province in China almost every year (Mukherjee 2012). In the seventeenth century, for instance, famines became common, especially in north China; worsened by unusually cold and dry weather nine million fatalities were caused by the famine in north China from 1876 to 1879.

Famine continued in China until very recently. In 1920 and 1921 in certain provinces at least 500,000 people died, and out of an estimated 48.8 million in these five provinces, over 19.8 million were declared destitute. Between two and three million died in Henan province in 1943 (L. Li 2011). The Great Leap Forward led to famine on a gigantic scale between 1959 and 1961, which killed around 30 million Chinese. This historical memory about huger and famine shapes the Chinese understanding of food security.

Secondly, grain self-sufficiency matters for political legitimacy. As an old Chinese saying goes, food is the paramount necessity of the people. In thousands years of history of China, rises and falls of the dynasties are closely linked to the production of grain, and the traditional Chinese worldview made the ruler responsible for producing enough grains for his people and providing relief aid in the event of famine. These rulers who ignored this responsibility would face losing the 'Mandate of Heaven', or the right to govern (Manning and Wemheuer 2011). Therefore, understandably, a regime's political support and legitimacy derives from its contribution to the food security of the people. When Chinese communist party took over the rein in 1949, Mao Zedong declared that 'not even one person shall die of hunger'. And the Chinese communist party considers providing enough food for the people as one crucial means to win political support. However, despite Mao's vow and the authority's efforts to build an open government system to address China's food problems, hunger was endemic and the fail of Great Leap Forward had led to the 1959–1961 famine, which was recognized as the worst in human history and killed around 30 million Chinese. In 1978, after the 10-years Cultural Revolution, the communist ideology lost its charm. Moreover, Chinese economy was on the blink of collapse and food was in short supply; the majority of the Chinese did not have enough to eat and 250 million out of 800 million rural residents were impoverished (Du 2006). The Chinese authorities faced serious political legitimacy crisis. To restore its political legitimacy, Chinese authorities started to undertake agricultural reforms to boost the grain production and feed its hungry population. With the introduction of Household Responsibility Systems and government supports, China's grain production, together with the productions of other food products, experienced phenomenal growth; since 1995 China has achieved self-sufficiency in grain and enjoyed grain surplus in following years. In 2001, the then premier Zhu Rongji claimed that for the first time ever in Chinese history, the Chinese Communist Party had succeeded in solving China's food problem, once for all.[2] This success has been portrayed by the Chinese government as a miracle, and presented as strong evidence that only the communist party could save China. Thus, for the Chinese authorities, the 'food problem' is of huge political importance. Grain self-sufficiency is a matter of national pride and it has profound impacts on the Communist Party's political legitimacy.

Thirdly, China's high degree of sensitivity towards grain self-sufficiency is also a product of its unique political structure. It may appear to the outside world that China is an authoritative regime with an all-mighty central government, yet the reality is that there are multiple disconnects between central and local government in China. Over the past three decades, and although China has made tremendous progress in agricultural liberalisation, the central government still plays a key role in this sector; and for historical and practical reasons, local governments have significant autonomy over implementing agricultural policies and allocating funds.

In order to achieve grain self-sufficiency, the Chinese central government has implemented a series of policies to ensure domestic grain production. To ensure grain security, China has set a 'red line' to guarantee its arable land never shrinks to less than 120 million hectares. Also, China has introduced the 95% grain self-sufficiency rate and the Rice Bag Governor Responsibility System to ensure grain production at the local level, to maintain high degree of grain self-sufficiency. These strict and rigid policies, while reflecting China's sensitiveness over its grain self-sufficiency, are also a result of China's domestic politics – the conflicts of interests between central and local governments. Although the central government is committed to ensuring grain security for the nation and promoting farmers' incomes, the local governments show little interest in the agricultural sector for two major reasons. First, agriculture does not help the local government's promotion system. Promotion of local government officials is strongly based on merit, especially their contribution to economic growth. However, agriculture, particularly the grain sector, generates little employment for the local economy and its contribution to GDP growth is negligible. Second, agriculture is less a contributor, more a liability to the local government's fiscal revenue. The local government officials' economic welfare is tightly linked to the total amount of fiscal revenue they can collect. After the agricultural tax reform in 2004, agriculture no longer contributes to local governments' fiscal revenue; instead, the local governments are required to contribute a large of portion of their fiscal revenue to support the agricultural sector, especially local grain production. The conflicts of interests between central and local governments' means that China's current food security system is very fragile, and it is an uphill task to maintain the high grain production level. Hence, in order to safeguard the country's food security, maintain high level grain production, the central government has to be very strict and sensitive towards the country's grain self-sufficiency rate.

Fourthly, China's sensitiveness towards grain self-sufficiency is driven by the desire to protect Chinese farmers. Despite the fact that with rapid industrialization and urbanization, the agricultural sector has taken a lesser and lesser share of China's GDP, the sector still employs more than one third of the country's labour force (Han 2012). Farming, particularly grain farming, still accounts for a major share of the farmer's annual income.

Furthermore, as the Chinese farmers have not received their fair share of the fruits of China's economic development, the income growth of the rural residents has lagged far behind that of their urban counterparts, and a large number of the rural residents, whose livelihoods are mainly dependent on grain farming, are living under the poverty line. Given the China's factor endowments, China's domestically produced grain cannot compete against grains from the United States, European countries and other major grain exporting countries, which enjoy comparative advantages in grain production and provide heavy subsidies to encourage their grain export. This means that once China starts importing grain from the international market, the livelihood of hundreds of millions of grain producers as well as Chinese grain processing enterprises in China will be adversely affected, which will in turn threaten China's social and political stability.

Trust deficit: memories of Cold War-era food weapons

China's sensitivity towards grain self-sufficiency is also influenced by China's interpretation of its external environment, as well as its understanding of the international food system.

To start with, China is concerned that food could be used as a foreign policy tool. As professor Katherine Morton (2012) states, 'In the contemporary era, concerns over the risk that food will be used as a foreign policy tool to undermine China's modernization drive continue to influence how food security is both understood and acted upon'. The experience of economic sanctions during the Cold War is still fresh in the memory of Chinese policy-makers. In 1959, when China suffered from the worst famine in history, the Chinese government desperately approached the international grain market to purchase grains to feed its starving population. However, although China was able to purchase some grains from Canada, it could not purchase enough grains from the international market to feed its people; this was due to the United States' food embargo against China. This painful memory sowed the seeds of distrust, and since then China has veered on the side of suspicion when it comes to the international grain market. In recent years, while geopolitical concerns are deeply caught in the struggle to address the global food security challenge, the debate in China over possible 'grain wars' with the United States has gained some momentum (People's Daily 2010; see also Financial Times 2008; Sullivan 2008). The words of Henry Kissinger – 'Who controls the food supply controls the people; who controls the energy can control whole continents; who controls the money can control the whole world' (Morgan 2011) – are taken as evidence by the Chinese that the United States wishes to use food to control the world. And when the quote is translated in to Chinese, it becomes 'if you control grain, you control the people'. This has led many Chinese commentators to argue that grain self-sufficiency should never be abandoned.

Next, China's sensitivity towards grain self-sufficiency has been a reaction to the international fear of the 'China threat' to global food security. In the mid 1990s, Lester Brown (1995), in his well-known book *Who Will Feed China? A Wake-up Call for a Small Planet*, claimed that an increasingly affluent China would starve the world, which added food as a referent in the narrative of China being a threat to global security. To adhere to its grand strategy of a 'peaceful rise', China's response was to boost the domestic supply of grain through investment and technology. In 1996, China issued a White Paper on its grain issue. In this White Paper, China claims that:

> The basic principle for solving the problem of grain supply and demand in China is to rely on the domestic resources and basically achieve self-sufficiency in grain. China endeavors to increase its grain production so that its self-sufficiency rate of grain under normal conditions will be above 95 per cent and the net import rate five percent, or even less, of the total consumption quantity. (China State Council 1996)

Since then, 95% of grain self-sufficiency rate has become the foundation for China's food security strategy, and over the large two decades, China has more or less achieved the target of maintaining a grain self-sufficiency rate above 95%. However, the 'China as a threat' narrative never stops. In 2008, when the global food crisis swapped the world, many from the west pointed their fingers at large developing countries such as China and India, accusing the rising demand from China and India as a significant cause of the global food crisis. While refuting this accusation, China introduced its first national grain security plan, in which China reiterated its aim to maintain grain self-sufficiency above 95%, and further claimed its aim to achieve 100% cereal self-sufficiency rate between 2008 and 2020 (China State Council 2008).

China's sensitivity over grain self-sufficiency has also, to a large extent, resulted from its concerns over the international grain market. Chinese leaders and scholars have repeatedly claimed that it is wishful thinking for China to rely on the international market to achieve food security for two major reasons. First, the capacity of the international market to regulate grain supply is limited. For example, the total volume of grain traded globally per year is about 250 million tonnes, which is less than half of China's total grain output; the total volume of rice traded globally is 25 to 30 million tonnes, which equates to only 15% of China's rice consumption per year (Han 2012). This shows that there are huge uncertainties and potential risks in the international food market. Third, the 'large country effect' is prominent in China. Specifically, any rise in global food prices would lead to higher import costs. Moreover, considering the huge scale of China's territory, procuring grain in the international market would be made uneconomical because of the great distances and high logistical costs involved, even if there were sufficient supply.

Furthermore, the international grain market is unstable and poorly constructed. The international grain trade, particularly the wheat, corn and soybeans trades, are tightly controlled by the United States and other developed countries, either through government or their multinational food enterprises such as Archer Daniel Midlands ADM, Bunge, Cargill and Louis Dreyfus. The international grain trade regime serves the interests of the exporting countries and is biased towards the grain importing nations. For decades, agricultural trade liberalization has mainly been targeted at opening the market for grain-export from the United States and other grain export giants, and reducing grain importing tariffs and other trade distorting barriers. Yet, it has done little to regulate or restrict the behaviours of the grain exporting countries. This presents a huge risk for the countries which rely on the international grain market for food, and it is a threat to global food security. A study on the 2007-2008 global food crisis, by the International Food Policy Research Institute (IFPRI), identified grain exporting countries' "export ban" to be the most decisive contributor, while noting that financial speculation, depreciation of the US dollar and reduction in grain stock were also factors to take note of (Headey 2011). This has led to even deeper distrust, on the part of the Chinese government, towards the international food regime.

Influenced historical memories of famine, concerned about its political legitimacy, troubled by conflicts of interest between central and local government and alarmed by the unreliability of the international grain market, China has been very sensitive towards the country's food self-sufficiency, grain self-sufficiency in particular. Yet, facing limited water and land resources, it is becoming ever more challenging for China to feed its increasingly affluent population. China is gradually looking outwards to search for food. However, China's agricultural 'Going-out' has quickly aroused concerns from the international community, thus facing a lot of resistances. The second part of the paper will address this issue.

China's overseas activities in agriculture

While China is determined to achieve food security through boosting domestic agricultural productions, China has being undertaking agricultural operations overseas in a variety of forms. Over the past three decades, China's overseas agricultural activities have expanded dramatically. To take China's agricultural Outward Foreign Direct Investment (OFDI) as an example, in 2010, China agricultural outward foreign direct investment reached USD 534 million and accumulated agricultural OFDI totaled USD 2.62 billion. In the same year, 468 Chinese agricultural corporations invested abroad and there were about 768 agricultural corporations registered by the Chinese in foreign countries (W. Chen 2012). Based on the flow of China's agricultural OFDI, the major destinations for China's agricultural investment are Russia, Southeast Asia, Europe and America.

Currently, China has built production bases for cereal, soybeans, rubber, palm oil, palm oil, sisal and other agricultural products in Russia, Southeast Asia, Central Asia, Latin America and other areas. China has set up agricultural technological demonstration centers in the Philippines, Cambodia, Indonesia, Malaysia and some African countries. China has established agricultural R&D exchanges and economic cooperation with major international agricultural and finance organizations, as well as over 140 countries and regions. Also, China has formed close to 60 bilateral agriculture or fishery cooperation working groups with over 50 countries and regions, and China is undertaking fishing operations in the exclusive economic zones (EEZs) of over 30 countries including Indonesia, Myanmar, Sri Lanka, Fuji, and Argentina and in the high seas of the Pacific, Atlantic and Indian Oceans (W. Chen 2012). By the end of 2010, the total number of Chinese distant water fishing (DWF) vessels topped 1991 – the largest in the world (see China's 12th Five-year Plan, nd). It has been estimated that China's distant water fishing sector provides employment for over 50,000 people and generates annual revenue reaching RMB 10 billion (Ji et al. 2010).

In addition, China has become one of the leading countries in the world in providing agricultural assistance and emergency relief to food insecure developing countries, particularly the poverty stricken African states. In terms of agricultural assistance, China mainly focus on the following areas, including:

> ... building farms, agro-technology demonstration centers, and experiment and promotion stations of agro-technology; constructing farmland irrigation and water-conservancy projects; supplying agricultural machinery and implements, farm produce processing equipment and related agricultural materials; dispatching agro-technicians and senior agricultural experts to pass on agricultural production technologies and provide consultations on rural development, and training agricultural personnel for recipient countries. (China State Council, 2011b)

By the end of 2009, China had aided 221 agricultural projects in other developing countries which consist of 35 farms, 47 agro-technology experiment and promotion stations, 11 animal husbandry projects, 15 fisheries projects, 47 farmland irrigation and water-conservancy projects, and 66 other types of agricultural projects, in addition to donating a large amount of agricultural equipment and materials to them (China State Council 2011b). In 2010, at the UN High-level Meeting on the Millennium Development Goals, China further pledged to establish 30 demonstration centers for agricultural technologies in other developing countries, to dispatch

3000 agricultural experts and technicians to these countries, and to invite 5000 agricultural personnel from these countries to China for training (Morton 2012). Moreover, China has emerged as one of the top donors of food in the world in recent years. Right after China officially made the transition from food recipient to food donor, China provided 577,000 tonnes of grain to the WFP. In 2011, as the first country joined the Strategic Alliance for South–South Cooperation lead by FAO, China donated US$30 million to a trust fund to assist developing countries' agricultural development. When the food security situation exacerbated in East Africa, China provided close to USD 70 million in food aid to help those countries to combat hunger (see *Chinanews* 2011).

However, in the past several years, in conjunction with the significant rise of China's overseas agricultural activities, wide suspicions and concerns have arisen about China's role in global food security. In particular, China's land acquisition abroad, pejoratively called 'land grabbing', has been taken as a threat to global food security, and its fishing operations in African waters have been criticized for causing overfishing and exacerbating the fragile food security conditions of African countries. While both statistical and empirical evidences tend to suggest that some of the claims about Chinese land grabs, particularly in Africa, has been overstated and politicized, there is a clear lack of constructive dialogue between China and the international community over China's overseas agricultural operations. The second part of this paper wishes to bridge this gap through reviewing the evolution of China's overseas agricultural operations, analyzing its motives and drivers, and uncovering the shortfalls in China's agricultural operations overseas.

Evolution of China's overseas agricultural activities

China's overseas agricultural operation is not a new phenomenon, although a full article merits a separate accounting (Zha 2010). In the 1960s, China started its overseas agricultural assistance programme. Between the early 1960s and mid 1980s, China's Guangdong Nongken Corp took over 20 agricultural assistance projects to countries such as Vietnam, Cambodia and Mali. From 1979 to 1987, China has sponsored 19 agricultural assistance projects, many of these more focused towards African countries. In those projects, China provided finance, seeds, and agricultural technicians to the respective countries, which in turn offered valuable insight for for China, when it came to overseas agricultural expansion. For instance, from 1960 to 1979, five friendship farms in Tanzania and Somalia were aided by Xinjiang Production and Construction Corps, and laid the foundation for the subsequent overseas crop plantation (Wang 2010).

Since the Reform and Opening up in 1978, while China has continued offering agricultural aid to foreign countries, it has also begun to undertake agricultural operations in foreign countries for profit. For instance, in 1989, China Nongken purchased 430,000 hectares of land in Queensland, Australia, to build a farm. This farm is mainly used for the cultivation of animal husbandry and as a vegetable plantation, the products of which are sold at the local market. In 1998, China's Xintian Corp (Xinjiang Production and Construction Corps) bought 1050 hectares of land in Mexico to plant rice. Since the 1990s, China's small and medium investors have voluntarily travelled abroad to acquire land for crop plantation. For example, private enterprises from the Zhejiang provinces traveled abroad to seek investment opportunities in the agricultural sector. So far, there are over 500,000 entrepreneurs from Zhejiang province undertaking business in agricultural sectors in over 40 countries or regions worldwide, leasing farm land over 200,000 hectares (GDCCT 2012). In addition, farmers from the Heilongjiang province crossed the borders to farm in Russia's Far East (Kramer 2012). There has been rapid inflow of Chinese farm labour in Russia, which reflects the growing agricultural ties between the two countries, one rich in land and resources, the other in people. One report said that every year there are over 20,000 Chinese farmers entering Russia through the border city of Tongjiang, Heilongjiang Province, and that this number is growing. Chinese farmers grow soybeans, corns and vegetables on Russian land and sell their agricultural produce at the local markets.

In the twenty-first century, with China's relations with foreign countries, particularly ASEAN nations and African countries, further strengthened, and stimulated by the rising global food prices since 2006, China's overseas agricultural activities have expanded notably. China's state-owned corporations and private enterprises began to acquire foreign land on a large scale. China's Chongqing Grain Group (CGG), one of China's largest state-owned grain companies, is one of the leading companies in China's agricultural overseas expansion. In 2009, CGG signed a contract with CCAN of Canada to purchase 6667 hectares of land in Saskatchewan, Canada through joint ventures with local firms to produce rape (Chongqing Municipal Government 2009). In 2011, CGG made a 2.5 billion investment in a Brazilian soybean base, which aims to send soybeans back to China to satisfy the country's rising demand for feed and edible oil. In 2012, CGG planned to work together with an Argentine Company to rent a 10,000 hectare soybean farm to produce soybeans. The announced investment was $10 million. The Beidahuang Nongken Group is another state-owned farming company, which is leading China's quest for expansion of its agricultural operations overseas. Since 2008, the company has been expanding its farming operations overseas. Currently, it owns land in Latin America, Africa, Russia and the Philippines. It plans to purchase 300,000 hectares of land in Argentina to grow crops to export to China. Not only investing in Africa, the Far East and South East Asia, the Beidahuang Nongken Group is now expanding its presence in Australia. In November 2012, it was reported that the company was planning to buy and lease more than

100,000 hectares of land as part of its USD 4 billion investment to create a supply chain to grow grain for export direct from West Australia to China (*The West Australian* 2012).

What is also noteworthy is that China's overseas agricultural expansion, particularly in reference to land acquisition in recent years, mainly occurs in the Asia Pacific. Contrary to common perception, China's land purchase or leasing numbers have been overblown by the media and some non-profit organizations. For instance, China's ZTE Agribusiness, which was reported to have bought three million hectares of land in the Democratic Republic of Congo to grow oil palm, was actually investing $880m in 200,000 hectares of land worldwide, of which 100,000 hectares were in the Congo, according to Standard Chartered (Vidal 2012).

China's overseas agricultural operation is not a new phenomenon but a continuous and lasting trend. In recent years, the rapid expansion of Chinese overseas agricultural operations has been encouraged by the Chinese government under the agricultural going-out strategy. As claimed by the Chinese authority, this strategy is not a sudden idea, but rather a scientific decision that China made after drawing upon the experiences of other countries, absorbing the research findings of its predecessors and assimilating the advanced cultural heritages and the achievement of civilization of the world over (Ministry of Agriculture of China 2009a). It is also a learning-by-doing process. For instance, in 2011, the Chongqing Grain Group (CGG) invested in 200,000 hectares of soybean production in Brazil to help secure supply, but after it made the first shipment of soybeans, the company met fierce resistance from local people and government. To overcome the obstacles, CGG changed its strategy from merely sourcing soybeans to building a soybean industrial base in Brazil, promising to not only to buy soybeans from local producers but also manufacture soy locally to expand local employment and contribute to the local fiscal revenue. Also, instead of directly purchasing land, CGG lent money to local soybean producers at discount rates, enabling them to expand their land and upgrade their equipment. In return, the company can exercise the option of buying soybeans at pre-determined rates (Xinhuanet 2012). This case illustrates how China's agriculture market players have grown, becoming more attuned and responsive to local sensitivities.

'Going-out' strategy: a partial assessment

China's growing agricultural activities in foreign countries should not be seen as separate from the country's grand 'Going-out' strategy. The pace of China's overseas agricultural activities is in consistence with the strategy. In 2000, the Chinese government officially introduced the 'Going-out' policy to enhance the global expansion of the Chinese companies. For the 'Going-out' strategy of China's agricultural sector, the initial focus was

Table 5 China's outward agricultural FDI and total FDI

	Agricultural OFDI	Total OFDI	Share	Accumulated agricultural OFDI	Accumulated total OFDI	Share
2004	288.66	5497.99	5.25%	834.23	44777.26	1.86%
2005	105.36	12261.17	0.86%	511.62	57205.62	0.89%
2006	185.04	21163.96	0.87%	816.7	90630.91	0.90%
2007	271.71	26506.09	1.03%	1206.05	117910.5	1.02%
2008	171.83	55907.17	0.31%	1467.62	183970.7	0.80%
2009	342.79	56528.99	0.61%	2028.44	245755.4	0.83%
2010	533.98	68811.31	0.78%	2612.08	317210.6	0.82%
Change	84.99%	1151.57%		213.11%	608.42%	

Source: 2010 Statistical Bulletin of China's Outward Foreign Direct Investment.

given to natural rubber, oil-bearing crops, cotton, vegetables and timer. The Chinese Central Government's Number 1 Document in 2007 called for the rapid implementation of China's agricultural 'Going-out'. This strategy covers a mix of goals which include promoting agricultural exports, foreign cooperation, external assistance, and direct investment in agriculture overseas (W. Chen 2012).

As shown in Table 5, the significant rise in China's overseas agricultural investment runs parallel with the dramatic expansion of China's overall investment abroad. Also, although from 2004 to 2010 China's agricultural outward foreign direct investment increased from 288.7 million to 534.0 million by 85%, China's total outward foreign direct investment increased by more than 115 times. The share of agricultural OFDI in China's total OFDI decreased from 5% to 0.78% from 2004 to 2012. A similar pattern has been observed with regards to the accumulated OFDI. What the above implies is that China's growing agricultural activities in foreign countries should be interpreted against the backdrop of China's rapid global expansion, and China's agricultural expansion is still very marginal compared with other sectors as such as mining, manufacturing, wholesaling and retailing and transportation.

In addition, China's agricultural 'Going-out' strategy runs in parallel with the country's agricultural 'bring in', both of which are considered to be of critical importance to China's efforts to modernize its agricultural sector. As the Chinese government claimed (Ministry of Agriculture of China 2009a):

> To keep up with the trend of economic globalization and regional integration and actively participate in the international division of labor and international competition, we should both 'bring in' and

'go global' to constantly upgrade the international competitiveness of Chinese agriculture.

China's agricultural modernization has lagged behind in China as compared with the country's remarkable process in industrialization and urbanization. The backwardness of China's agriculture sector not only threatens the country's food security, but also holds back China's overall modernization, in addition to undermining the sustainable development of the rural economy and society. Against this backdrop, renewed attention has been given to the development of China's agricultural sector. Since 2003, for nine consecutive years, China's Number 1 Document has put the issue of agriculture, farming and rural affairs at the top of the central government's agenda. Shortages in capital and technological inputs are frequently identified to be the main obstacles against further expansion of the country's agricultural sector. While the Chinese government is increasing its fiscal expenditures towards agriculture, the country also strives to attract foreign investment to modernize its agricultural sector. As Table 6 shows, from 2000 to 2011, FDI in China's agricultural sector expanded phenomenally, and this has made a great contribution to the development of the country's agricultural sector. Japan, Singapore, and other countries have leased large areas of land to produce food to meet their domestic demands. China considers FDI beneficial to the country's agricultural development as foreign investors bridge the financial gap, create jobs opportunities for farmers, and bring advanced technological and management know-how, as well as market access. Therefore, learning from its own experience, China feels that its agricultural expansion overseas is beneficial to both itself and the host countries.

Table 6 China's use of FDI in the agricultural sector

Year	Number of projects	Value, USD million
2000	821	676
2001	887	899
2002	975	1027
2003	1116	1000
2004	1130	1114
2005	1058	718
2006	951	600
2007	1048	924
2008	917	1191
2009	896	1429
2010	929	1912
2011	865	2009

Source: National Bureau of Statistics of China, multiple years.

Multiple drivers

The international community's sensitivity over China's overseas agricultural expansion lies in the perception that China is grabbing land from foreign countries – particularly countries in Africa which are mostly food insecure – to grow grain and other agricultural products to ship back to China. Yet, the Chinese government has claimed that China has never shipped even a single grain from Africa back to China. If this is the case, the question arises as to what the driver is for China's overseas agricultural expansion, if not to produce grains for domestic consumption?

It is undeniable that a food security concern is one of the major drivers for China's overseas agricultural expansion. Although the Chinese government still firmly believes that grain self-sufficiency is the fundamental solution to China's food security, it realizes that China's food security is increasingly interlinked to that of the international food market, and also that – this being so – China needs to utilize the international resources to better safeguard the country's food security (Changfu 2012). Chinese state-owned farming groups' investment in Argentina, Brazil, Canada and other countries for soybeans and rape production comes mainly out of concerns of China's overreliance on the international market for soybeans and oilseed; and the expansion of China's distant water fishing is also a means to meet China's rising demand for aquatic products. However, when it comes to the core of China's food security – grain security/cereal security – to be precise, so far, China's overseas agricultural expansion does not intend to plant cereals abroad for domestic consumptions, though it seems to be a long term trend. There are three reasons for this. Firstly, unlike the production of soybeans and other agricultural productions, China's cereal production is sufficient to meet domestic demand. The demand and supply gap is very marginal; hence, so far there is no need for China to produce cereal abroad for domestic consumption. Secondly, it is not economically viable for Chinese companies to produce cereal abroad and ship it back to China. According to a report by the Standard Charter Bank, domestic infrastructure bottlenecks contribute to high transport costs and mean that, even given high grain prices, exporting grain back to China does not make economic sense. Therefore, cereal as well as other agricultural products produced in China's overseas farmers are mainly sold at the local market or exported to European and other developed countries. Thirdly, the Chinese government still tightly controls the export and import of grains. A Chinese company has to go through a series of administrative procedures if it wishes to export grains produced abroad to back to China. Of course, shipping grain back to China is not the only way to contribute to China's food security. As echoed by Chen Xiwen, deputy head of China's central agricultural working group, if China's overseas agricultural operations could help to release the potentials of global grain production, the increase in global grain supply could in itself be a strong support to China's food security.This will be beneficial to all countries in the world.

Next, as admitted by Chinese Agricultural Minister Hang Changfu (2012), China's agricultural modernization, as compared with industrialization and urbanization, has lagged behind, and this is due to natural and historical factors. China's agricultural sector, accounting for close to 40% of the country's total employment, only contributed towards 10.2% of the GDP in 2010, and the agricultural trade deficit exceeded 30 USD billion in the same year (C. Han 2012). This means that large numbers of people are still held up in rural areas, creating a large surplus of agricultural labour. China's agricultural sector is still dominated by small household farming, of which farming methods are pretty primitive. To pursue a modern agriculture pathway, opening up the country's agriculture sector, drawing upon capital, technology, and management experiences from the outside world is important. As evidenced in an official report on international cooperation and exchange in agriculture published in 2009:

We should make the best of the opportunities brought about by globalization to use foreign capital, introduce technology, varieties and management expertise and to upgrade industrial structure so as to enhance our comprehensive competitiveness and implement the strategy of 'agriculture and agricultural products going global. (Ministry of Agriculture of China 2009a).

Moreover, as it has been repeatedly advocated, China also aims to promote the export of Chinese agricultural products though agriculture 'going-out'. As it has been said, China's agricultural 'going-out', in the broad sense, also includes agricultural products going out. China's labour-intensive agricultural products enjoy a certain advantage, and its agriculture is also in an advantageous position as compared with some countries. However, the country's agricultural export is supplied in small batches, which involves many varieties with the small and medium sized enterprises as the major players. In addition, China's agricultural export market is too concentrated and is facing more and more trade barriers. As a result, Chinese agricultural export is challenged by difficulties in transportation and sales, high costs, thinly-spread profits and weak profit motivation (Ministry of Agriculture of China 2009a). Furthermore, Chinese agricultural enterprises are lack independent branding and the motivation and initiative to tap a new market. Therefore, China's agriculture-going out could contribute to China's agricultural export through smoothing supply chain management, reducing trade barriers, building up the brand names of China's agricultural products and other means.

China's overseas agricultural expansion is also driven by diplomatic purpose. In an official document published by the Ministry of Agriculture in

2009, it stated that China 'should unleash the advantage of agricultural international cooperation in diplomacy to upgrade the "soft power" of China' (Ministry of Agriculture of China 2009b). Agriculture has always been an important tool for China's foreign policy. Since the 1960s, China has used agricultural assistance to foreign countries, particularly countries in Africa, to enhance China's relations with the outside world and to create a favourable international environment for China's development. With over 30 years of rapid development, though still facing challenges, China's agricultural sector has advanced notably. The development paths of China's agricultural sector as well as China's food security strategy are very valuable references for other developing countries which have suffered from food insecurity. In the areas of hybrid rice plantation, aquaculture, biotechnology, farm produce, machinery, and agricultural fiancé, China also has a lot to offer to developing countries, which could contribute to the development of their agricultural sectors. As food security emerges as one of the top threats to global stability and prosperity, China believes that the expansion of China's overseas agricultural operations contribute to the global efforts to fight hunger, which can increase China's international influence, and create image of being a responsible global power.

Finally, although the Chinese government voices many grand objectives while promoting the country's overseas agricultural expansion, the policy implementers – either the state-owned enterprises or private companies or individual farmers – are driven mainly by profit. They do not care much about the country's food security, and their investment decisions are shaped largely, if not entirely, by market forces. Even these state-owned farming companies have become more and more profit oriented. In pursuit of profit, they determine their own expansion path in foreign countries. This is the main reason why they tend to sell the agricultural produce at the local market, or export to the European countries, given that it is not profitable for them to ship overseas produces back to China.

Overseas agricultural operations, particularly with regards to purchase or leasing land in foreign countries, is not just a unique Chinese phenomenon. As matter of fact, Japan, South Korea, and Gulf countries are the leaders in purchasing or leasing land in developing countries, and American and European firms have long been champions in expanding their presences on the foreign market (FAO 2012). As mentioned above, China's agricultural going-out strategy was introduced after China's in-depth study of the experiences of other countries, particularly its Asian neighbours such as Korea and Japan. Japan's overseas' farm land is three times that of its domestic arable land, and South Korea has rented half of Madawaska's arable land (GDCCT 2012). On the contrary, China's overseas' land purchase or lease is quite marginal, yet the international community voiced far more concerns over China's 'land grabbing'. The reasons why China's overseas agricultural expansion has drawn so much international suspicious are twofold. On the one hand, the 'China factor' has a big impact. As the most populous country in the world, China's food security condition is always a top concern with regards to global food security. However, there is a lack of transparency in China's food security conditions. Although China claims that it has maintained 95% of grain self-sufficiency over the last decade, and that it has ample grain reserves, there are suspicions that China's grain production – as well as the amount of grain reserved – could be overstated. Hence, China's overseas agricultural operations inevitably invite questions as to whether the country is outsourcing its domestic food problems to other countries. As the most populous country in the world, and with the largest foreign exchange reserve, the international community is highly concerned about any potential shifts in China's food security strategy. On the other hand, the global sentiment towards foreign countries overseas' agricultural operation, particularly land grabbing, has shifted. For decades, world food prices had been kept artificially low as the world food market was flooded with cheap grains from the United States, European countries and other grain exporters, where the governments provided heavy subsidy for grain production and export. Low food prices sidelined global food security problems, and led to inattention to the agricultural sector, particularly in developing countries. Against that backdrop, investments from Japan, South Korea, and Gulf countries in the developing countries' agricultural sector – through land purchasing or leasing, or other channels – were overlooked or even welcomed. However, by the time China tried to follow the path of its Asian neighbours to expand agricultural operations overseas, the international environment had changed. With the outbreak of the global food crisis in 2006, food security was back at the top of global political agenda, and renowned attention has been given to food productions in poverty-stricken countries such as the Sub-Saharan region. In this context, the expansion of China's agricultural operations in developing countries was viewed with concern and suspicion.

Conclusion

With dramatic rise in food prices, renewed attention is being given to global food security, which has emerged as one of the most acute problems of our time. The central role of China in the global food security is an issue for agricultural and more generally macro-economists to debate. With rapid globalization and trade liberalization, while the concept of food security has changed dramatically from being production centered to being more concerned about accessibility, affordability and availability, and utilization of food to all, food self-sufficiency and grain self-sufficiency in particular is still paramount in the Chinese context. Notwithstanding the increasing unsustainability of China's agricultural sectors in addition to the huge economic costs suffered by the Chinese farmers, the Chinese are determined to achieve self-sufficiency in supplying farm produce, especially grain. The reasons for China's sensitiveness towards grain self-sufficiency are twofold. On the one hand, China's sensitiveness towards grain self-sufficiency is a domestic construct. It is influenced by historical memories of famine, concerns over political legitimacy, and conflicts of interest between central and local government. On the other hand, China's sensitiveness towards grain self-sufficiency is also shaped by China's interpretation of its external environment, as well as its under-standing of the international food system.

Yet, fully aware that the country has a severe shortage of agricultural resources in per capita terms, especially in land and fresh water supply, China is also increasingly expanding its agricultural presence overseas while upholding its long-standing policy of grain self-sufficiency. However, there seems to be a lack of effective dialogue between epistemic communi-ties in China and outside over China's overseas agricultural activities in recent years. To understand the causes for this lack of effective dialogue, this paper reviews the revolution of China's overseas agricultural activities, the recent contexts as well as its multiple drivers. This paper finds that: first, China's agricultural expansion overseas is not a new phenomenon, but has roots dating back to the 1960s; second, the recent surge of China's agricul-tural expansion overseas is part of the country's grand 'Going-out' strategy and agriculture also takes a very small share in China's overall 'Going out' efforts; third, China's agricultural 'going-out' is in parallel with the country's agricultural 'bring in', both of which are considered of critical importance to China's efforts to modernize its agricultural sector; fourth, China's overseas agricultural expansion is not driven by the desire to pro-duce grains for the country's domestic consumption; rather, it is a compli-cated process involving a wide range of players and driven by multiple objectives including economic incentive, efforts to modernize its agricul-ture, and diplomatic goals. The international community's insufficient understanding of the nature and the complexity of China's overseas agri-cultural expansion is one of the major factors leading to this lack of effec-tive dialogue with China on the issue. Meanwhile, what should not be overlooked is that China's overseas agricultural expansion, particularly in recent years, is a learning-by-doing process. The lack of experience of Chinese government and China's agribusiness firms as well as its obsolete business model in undertaking cross border agricultural operations led to resistances of local community as well as a negative impression of interna-tional observers towards China's overseas agricultural expansion.

As the most populous country in the world and being the leading pro-ducer and consumer of food products, it is critical for China to integrate itself into the global food system to safeguard food security for both China and the world. Considering the dramatic changes in diet and the food pref-erences of the Chinese as well as the huge environmental, economic and social costs, China needs to replace the increasingly obsolete political promise of ensuring grain self-sufficiency with a grand food security concept that focuses on availability, accessibility, affordability and utilization of food. It is in the long term interests of China and the world for China to adjust its agricultural plantation structures. Furthermore, the role of agriculture should be highlighted in addressing global food insecurity, particularly in the developing countries. A thriving agriculture sector is the best guarantor to global food security. After decades of under-investment in the agricultural sector word wide, there is an urgent need for capital flow into the agricultural sector to boost global food production. As the second largest economy with largest foreign reserve in the world, in addition to being a leader in agricultural technology and management as well as successful experience in transforming its agricultural sector, China's overseas agricultural expansion, although it needs to be carefully monitored, should not be feared by the international community. It is important for China to adopt an inclusive strategy in its overseas agricultural expansion which takes full consideration of China's rising demand for food, the interests of the local community, and environmental sustainability as well as the food security concerns of host countries. Only then could a win–win outcome could be achieved and China's food system serve as a positive model to the world.

Acknowledgements

We are thankful to the editor of *The Pacific Review* for challenging us to think through this complex topic and the reviewers for useful comments. Errors and opinions are our sole responsibility.

Notes

1 Xinhuanet: http://news.xinhuanet.com/food/2013-03/12/c_124444920.htm.
2 See Zhu Rongjie's speech at the 6th World Chinese Entrepreneurs Convention, September 17–19, 2011, Nanjing.

References

Brown, L. (1995) *Who Will Feed China? A Wake-up Call for a Small Planet*, New York: W. W. Norton.
Carter, C. A. and Rozlle, S. (2002) 'Will China's agricultural trade reflect its comparative advantage?' in R. Gale (ed.) *China's Food and Agriculture: Issues for the Twenty-first Century*, Washington, DC: USDA, pp. 27–30.
Changfu, H. (2012) *Han Changfu: To Create New Dimensions in Agricultural Economy Following the Scientific Development Concept*, July 2; accessed at http://www.gov.cn/jrzg/2012-07/02/content_2174953.htm, 2 December 2012.
Chen, W. (2012) 'China's agricultural going-out: current status, problems and solutions', *International Economic Cooperation*, January, 32–37 [in Chinese].

Chen, X. (2012) *2012 China High Level Agricultural Development Forum held in Agricultural University of China*, May 23; accessed at http://finance.chinanews.com/cj/2012/05-23/3909375.shtml, 2 December 2012.

Cheng, F. and Beghin, J. C. (2000) *Food Self-suficiency, Comparative Advantage and Agricultural Trade: A Policy Analysis Matrix for Chinese Agriculture*, Working Paper, Ames: Iowa State University.

China's 12th Five-year Plan on Fishery Development (nd); accessed at http://www.moa.gov.cn/zwllm/ghjh/201110/t20111017_2357716.htm, 23 April 2012.

Chinanews. (2011) 'China provides Africa the largest food assistance since 1949', *Chinanews*, September 25; accessed at http://www.chinanews.com/gn/2011/09-25/3351368.shtml, 2 December 2012.

China State Council. (1996) *The Grain Issue in China*, White Paper, Beijing: Information Office of the State Council.

China State Council. (2008) *Mid- and Long-term Grain Security Plan*, Policy Guideline, Beijing: Information Office of the State Council.

China State Council. (2011a) *White Paper On China's Peaceful Development*, Beijing: China State Council.

China State Council. (2011b) *China's Foreign Aid*, White Paper, Beijing: Information Office of the State Council of China.

Chongqing Municipal Government. (2009) *Chongqing Grain Group Investing USD 2 Billion Abroad to Farm*, March 28; accessed at http://www.cq.gov.cn/today/news/139012.htm, 23 October 2012.

Du, R. (2006) *The Course Of China's Rural Reform*, Research Paper, Washington, DC: The International Food Policy Research Institute.

FAO. (1996) 'Rome Declaration on World Food Security and World Food Summit Plan of Action', *World Food Summit 13–17 November 1996*, Rome: FAO.

FAO. (2012) *Trends and Impacts of Foreign Investment in Developing Country Agriculture*, Rome: FAO.

Financial Times (2008) 'How China deal with the global food crisis', *Financial Times*, May 8; accessed at   http://www.ftchinese.com/story/001019233, 12 December 2012.

GDCCT. (2012) 'Going farming abroad', *GDCCT* 1(1): 16–20.

Han, C. (2012) 'Accelerating the modernization of agriculture.', *Qiushi Journal* 4(1): 46–52.

Headey, D. (2011) 'Rethinking the global food crisis: the role of trade shocks', *Food Policy* 36(2): 136–146.

Ji, X., Liu, S. and Task Force. (2010) 'To support distant water fishing as a strategic industry', *China National Conditions and Strength*, September, 7–11 [in Chinese].

Kramer, A. E. (2012) 'Nation rich in land draws workers from one rich in people', *New York Times*, September; accessed at   http://www.nytimes.com/2012/09/11/business/global/in-russia-chinese-run-farms-solve-each-sides-needs.html?pagewanted=all, 23 November 2012.

Li, L. (2007) *Fighting Famine in North China*, Stanford: Stanford University Press.

Li, X. (2011) 'Virtural land import is the approach to safeguard current and future China grain security', *Agricultural Outlook*, October: 28–31 [in Chinese].

Lu, F. (1998) 'Grain versus food: a hidden issue in China's food policy debate', *World Development* 26(9): 1641–1652.

Mallory, W. H. (1926) *China: Land of Famine*, New York: American Geographic Society.

Manning, K. E. and Wemheuer, F. (2011) *Eating Bitterness*, Toronto: UBC Press.

Mao, Y. and Zhao, N. (2011) *Which China's Grain Security Should Depend on: Planning or Market?*, Beijing: IPPH.

Ministry of Agriculture of China. (2009a) *International Cooperation and Exchange in Agriculture Shall Persist with 4 Fundamental Concepts and Beliefs*, Policy Report, Beijing: Ministry of Agriculture of China.

Ministry of Agriculture of China. (2009b) *Unleash the Advantage of Agricultural International Cooperation in Diplomacy*, Policy Report, Beijing: Ministry of Agriculture of China.

Morgan, I. (2011) *The American Economy and America's Global Power*, Special Report, London: LSE Ideas.

Morton, K. (2012) *Learning by Doing: China's Role in the Global Governance of Food Security*, Working Paper, Indiana: Indiana University.

Mukherjee, A. (2012) *Food security in Asia*, New Delhi: Sage.

National Bureau of Statistics of China. (nd) *China Statistics Year Book*, Beijing: National Bureau Statistics of China, Mutiple Years.

People's Daily (2010) 'The United States has waged smokeless grain war against China', *People's Daily*, June 3; accessed at http://world.people.com.cn/GB/157578/11767832.html, 12 December 2012.

South China Morning Press. (nd) 'China must invest abroad food security forum told', *South China Morning Press*; accessed at http://www.scmp.com/business/economy/article/1133255/china-must-invest-abroad-food-security-forum-told, 12 December 2012.

Sullivan, K. (2008) Washington Post Kevin Sullivan. 'Food crisis is depicted as "silent tsunami"', *Washington Post*, April 23; accessed at http://www.washingtonpost.com/wp-dyn/content/article/2008/04/22/AR2008042201481.html, 12 December 2012.

The West Australian. (2012) 'Chinese buy farms for food', November 30; accessed at http://au.news.yahoo.com/thewest/a/-/newshome/15517531/chinese-buy-farms-for-food/, 1 December 2012.

US International Trade Commisssion. (2011) *China's Agricultural Trade: Competitive Conditions and Effects on US Exports*, Washington, DC: USITC.

USITC. (2011) *China's Consumption of Agricultural Products Increasing Substaintially as Income Rise, Says USITC*, March 22; accessed at http://www.usitc.gov/press_room/news_release/2011/er0322jj1.htm, 23 October 2012.

Vidal, J. (2012) 'Chinese food security may be motivating investments in Africa', May 12; accessed at http://www.guardian.co.uk/global-development/2012/may/10/chinese-food-security-investments-africa?newsfeed=true, 23 October 2012.

Wang, Y. (2010) 'Zhongguo de Haiwai Nongzuowu Zhongzhi: guimo yu zhenglun' [China's involvement in overseas agricultural plantation activities: scope and debates], *Guoji Zhengzhi Yanjiu* [International Politics Quarterly] June: 10–38.

Xinhuanet. (2012) 'Xinhua insight: twists and turns for Chinese SOEs abroad', September 28; accessed at http://news.xinhuanet.com/english/china/2012-09/28/c_131879656.htm, 1 December 2012.

Xu, D. and Li, X. (2010) *Jingji Mingmai Xi Sannong*, Beijing: China Machine Press.

Ye, L. and Van Ranst, E. (2009) 'Production scenarios and the effect of soil degradation on long-term food security in China', *Global Environmental Change* 19(4): 464–481.

Zha Daojiong, Guoji Zhengzhi Yanjiu yu Zhongguo de Liangshi Anquan [International Studies Research and China's Food Security], Guoji Zhengzhi Yanjiu [International Politics Quarterly], June 2010, pp. 1–9.

Supermarkets, iron buffalos and agrarian myths: exploring the drivers and impediments to food systems modernisation in Southeast Asia

J. Jackson Ewing

Abstract Southeast Asian food systems are changing rapidly. Populations are growing and urbanising, production and consumption choices are shifting, and food value chains are experiencing a myriad of ripple effects from rural hinterlands to city marketplaces. These systemic changes are inconsistent, however, and variable challenges define key sectors. Distribution chains, wholesaling, food processing, retail and supermarkets, and other midstream and downstream segments of regional food systems are undergoing transformative and largely unhindered change. On-farm modernisation and trade liberalisation are occurring more haltingly. Previous advances in food production technology and methods have lost momentum, and much of the region faces confronting questions about how to produce adequate and appropriate food in light of shifting demographics, environmental stress, land scarcities, market manipulations and other defining regional characteristics. This paper juxtaposes these challenges with remarkable distribution chain evolutions, and focuses upon three impediments to further shifts in regional food systems: (1) the perpetuation of agrarian mythologies, (2) push-back against rice market integration, and (3) regulatory barriers to the adoption of genetically modified (GM) plants. These seemingly disparate dynamics actually have points of convergence, and are unified in their negative overall impacts on regional food security. This paper explores reasons behind the pervasiveness of these impediments and argues for supply-oriented improvements in the regional food systems.

Introduction

There is a disconnect between value chain and food supply modernisation efforts in Southeast Asian. Distribution chains, wholesaling, food processing, retail and supermarkets, and other midstream and downstream segments of regional food systems are undergoing transformative change (Reardon et al. 2013). These changes, which some authors call a food systems 'revolution' (Reardon and Timmer 2012), have accelerated over the past two decades and are likely to continue to do so particularly in Southeast Asia's least developed countries.

On-farm modernisation is occurring more haltingly. Previous advances in food production technology and methods have lost momentum, and much of the region faces confronting questions about how to produce adequate and appropriate food in light of shifting demographics, environmental stress, land scarcities, market manipulations and other defining regional characteristics. Compounding these questions are a series of impediments to food supply that are paramount to the region's food future.

These impediments are the focus of this paper, which proceeds in two primary sections. The first section investigates changes in regional food value chains and asks what these changes mean for food security and for food supply requirements. It then briefly frames a debate on agricultural modernisation and argues for its judicious progress in Southeast Asia. The second section explores why such regional modernisation is progressing slowly on the supply side, and presents three key impediments to improving supply resilience: (1) so-called 'agrarian myths' that perpetuate rural stereotypes, (2) push-back among key regional players against market integration in the rice sector, and (3) regulatory barriers to the adoption of genetically modified (GM) plants. These seemingly disparate dynamics actually possess points of convergence, and are unified in their negative impacts on regional food security. The subjects of the paper's two main sections are closely interlinked but clearly not moving in tandem. Growing urbanisation and the modernisation of supply chains are changing both the makeup of rural spaces and the expectations that will be placed upon them. Supply-oriented improvements in regional food chains are needed, and require policies that respond to rather than lament inevitable and already occurring changes to the region's historically agrarian character.

Food systems modernisation in Southeast Asia
Urbanisation

The significance of urbanisation in Southeast Asia is difficult to overstate. Throughout the region's history the lure of social connectivity and economic opportunity has brought people to cities and peri-urban areas (Reid 1999), and these movements have hastened in real and relative terms during the twentieth and twenty-first century. Cities offer logical destinations for many people compelled to move because of protracted environmentally-related challenges (such as droughts), everyday rural hardships and/ or abrupt events (such as storms or violence), the draw of greater social and economic opportunity in cities, or various combinations of many such forces (Ewing 2012). As centres of culture, commerce, trade and family relations, cities are places where the immediate and longer term needs of such populations can be most readily met.

The overall rapidity and scale of urbanisation in Southeast Asia and China is without precedent historically (Rimmer and Dick 2009). Southeast Asia's urban population has swelled from roughly 15% of the total in 1950 to almost 42% by 2010, and increasing trends continue (ISEAS 2009). Much contemporary urbanisation is occurring in the least urbanised states such as Laos and Cambodia even as the cities of these countries struggle to manage rapid influxes of people. Large megacities such as Jakarta, Manila and Bangkok continue to swell while many small and medium-sized cities and towns, which house roughly 67% of the region's urban populace, are growing even faster (ISEAS 2009).

Perhaps unsurprisingly, urbanisation is fundamentally impacting regional food systems.[1] Food systems all have the fairly uniform and straightforward goal of feeding people, and modern urbanisation in Southeast Asia is the latest dynamic to alter how this is achieved (for historical examples of food systems evolutions, see Braudel 1979 and Greif 1993). However, off-farm transportation, logistical, wholesale and retail practices in Southeast Asia, along with much of the rest of the developing world, are evolving at a rate never before seen. This 'revolution' in food systems has been underway in Southeast Asia in various forms for over three decades, and comes on the heels of similar, if slower, food system changes in the United States and Europe (Reardon and Timmer 2012; Reardon et al. 2010). Complex and systemic changes are marked by the consolidation of distribution and marketing practices, an explosion of increasingly competitive supermarkets, large wholesale and retail actors, and an increase in consumer choice and the consumption of processed food. These rapid shifts have debunked to a degree previous assessments (Goldman 1974) that developing and largely agrarian economies were anathema to such changes, and would necessarily continue to support traditional food markets (Reardon et al. 2003).

Origins

Such off-farm changes, while far from regionally uniform, have key characteristics that are relevant across much of Southeast Asia. They were spurred by influxes of foreign direct investment which accompanied wider economic liberalisation trends during the 1990s and 2000s (Reardon and Timmer 2012; Traill 2006).[2] An initial wave of investment into food processing came from western corporations such as Nestlé, Kraft and Danone that were seeking markets with strong growth opportunities, and later from multinationals from within the region such as Thailand's Charoen

Pokphand (CP), the Philippines' San Miguel and Del Monte Asia (Gehlhar and Regmi 2005; Timmer and Reardon 2012).[3] Logistical and market advances have followed, and a growing segment of Southeast Asia's population is accessing more of their calories from processed foods that have traversed modern supply routes. Impacts have been pronounced. By the early 2000s Nestlé was supplying over one-third of packaged goods in the Philippines, with Unilever enjoying a similar role in Indonesia (Bolling and Gehlhar 2005). This reflects a global trend in which economic growth is accompanied by greater expenditures on processed food: the share by packaged food in low-income countries being 7% of the total compared to 30% of totals in lower-middle-income countries and 45% in upper-middle-income countries (Gehlhar and Regmi 2005; Wilkinson and Rocha 2009).

Not coincidentally these changes have occurred in concert with previously-discussed urbanisation trends. Urban spaces provide transportation options for accessing supermarkets, housing that is more likely than rural counterparts to have refrigeration, and greater exposure to advertising (Reardon and Timmer 2012). Supermarkets also reduce shopping commitments through aggregating a range of goods in a single location; which is conducive to the greater female employment that exists in urban spaces and is emancipating for those unable or not desirous to shop regularly or in multiple locations. Moreover, these emergent avenues for accessing food can exist complementarily with more traditional wetmarkets, with consumers opting to buy processed food and staples from chain stores and fresh produce through more familiar channels.

The impetuses for accessing and creating emergent food market follow demand–supply dynamics in the region's urban and increasingly peri-urban spaces. Namely, there is a demand by consumers for both a variety of goods (from processed to fresh foods) and services (receipts, lighting, air conditioning, product information, etc.), and a parallel supply of these goods and services by firms that necessitate logistical advances (distribution facilities, vehicles), equipment (cold storage), real estate and the investment to underpin it (Reardon et al. 2003). These symbiotic relationships and convergent interests have led to transformative food product systems in Southeast Asia that respond to consumer desires and utilise new technologies and capacities (for detailed examples of how this can occur, see Goodhue and Rausser 2003).

Impacts

While the key elements of off-farm food systems modernisaiton are increasingly clear, uncertainty remains concerning how the evolution of food value chains is affecting poverty, environments, health and other development imperatives (Gómez et al. 2011). Ewing and Ong have argued, for example, that the increased consumption of processed food in the wider Asia-Pacific is bringing with it a range of health problems (2011), and moves to more meat-heavy diets in particular are increasing the ecological footprint of agricultural production in the region and beyond (Ewing and Ong 2011; Friel and Baker 2009). Work is needed to build knowledge about how supply-chain shifts in Southeast Asia impact multiple elements of food systems performance, including economic and social costs, distributional equity, energy use, environmental footprints and consumer and farmer health and safety (Gómez et al. 2011). These issues speak to fundamental food supply questions facing the region and are explored in the following section.

Uncertainties notwithstanding, however, it is clear that Southeast Asia's supply chain revolution is proceeding at a pace and scale that makes it paramount for regional food security calculations. Retail data reveal that late adopters grow supply chains even more rapidly. East Asian countries that were early to modernise food markets had a compound growth rate in retail food sales of 11.2% from 2001 to 2009, compared to a growth rate of 17.9% for the 'second wave' countries of Indonesia, Malaysia, the Philippines and Thailand and a rate of 40.9% for the most recent modernisers of Vietnam, China and India (Reardon et al. 2010).[4] In each of these cases, growth in retail food sales outstripped relatively high-levels of GDP growth. This has predictive value for anticipating the trajectory of Southeast Asia's less developed economies in Myanmar, Cambodia, Laos and Timor-Leste. Unlike the previous experiences of Europe and the United States, however, the Southeast Asia's supply chain revolution has not been accompanied, at least during these initial decades, by a large-scale consolidation of food suppliers. Rather, small-scale farming persists in Southeast Asia with only limited signs of abatement, and persistent poverty continues to afflict many food producers and poor urban consumers (Teng et al. 2012). This disconnect has implications, particularly for growing urban populations that are highly susceptible to food supply deficits.

Supply shifts: looking back

Green Revolution technologies and the effective prioritisation of the food sector during the latter half of the twentieth century brought Southeast Asia from the precipice of acute food insecurity to levels at which far fewer citizens lack access to sufficient and adequately nutritious foods (Hazell and Haddad 2001; Hazell 2009). Regional wheat, rice and maize yields grew at annual rates of 5.43, 3.25 and 4.62% respectively between 1967 and 1982, primarily as the result of the planting of faster-growing varieties, access to more effective and widely used irrigation systems and greater profitability levels for grain farmers (Hazell 2009). Yield increases occurred with only negligibly greater areas of land under cereal cultivation, and were the key to providing millions of people with access to affordable sources of nutrition. In a compelling indicator of food security success in the wider Asia-Pacific, at the same time that there was a 60% increase in Asia's population (between 1970 and 1995), caloric availability per person increased nearly 30% and wheat and rice became cheaper in real terms (ADB 2000; Hazell 2009).

These resounding achievements help explain why regional experiences are held up as an example of food security progress from which other regions can gain lessons (FASID 2003). It is important to recognise, however, that within this larger success story there are pervasive conditions of undernourishment which continue to plague the lives of individuals and the progress of communities in pockets throughout the region. The Global Hunger Index released by the International Food Policy Research Institute (IFPRI) reveals the details of this reality, finding 'moderate' hunger levels in Thailand and Malaysia, 'serious' hunger levels in Indonesia, the Philippines, Vietnam and Myanmar, and 'alarming' levels of hunger in Cambodia, Lao PDR and Timor-Leste (Von Grebmer et al. 2010).[5] Furthermore, the Green Revolution has been singled out for exacerbating food access inequalities (particularly in Latin America), and environmental decline (Horlings and Marsden 2011). Some suggest that runaway agrotechnologies driven by corporate interests will lead to greater food access inequalities and ecological stresses in the future. That said, as with the period preceding the Green Revolution, the region again finds itself in need of pronounced improvements in food supply systems.

Supply shifts: looking forward

Previously-explored rural to urban population shifts reveal the need for more food to be produced by rural communities that continue to decline in size relative to their city-dwelling neighbours. This is true both domestically, where rural hinterlands feed urban centres, and internationally, where countries with high rural agricultural capacities supply countries with significant food importing needs (Ewing 2011a). Globally, arable land has shrunk from 0.45 hectares (ha) per person in the mid twentieth century to 0.25 ha per person in 1997 (Spiertz 2010). While perhaps alarming on the surface, this trend is unsurprising given the world's rapid population growth, mercurial gains in global economic production and the attendant land conversions that these changes wrought. Reductions are set to continue and estimates suggest that arable land per person will drop to 0.15 ha by the mid twenty-first century (Spiertz 2010).

Land-use changes progress as cities expand and prime agricultural lands are converted into residential and industrial areas. As cities struggle to absorb ever increasing numbers of people, more informal housing arises and populations of urban poor swell. These populations are exceedingly vulnerable as they spend a major part of their income on food. As such, there is the need to grow more varied food in greater quantities without significantly expanding land use (particularly into forested areas), exhausting key inputs such as water or topsoil or amplifying pollution problems (Ewing 2011b). There is strong disagreement about how this should be done.

Development precedents from outside of the region suggest a consolidation of agricultural production strategies and land holdings may be in the offing. In Asia, however, despite the rapid modernisation of food supply chains and the expansion of plantation farming in some commodities, the average farm size is actually becoming smaller (Timmer 2010b). Factors contributing to this phenomenon include growing competition for land, non-rural employment opportunities developing slowly, and government protection of small-scale farming in Southeast Asia. Shrinking farm sizes have implications for innovation in productivity, given that increased utilisation of mechanised technologies – typically associated with increasing farm sizes – is challenging to implement on very small scales. Southeast Asian farmers will therefore increasingly rely on biological and chemical technologies instead more modern approaches to improving yield growth and controlling pests and disease.

Such modern approaches are subject to controversy, as critiques call attention to the high greenhouse gas emissions released by some food producing and distribution practices, the degradation and depletion of vital freshwater systems to meet agricultural needs and the large-scale conversion of formerly valuable ecosystems to support corporate farming operations (Horlings and Marsden 2011). Arguments point out that decades of agricultural intensification have had serious side-effects, with the overuse of nitrogen-based fertilisers and high inputs of phosphorus, insecticides, fungicides and heavy metals all creating lasting problems for soil and freshwater systems, and overall nutrient flows throughout food chains (Stoate et al. 2001). Working from these critiques, many in the environmental sector and beyond now advocate a return to, or perpetuation of, more 'traditional' and often small-scale farming techniques (Horlings and Marsden 2011).

Critiques in the name of environmental stewardship also extend forcefully into issues associated with GM plants (Azadi and Ho 2010). GM plants have had their genetic material altered in a way that does not occur naturally by mating and/or natural recombination. Fears concerning growing influxes of undesirable insects, detrimental effects on beneficial insects, the potential introduction of new plant pathogens, the spread of herbicide-resistant genes to other plants, and adverse consequences for plant biodiversity are among the most prevalent cautionary issues raised regarding GM plants. Like other areas of agrotechnology, these scientific concerns over GM combine with a range of socially based arguments that question the domination of GM seed banks by a relatively few monopolistic companies, the safety of consumers and the ethics of genetic modification more broadly (Azadi and Ho 2010; Horlings and Marsden 2011).

Critiques of the agricultural expansion record during past decades illuminate many pitfalls that should be considered when formulating future food production strategies. They do not, however, justify retreating from technological progress in food production sectors. The impressive growth in food yields during past decades have no doubt been accompanied at times by social injustices, gross environmental oversights and instances of outright negligence. These experiences, however, must not be allowed to undermine the potential value of agrotechnologies for both food production and environmental stewardship. Agrotechnology provides environmentally prudent tools for reducing water usage through targeted low-volume irrigation systems, combating soil erosion through less invasive tilling practices and increasing yields per ha so that fewer areas of land require conversion to agriculture (Tilman et al. 2002). Technologies can also help to sequester increasing levels of atmospheric carbon, lessen emissions of powerful greenhouse gases such as methane, and have the second-order effect of cutting transportation emissions through creating food production possibilities in new locations. Regarding climate change adaptation, emerging farming techniques and more robust crop varieties can create greater resilience to predicted changes in surface temperature, precipitation patterns and growing seasons.

Low-impact 'precision' farming technologies and practices, when applied in appropriate ecological and social settings, have the potential to contribute to food security while maintaining responsible environmental principles. Reasoned approaches that apply modern technological offerings – such as soil sensors that gauge the need for water and nutrients and judiciously apply them, information technologies that monitor complex farm systems and provide relevant information to farmers in real time, and labour-reducing farm machinery – can all enhance resource-use efficiencies and produce greater quantities and qualities of food. These tools are needed to improve the robustness of Southeast Asian food supplies.

The following section explores three key forces impeding such improvements. The first force is the perpetuation of 'agrarian mythologies' that romanticise rural farming life. These narratives, while at times well-meaning, tend to originate from outside of farming communities and can misrepresent the stated and observable interests of farmers. The second force relates to market integration, and reveals a distrust in trade and focus of self-sufficiency goals. While ostensibly steeped in food security logic, these approaches can paradoxically make national food systems less resilient. The third force concerns the difficulties of regulating biotechnology in the region. While showing promise for creating more efficient and effective agricultural systems, these technologies are plagued by bureaucratic hurdles that defy straightforward responses. Taken together, these impediments to food supply modernisation present confronting regional challenges.

Impediments to food supply modernisation
Romanticising the rural in Southeast Asia

The Green Revolution, and to a degree the technological efforts pursued since, undervalued the importance of indigenous knowledge and experience in Southeast Asian farming systems. Traditional farming systems were viewed by many to be unproductive, wasteful, environmentally destructive and predicated upon pedestrian and at times mystical assumptions and belief systems. Fortunately, a wave of subsequent research spread across Southeast Asia with the objective of learning about what farmers thought about the recent changes to agriculture and how they viewed local conditions (Rambo 1984). This wave revealed, unsurprisingly, that local people often possessed vast knowledge about a multitude of aspects of their agricultural environments, and that such knowledge had at times escaped those from science and policy communities (Jamieson et al. 1998). This essential recognition has created a greater appreciation for indigenous and existing knowledge and practices, and been a boon for Southeast Asian agriculture.

However, to borrow from Rambo, 'the pendulum may have swung too far' (Rambo 2009: 5). Some civil society actors, members of academic and epistemic communities and policymakers now romanticise traditional agrarian systems to an extent that is detrimental to the future of food security in Southeast Asia. This romanticisation rests on a number of problematic assumptions. Namely, there is a pervading and often misleading sense that traditional, agroecological and/or organic farming methods are environmentally benign or even beneficial. While this may be true in certain times and locales, it should not be assumed to be so, and a number of 'traditional' farming methods can create significant environmental strains and use scarce resources inefficiently. There are also problematic suppositions concerning the implicit value of indigenous knowledge and techniques, and a tendency to not always hold them to the same levels of scrutiny as those faced by emergent techniques and practices (Rambo 2009). This risks an *a priori* positive viewing of all community-based agricultural.

Such problems are compounded by the often monolithic and static assumptions underlying praise for rural sectors, which is not conducive to the rapid demographic, economic and environmental dynamism that defines the Southeast Asian context. As such, romantic visions of traditional agriculture often misrepresent the interests and desires of rural populations. Ideas that agrarian populations are (or should be) satisfied with traditional farming lifestyles and opportunities need to be closely scrutinised; particularly given the fact that they often originate from outside the farming communities themselves (Rambo 2009).

The 'agrarian myth' concept refers to the belief that culturally-grounded, small-scale farming is the most desirable form of community life in rural settings (Brown 2003; Dayley 2011). The application of agrarian mythologies to developing world farmers has increased in the face of distrust towards economic and social elements of globalisation, and contributed to ideas that a seemingly homogenous group of rural 'peasants' wish to return to the cultural and economic practices of simpler times (Brass 2000). This nostalgic vision of traditional life speaks to rural identities that are intrinsically tied to physical spaces and a 'contentedness' found not through material gain but through communal relationships with nature. It assumes that rural farmers may desire little beyond a self-sustaining cycle of food production and consumption, shelter, basic necessities and a tranquil village existence (Brass 2000). Such myths, however, are not 'progressive', but rather 'inhibit farmer autonomy' and disparage 'developments in agricultural science, production technology, and market exchange' (Dayley 2011: 342).

Perhaps more importantly, agrarian myths in Southeast Asia and elsewhere can misrepresent both the stated and observed preferences of rural people. These myths are often propagated by city-dwelling members of civil society groups, government, academe and other parties not responsible for their own food production. The case of agrarian myths in Thailand is useful for drawing out these dynamics, which impact food production narratives and strategies in various ways throughout the region.

'Fish in the water and rice in the fields': Thailand's agrarian myth

Thailand's agrarian myth is rooted in historical imagery about previous periods of rural 'contentment', romantic visions of village life that underpin national identities and an assumed 'sufficiency ethic' that suggests that rural farmers desire little by way of material gain (Dayley 2011).[6] Dominant Thai histories posit that a thirteenth century king called for idyllic sufficiency communities with 'fish in the water and rice in the fields', and these humble origins contribute to what has become a modern village-based Thai identity (Dayley 2011: 344; see also Hirsh 2002). Subsequent rural norms have retained a focus on such simplicity, the narrative goes, so that contentment relies on little more than steady access to the basic accoutrements of life (Dayley 2011; Scott 1976).[7]

Thai agrarian myths enjoy support from the monarchy, a selection of Thai intellectuals, activists, some military and government leaders and Buddhist fundamentalists. The myths have found their way into policy approaches such as the monarchy's 'new theory agriculture' that calls on the country's small-scale cultivators to seek total self-reliance by dividing up their limited land among water storage, rice cultivation, growing fruits and other crops, animal husbandry and housing (Priyanut 2004). Moreover, these rural farmers should avoid any agricultural debt, use no chemical herbicides or pesticides and farm for self-sufficiency rather than commercial purposes (Ampol 2004; Priyanut 2004). The less top-down proselytisers of Thailand's agrarian myth, meanwhile, argue that power in the country should be redistributed to local communities and that farmers should revive sufficiency ideals that have been lost through commercial agriculture (Dayley 2011; International Network of Engaged Buddhists 2007).

These positions and ostensible goals are at odds with empirical realities in Thailand. As Dayley points out in a cogent analysis of Thai agrarian myths, 'farmer behaviour over the past 50 years or so belies any serious predisposition toward the sufficiency ethic or belief in the Thai agrarian myth' (2011: 351).[8] Over this period, the expectations of Thai farmers have grown as urbanisation, capitalism and a state-led push to commercialise agriculture made them more aware of their relative poverty compared to city-dwellers (Wyatt 1984). Like so many other members of Thai society, farmers seek material betterment and upward mobility. On the farm they overwhelmingly reach for techniques and technological inputs (often far from the traditional) that can save labour, reduce costs and raise production (Dayley 2011). Thai farmers have been seeking high-yielding seed varieties, mechanisation, irrigation, chemicals and double cropping since they became available in the 1970s and 1980s (Falvey 2000; Siriluck and Kammeier 2003), and when asked have expressed curiosity over the possibilities of GM plants (Dayley 2011). Older farmers harbour not nostalgia for the past but rather opine about how labour intensive things used to be before fertiliser, 'iron buffalos' (hand tractors) – which are never 'stubborn' – and harvesting tools came to save time and energy (Dayley 2011: 353; see also Seri and Hewison 2001).

Beyond such opportunity costs, agrarian myths – however misguided – are not benign. Political divisions over agrarian management have contributed to an at-times violent schism in Thailand. The benefits of agricultural modernisation during the early decades of the Green Revolution were not evenly distributed, and the resulting animosity created by the new rural 'haves' and 'have nots' helped fuel resentment towards the government and insurrectionist activities (Pasuk and Baker 1998). Today, divisions between coalitions loyal to the monarchy and those supporting the populist Thai regime also break on their approaches to Thailand's agrarian character. In both cases the well-being of rural communities is often at the centre of debate but consultation with the communities themselves, and a willingness to recognise results that run counter to prevailing narratives, is found lacking.

Agrarian myths, which exist to varying degrees and in various forms elsewhere in Southeast Asia, present a number of ethical reasons for pause. It should not come as a surprise that many among the regional rural populace desire similar comforts to those that they see being enjoyed elsewhere. Regional urbanisation trends exist in part as a response to such desires. Significant moral hazard exists when those not involved in food production make romantic assumptions about the draw of traditional rural lifestyles and the agricultural methods that such lifestyles necessitate.

While unique in its detail, Thailand's agrarian myths are not outliers. On international levels groups such as Greenpeace and Friends of the Earth are unrelenting and largely undeciphering in their critiques of modern agricultural approaches and romanticisation of the traditional (Miller and Kershen 2013). The influential La Via Campesina International Peasant Movement has also proven a major player in this space, seeking to protect rural farming populations from the dangers of liberal markets and exploitative practices.[9] The organisation trumpets 'food sovereignty' as a rival concept to the widely used definitions of food security,[10] and advocates for countries, communities and individuals to gain power over the food systems affecting them. Protecting farmer interests and warding off exploitation are laudable goals. The problems arise from the wholesale disavowal of 'destructive neoliberal practices' called for by La Via Campesina or the emotive Greenpeace campaign against 'genetic pollution' (La Via Campesina 2011; Greenpeace 2013). As the Thai case demonstrates, such agendas do not necessarily jibe with the interests of small and medium-scale farmers, and are influencing debates on the future of developing world agriculture in ways that can be detrimental to the well-being of both producers and consumers.

The following section explores ways that implied food sovereignty notions, and fear of import dependencies, are influencing key policies in Southeast Asia. While logical on the surface from a food security standpoint, these policies create a tenuous situation that is impeding regional food supply progress and resilience.

Market integration shortcomings: examples from the rice sector

Lessons from the 1980s and 1990s suggest that advocating completely free trade, market integration and liberalisation in the rice sector without government oversight would be unwise (Trethewie and Ewing 2012). During these decades, there was a push by analysts and donors for minimal government intervention in the food and agricultural sectors, based on the determination that market forces, when left alone, would secure food supplies. The resulting problems – lack of implementation of agrotechnology, lack of investment in agriculture, shortage of funds and support for R&D, absence of governments from food security discussions and decision-making, and slow yield growth – took the luster off of market fundamentalist arguments.

However, the political penetration of the rice sector in subsequent years, and particularly since the 2007–2008 price crisis, is proving detrimental for regional rice supply resilience. Macroeconomic forces have the capacity to undermine access to affordable food in fundamental ways, particularly when factors coalesce to lead to rapid food price increases. The 2007–2008 events help illuminate this point. International prices for wheat climbed in response to a period of decreased production and corn prices rose primarily because of crop diversions to the biofuel industry. Rice, however, faced no similar constraints and rice production actually increased as the food crisis deepened (Timmer 2010c). The prices of rice in Asian markets still spiked, however, as rice exporting countries such as India and Thailand reduced rice exports and imposed minimum export prices in order to supplement domestic food markets during the period of price instability for other staples (in this case, wheat and corn). Importing countries, most notably the Philippines, responded by trying to rapidly increase rice stocks through purchases on the international market, which in turn drove the prices ever higher in a compounding cycle of panic buying and climbing prices. 'Nervousness' in Asian rice markets led to skyrocketing prices that saw rice move from USD375 per tonne at the beginning of 2008 to over USD1,100 per tonne by April of that year (Timmer 2010c).

Such price volatility is not unique to the modern period nor is it confined to international markets. Staple grains in Southeast Asia, especially rice, are particularly difficult to stabilise because of the myriad stakeholders involved. Hundreds of millions of small-scale farmers and millions of traders, processors, retailers and consumers all interact in a system that affects decisions about how much grain is grown, sold, stored and consumed (Timmer 2010b). When prices appear to be increasing and/or set to increase more, everyone from the individual family to the farmers, grain harvesters, millers, traders and governments attempt to rapidly gain access to more. These decisions affect both domestic and international pricing and can leave countries, producers and consumers all grappling with uncertainties about the future prices and availability of some of Southeast Asia's most essential crops. Such uncertainties are neither new (rice and cereals also fluctuated greatly during the early 1980s) nor are they fading, with pronounced price increases defining much of the 2010–2012 period.

Such food price increases impede access to adequate food for the most vulnerable populations of the Southeast Asia, and fuel drives towards greater sufficiency in domestic supply and an attendant opacity in regional markets. These systemic forces have the capacity to abruptly affect the quality of life of millions of individuals and have potentially acute implications regional food security (Wailes 2005). Nowhere are these forces more apparent than the rice sector, which unsurprisingly commands unrivalled political attention among crops in Southeast Asia.

Rice importers and exporters in Southeast Asia have long practised strong protectionist policies. This has been the source of considerable political tension and has been a major barrier to free trade in the region. The food price crisis of 2007–2008 worsened these conditions, and deepened existing distrust between exporting and importing players. It also triggered strong long-term policy responses that sought to secure domestic supplies and stable prices by fragmentation, rather than integration, of the international market (Trethewie 2013). Thailand implemented a rice mortgage intervention program with the objective of driving up international rice prices in 2011, when it was the world's largest rice exporter. The scheme, which has well-exceeded the scale of previous interventions in the region, includes income guarantee for rice farmers, a buy-in rice scheme and tighter control over trade, with a preference for government-to-government deals and minimal private sector activity. Rather than increasing prices, the scheme has led to a decrease in demand for Thai rice. As a result, the country is holding unmanageably high stocks and experienced a drop in exports of 37% in 2012.

Thailand is also pursuing the development of a rice exporters' cartel involving Vietnam, Cambodia, Myanmar and Laos. The objective is to control rice exports in the region and drive up prices in the international rice market by 10% each year. This would shift the dynamics of competitiveness in Southeast Asia and widen the chasm between the region's mutually dependent importers and exporters. Although the cartel is unlikely to materialize – the countries involved have failed to come to an agreement and there is external pressure to conform to international trade principles – the pursuit of a cartel speaks volumes about exporters' hesitancy towards market integration (Trethewie 2013).

A responding and potentially more significant strategic shift in the longer term is the response of rice importing countries to secure their domestic rice needs (Trethewie and Ewing 2012). These importing countries seek to increase production in order to become less reliant on the world market; even if this strategy is neither economically viable or an efficient use of resources. The Philippines and Indonesia, which were two of the world's largest rice importers pre-crisis, have both pursued substantial rice production initiatives and pledged to be self-sufficient in coming years, with the aim of becoming net exporters soon after.

In the context of an opaque, thin and relatively unstable rice trade, the push by the Philippines and Indonesia towards self-sufficiency seems a logical move for securing domestic supplies and stabilising domestic rice prices. Both Indonesia and the Philippines are already significant producers of rice, being respectively the third and seventh largest producers of milled rice globally in 2011, but their roles as the world's largest rice importers are fundamental to regional trade characteristics. Their moves toward self-sufficiency will reduce the already thinly traded rice quantities in Southeast Asia to a degree that will erode the robustness of the regional rice market (Trethewie and Ewing 2012).

In 2011, the Philippines' National Food Authority (NFA) announced that it would no longer be directly involved in importing rice through government-to-government deals and would engage the private sector to conduct all imports, as long as a minimum target is reached. The NFA will instead focus on domestic procurement and will in turn support rice producers in meeting growing demand. The government says it is on track to reach self-sufficiency by 2013 and become an exporter of rice soon after.

Indonesia has begun to advocate a decrease in household consumption of rice, encouraging increased consumption of alternatives such as cassava. It has also undertaken strategies to increase rice production, including the allocation of new farmlands and the improvement of irrigation infrastructure in order to become self-sufficient by 2014 and an exporter of rice by 2015. These are not entirely new objectives given that both countries have been aiming for self-sufficiency for some years, but the strategy has taken on new momentum post-crisis.

These strategies designed to secure sufficient local supplies and stabilise domestic rice prices through self-sufficiency will come at substantial economic cost to both countries. Rice as a share of agricultural output in Southeast Asia has fallen from 40.2% in 1961 to 32% in 2007, while its share in the region's gross domestic product (GDP) has decreased from 14.5% in 1961 to just 3.8% in 2007 (Timmer 2010a). Rice has also decreased in profitability, with the importance of rice production to the livelihoods of millions of smallholder farmers increasingly in flux. Many rice farmers are choosing to diversify production to include or exclusively produce other crops in order to generate a larger income. There is also pressure, particularly in Indonesia, for farmers to use or sell land for the farming of lucrative crops such as rubber and oil palm (Ewing 2011b). Furthermore, government interventions to achieve self-sufficiency by supporting farmers may in the long term stifle the emergence of the next stage of structural transformation and development in which it becomes more cost-effective for rice to be grown on larger farms. On the supply side, government strategies to support local rice production for domestic consumption, in conjunction with limited or no imports, typically result in higher rice cost for local consumers to cover minimum prices for farmers. Beyond the short-term costs of funding infrastructure and programmes to increase production, the gradual decline in the importance of rice – as a key staple food, economic force and livelihood provider in Asia (Timmer, 2010a) – should be considered.

Given the potential economic disadvantages, it is evident that the Philippines' and Indonesia's actions are primarily strategic. The characteristics of the region's rice economy therefore need to be understood in order to explain why countries would knowingly take such economic risks in order to secure supplies. Ultimately, the way the rice industry is structured makes it a more unstable commodity than others (Timmer 2010b). Rice price formation is impacted not only by governments and traders, but also by the decisions of millions of smallholders and consumers. Relatively little data is publicly available on quantities, trades and prices, leading to decisions being made on unreliable information.

The bold agricultural policy responses of the Philippines and Indonesia to secure supplies, provide resilience against shocks, and stabilise domestic prices, albeit at high economic cost, therefore reflect an understandable lack of trust in the rice market and fear of market integration. Perhaps the strongest argument for Indonesia and the Philippines to resist isolationist self-sufficiency, however, and to continue to participate in the world rice market, is that it would help promote stability during localised shocks (for example as the result of storms, drought or pests). While no existing studies examine the costs and benefits of these countries' strategies as they move towards self-sufficiency, general literature on rice trade liberalisation and studies of other countries suggest that participation in the world market rather than self-sufficiency strategies serve to better secure domestic supplies (Timmer 2010a), particularly in the case of local market shocks (Tanaka and Hosoe 2011).

Greater market integration and trust in the rice sector would be a boon to regional food security. However, it requires a modicum of regional cooperation that has so far been found wonting. A similar cooperation deficit drives the third major impediment to modernising food supply in Southeast Asia, which is a milieu of regulatory barriers to biotechnology adoption.

The regulatory hurdles of biotechnology

Regulatory hurdles have proven crippling for GM adoption in Southeast Asia. The case of so-called 'Golden Rice' has become something of a rallying cry for those lamenting the influence of wholesale anti-GM positions. Significant GM-oriented research has focused on improving the vitamin and nutrient content of diets in developing countries (Davies 2007: 123). Golden Rice and the subsequent Golden Rice II are varieties that have been genetically enhanced to synthesise beta-carotene so that they can serve as a fortified staple food to be consumed in areas where there is a shortage of dietary vitamin A. The potential for Golden Rice has been recognised internationally, particularly after the Bill and Melinda Gates Foundation funded the improvement of Golden Rice to increase its pro-vitamin A, vitamin E, iron, zinc and protein quality through GM technology (Pucie 2005). Moreover, the vision for Golden Rice was that it would be a 'public good' and free of any profit-driven charges to producers or consumers in developing countries (Potrykus 2010). Impediments to rolling out the product in much of Asia have been pervasive.

A number of hurdles have largely kept Golden Rice in the lab since the early 2000s. Almost all of these, however, can be subsumed in the eyes of one of its founders, plant scientist Ingo Potrykus, under 'the political dimension of GE [genetically engineered crops] and particularly its effect on GE-regulation' (Potrykus 2010: 467). Potrykus laments that the regulations on GM use and expectations of regulatory authorities 'are so demanding that even with the best support it takes ten years to prepare for and assemble all the data required', and this incurs 'exorbitant' costs (Potrykus 2010: 467). Potrykus itemises the different phases of meeting

GM regulatory requirements, along with their putative time needs, to paint a picture of a decade of futility. The author spreads blame widely for these shortcomings, but originates his criticising the unfairly negative attitudes towards GM technology by European countries, influential NGOs, a small swathe of the public and much of the media and development community (2010). Miller and Kershen go further still, calling it a 'moral outrage' that intransigent activists have provided 'political cover' for risk-averse regulators to stall approvals (2013: 4). The authors contend that intellectual and economic problems were solved during the early 2000s and that governments have placed 'endless regulatory obstacles' in the path of approval (Miller and Kershen 2013: 4).

It is unsurprising that as a scientist directly involved with the Golden Rice project such as Potrykus would weary of seemingly overbearing regulatory requirements. Miller and Kershen, meanwhile, steep their argument on the moral failings of *not* bringing potentially beneficial GM technologies to bear rather than through a detailed look at the impediments to agrotechnological embrace. Escalar et al. do pursue such an analysis, however, revealing that the Golden Rice case is in some ways emblematic of larger challenges for the regional management and regulation of GM products (2012).[11] The authors argue that regulatory uncertainties and unpredictability are disruptive for trade and create market constraints that can increase food prices (Escalar et al. 2012). Moreover, in an echo of more cutting critiques, the authors cite 'unnecessary' regulatory requirements as creating superfluous costs and impediments for farmers attempting to access GM inputs. A wider look sees inconsistencies in GM policies across the region proving detrimental to their adoption, and as such impeding potential gains that could otherwise be realised.

Overall, this is a picture of a region behind. Almost all traded soybeans, roughly half of traded maize and large portions of traded oils are GM, and with 29 countries and 16 million farmers growing GM globally it is detrimental for Southeast Asian countries to be situated in a region with ineffectual regulatory frameworks. As a result, Southeast Asia is only scratching the surface of what is possible with bourgeoning genetic advances. Environmental and socioeconomic hurdles for GM adoption are formidable but not insurmountable. Existing and planned GM plants reflect fairly simple genetic modifications, such as the insertion of genes for herbicide resistance and others that act as pest insect toxins. Assertions that such modifications create pronounced risks from emergent pathogens, expand herbicide-resistant genes in unwanted plants, and have detrimental consequences for plant biodiversity do not enjoy strong empirical support (Spiertz 2010). Public health concerns have also largely failed to materialise in countries that deploy GM products on a large scale, and such issues can be all but negated through extensive testing (Davies 2007). The key to harnessing the potential of GM is thus to gain public trust in these products through transparent monitoring processes and effective communication, and to put economic structures in place that will encourage their usage. If done successfully, such advances would help Southeast Asia meet its nourishment needs without compromising environmental and resource endowments needed for the future.

Conclusion

Advanced production methods, greater market integration and value chain modernisation are, even in tandem, far from a panacea. Industrial farming and the corporatisation of food chains elsewhere in the world have laid bare a host of environmental, health and social ills that Southeast Asia would do well to avoid. However, it is a key contention of this paper that changes in supply systems and off-farm value chains are not progressing in Southeast Asia in a complementary fashion, and this necessitates new research and policy considerations. Cities are swelling and food chains evolving at the same time that farm sizes are shrinking land available for cultivation declining. Economic opportunities are bourgeoning in some locales while faltering in others, with increasing connectivity ensuring that the contrast between haves and have-nots has never been more apparent. Decades of underwhelming public commitment to agricultural investments have hindered the ability of farmers to pull themselves out of poverty, cope with price volatility, or deal with environmental and economic shocks. Tools that could help these farmers become more resilient to changing regional conditions are being impeded by outmoded visions of a traditional agrarian region, national rice policies that increase vulnerabilities for producer and consumer alike, and regulatory impediments to key technological inputs.

The rural to urban shifts currently underway in Southeast Asia lay bare food supply systems that are behind corresponding responses. Evolving these supply systems requires combining food supply productivity goals with wider objectives towards poverty reduction, the facilitation of labour shifts and rural development advances. This clearly necessitates looking beyond the farm, and certainly beyond the perpetuation of often grueling rural farming paradigms, to providing soft and hard infrastructure, better education, effective healthcare and other essential services. It is in this space that there is the greatest chance for symbiotic relationships between growing urban centres and the rural peripheries that they depend on so heavily. Such symbioses need not be confined to state boundaries, with regional market integration for rice and other crops offering promise for greater overall supply resilience.

Urban centres of trade, governance, finance, culture and research owe it to their rural counterparts to erode the barriers to agricultural inputs, move past stereotypical peasant narratives, and create regional systems of trade that can fortify food security for rural and urban populations alike. Doing so will not only help ensure their own consistent and affordable supply of the foods which they desire, but also help the rural hands that feed them.

Notes

1 Food systems are defined here as the collection of interactive inputs and products that exist along the chains from farms to consumers. These include farming inputs, farm activities, logistics, processing, transport, sale and so forth.
2 Traill (2006) found that the most important explanatory variables for the penetration of modern retail to be GDP per capita and openness to retail FDI.
3 Some investment scales are significant, with CP recently basing the largest shrimp processing firm in the world in Indonesia.
4 These data come from the group Planet Retail; http://www1.planetretail.net/.
5 The International Food Policy Research Institute's (IFPRI) Global Hunger Index tracks hunger through a multidimensional variable calculation that combines the proportion of undernourished persons as a percentage of population, the prevalence of underweight children under the age of 5-years-old and the mortality rate of children under 5-years-old.
6 Dayley's typology has five elements, three of which are condensed here into the notion that village imagery underpins Thai identity culture.
7 The 'sufficiency ethic' concept was introduced in Scott (1976).
8 Dayley bases this and other assertions on, among other things, over 100 field interviews. For more details on the methods of this study, see Dayley (2011: 357–358).
9 La Via Campesina describes itself as 'an international movement which coordinates peasant organizations of small and middle-scale producers, agricultural workers, rural women, and indigenous communities from Asia, Africa, America, and Europe'. More information can be found at http://viacampesina.org/en/index.php/organisation-mainmenu-44.
10 For the UNFAO's widely utilized conceptualisation of food security, see ftp://ftp.fao.org/es/ESA/policybriefs/pb_02.pdf. The World Food Summit in 1996 gave the most widely-used definition as: 'Food security exists when all people, at all times, have physical and economic access to sufficient, safe and nutritious food that meets their dietary needs and food preferences for an active and healthy life' (World Food Summit 1996).
11 Escalar et al. (2012) pursue this analysis for APEC countries as opposed to only those in Southeast Asia, but many of their points retain regional relevance.

References

Ampol, S. (2004) 'His Majesty's philosophy of Sufficiency economy and the royal development study centres', The Ministerial Conference on Alternative Development: Sufficiency Economy; accessed at http://www.sufficiencyeconomy.org/old/en/files/15.pdf, 31 October 2013.

Asian Development Bank (ADB) (2000) *Rural Asia: Beyond the Green Revolution.* Manila: Asian Development Bank.

Azadi, H. and Ho, P. (2010) 'Genetically modified and organic crops in developing countries: a review of options for food security', Biotechnology Advances 28(1): 160–168

Bolling, C. and Gehlhar, M. (2005) 'Global food manufacturing reorients to meet new demands'. See Regmi, A. & Gehlhar, M. (eds.). New Directions in Global Food Markets. Agriculture Information Bulletin Number 794. Washington DC: USDA, pp. 62–73.

Brass, T. (2000) *Peasants, Populism and Postmodernism: The Return of the Agrarian Myth.* London: Frank Cass

Braudel, F. (1979) *The Wheels of Commerce*, New York: Harper and Row

Brown, R. (2003) 'Agrarian myth', in K. Christensen and D. Levinson (eds) *Encyclopedia of Community: From the Village to the Virtual World.* pp. 28–30. Thousand Oaks, CA: Sage.

Davies, K. M. (2007) 'Genetic modification of plant metabolism for human health benefits', *Mutation Research* 622(1-2): 122–137.

Dayley, R. (2011) 'Thailand's agrarian myth and its proponents', *Journal of Asian and African Studies* 46(4): 342–360.

Escaler M., Teng P. P. S. and Powell, A. D. (2012) 'The involvement of nano-drug delivery in biosafety issues', *Biosafety* 1(3): 1–7.

Ewing, J. J. (2011a) 'Food production and environmental health in Southeast Asia: the search for complementary strategies', *NTS Policy Brief* (May): 1–6.

Ewing, J. J. (2011b) 'Forests, food and fuel: REDD+ and Indonesia's land-use conundrum', Asia Security Initiative Policy Series, Working Paper No. 19.

Ewing, J. J. (2012) 'Contextualising climate change as a cause of migration in Southeast Asia', in L. Elliott (ed.) *Climate Change, Migration and Human Security in Southeast Asia.* pp. 13–27. Singapore: RSIS.

Falvey, L. (2000) *Thai Agriculture: Golden Cradle of Millennia.* Bangkok: Kasetsart University Press.

Foundation for Advanced Studies on International Development (FASID). (2003) *FASID Forum X: Green Revolution in Asia and Its Transferability to Africa (8–10 December 2002).*Workshop Report, Tokyo.

Friel, S. and Baker, P. I. (2009) 'Equity, food security and health equity in the Asia Pacific Region', Asia Pacific Journal of Clinical Nutrition 18(4): 620–632.

Gehlhar, M. and Regmi, A. (2005) 'New directions in global food markets', *Agriculture Information Bulletin* 794, Economic Research Service, US Department of Agriculture, Washington, DC.

Goldman, A. (1974) Outreach of consumers and the modernization of urban food retailing in developing countries, *Journal of Marketing* 38(4): 8–16.

Go´mez, M. I., Barrett, C. B., Buck, L. E., De Groote, H., Ferris S., et al. (2011) 'Research principles for developing country food value chains', *Science* 332(6034): 1154–1155.

Goodhue, R. E. and Rausser, G. C. (2003) 'Value differentiation', *Journal of Agriculture Resource Economics* 28(3): 375–395.

Greenpeace (2013) 'Say no to genetic engineering'; accessed at http://www.greenpeace.org/international/en/campaigns/agriculture/problem/genetic-engineering/, 31 October 2013.

Greif, A. (1993) 'Contract enforceability and economic institutions in early trade: the Maghribi traders' coalition', *American Economic Review* 83(3): 525–548

Hazell, P. B. R. (2009) *The Asian Green Revolution.* IFPRI Discussion Paper 00911, Washington, DC: International Food Policy Research Institute (IFPRI).

Hazell, P. B. R. and Haddad, L. (2001) *Agricultural Research and Poverty Reduction.* Food, Agriculture, and the Environment Discussion Paper No. 34, Washington, DC: International Food Policy Research Institute (IFPRI).

Hirsch, P. (2002) 'What is the Thai village?', in C. Reyolds (ed.) *National Identity and Its Defenders: Thailand Today.* pp. 262–276. Victoria: Monash University Centre of Southeast Asian Studies.

Horlings, L. G. and Marsden, T. K. (2011) 'Towards the real green revolution? Exploring the conceptual dimensions of a new ecological modernisation of agriculture that could "feed the world"', *Global Environmental Change* 21(2): 441–452.

International Network of Engaged Buddhists. (2007) 'Two social alternatives on the future of Thai society'; accessed at http://www.inebnetwork.org/web/

index.php?option=com_content&task=view&i=33&Itemid=40, 15 August 2013.

Institute of Southeast Asian Studies (ISEAS). (2009) *Urbanisation in Southeast Asian Countries*. Singapore: ISEAS.

Jamieson, N. L., Le Trong Cuc and Rambo, A. T. (1998) *The Development Crisis in Vietnam's mountains*. East–West Center Special Reports 6, Honolulu: East–West Center.

Miller, H. I. and Kershen, D. L. (2013) 'Politics and the poor man's plate', *Defining Ideas* January: 1–5.

Ong, S. E. and Ewing, J. J. (2011) 'Brave new world? Assessing the health risks of modern food systems in Asia', *NTS Alert*, June (2), Singapore: RSIS Centre for Non-Traditional Security (NTS) Studies for NTS-Asia.

Pasuk, P. and Baker, C. (1998) *Thailand's Boom and Bust*. Chiang Mai: Silkworm Books.

Potrykus, I. (2010) 'Lessons from the "Humanitarian Golden Rice" project: regulation prevents development of public good genetically engineered crop products', *New Biotechnology* 27(5): 466–472.

Priyanut, P. (2004) 'Research note: sufficiency economy', *ASEAN Economic Bulletin* 21(1): 127–134.

Pucie, C. (2005) 'Grand challenges in global health initiative selects 43 groundbreaking research projects for more than $436 million in funding', *Bill and Melinda Gates Foundation*, 27 June; accessed at http://www.gatesfoundation.org/pressreleases/Pages/fundinggroundbreakingresearch050627. Aspx, 14 August 2013.

Rambo, A. T. (United Nations Development Programme, East-West Environment and Policy Institute) (1984) 'Why shifting cultivators keep shifting: understanding farmer decision-making in traditional agro-forestry systems', in *Community Forestry: Some Aspects*. Bangkok: Food and Agricultural Organization of the United Nations; United Nations Development Programme; Environment and Policy Institute, East-West Center, pp. 73–81.

Rambo, A. T. (2009) 'Are the farmers always right? Rethinking assumptions guiding agricultural and environmental research in Southeast Asia', *AsiaPacific Issues*, 88. Honolulu: East-West Center, pp. 1–12.

Reardon, T., Chen, K., Minten, B. and Adriano, L. (2013) *The Quiet Revolution in Staple Food Value Chains: Enter the Dragon, the Elephant and the Tiger*. Mandaluyong City, Philippines: Asian Development Bank.

Reardon, T. and Timmer, C. P. (2012) 'The economics of the food system revolution', *Annual Review of Resource Economics* 4(14): 225–264.

Reardon, T., Timmer, C. P., Barrett, C. B. and Berdegue, J. A. (2003) 'The rise of supermarkets in Africa, Asia, and Latin America', *American Journal of Agricultural Economics* 85(5): 1140–1146.

Reardon, T., Timmer, C. P. and Minten, B. (2010) 'The supermarket revolution in Asia and emerging development strategies to include small farmers'. *Proceedings of the National Academy of Sciences*. USA 109(31).

Reid, A. (1999) *Charting the Shape of Early Modern Southeast Asia*. Chiang Mai: Silkworm Books.

Rimmer, J. R. and Dick, H. W. (2009) *The City in Southeast Asia: Patterns, Processes, and Policy*. Singapore: NUS Press.

RSIS Centre for Non-Traditional Security (NTS) Studies. (2011) *International Conference on Asian Food Security 2011 – Feeding Asia in the Twenty-first Century: Building Urban–Rural Alliances (10–12 August 2011)*. Report, Singapore.

Scott, J. C. (1976) *The Moral Economy of the Peasant: Subsistence and Rebellion in Southeast Asia*. New Haven: Yale University Press.

Seri, P. and Hewison, K. (2001) *Village Life: Culture and Transition in Thailand's Northeast*. Bangkok: White Lotus Books.

Siriluck, S. and Kammeier, H. D. (2003) 'Government policy and farmers' decision-making: the agricultural diversification programme for the Chao Phraya River Basin (1993–95) revisited', in F. Molle and S. Tip-pawal (eds) *Thailand's Rice Bowl: Perspectives on Agricultural and Social Change in the Chao Phraya Delta*. Bangkok: White Lotus, pp. 245–260.

Spiertz, H. (2010) 'Food production, crops and sustainability: restoring confidence in science and technology', *Current Opinion in Environmental Sustainability* 2(5-6): 439–443.

Stoate, C., Boatman, N. D., Borralho, R. J., Rio Carvalho, C., de Snoo, G. R. and Eden, P. (2001) 'Ecological impacts of arable intensification in Europe', *Journal of Environmental Management* 63(4): 337–365.

Tanaka, T. and Hosoe, N. (2011) 'Does agricultural trade liberalization increase risks of supply-side uncertainty? Effects of productivity shocks and export restrictions on welfare and food supply in Japan', *Food Policy* 36(3): 368–377.

Teng, P., Escaler, M. and Ewing, J. J. (2012) 'Feeding Asia in the twenty-first century: building urban–rural alliances: summary of the main findings of the international conference on Asian food security held in Singpaore on 10–12 August 2011', *Food Security* April: 141–146.

Tilman, D., Cassman, K. G., Matson, P. A., Naylor, R. and Polasky, S. (2002) 'Agricultural sustainability and intensive production practices', *Nature* 418: 671–677.

Timmer, C. P. (2010a) *The Changing Role of Rice in Asia's Food Security*. ADB sustainable development working paper series No. 15, Manila: Asian Development Bank (ADB).

Timmer, C. P. (2010b) 'Rice and structural transformation', in S. Pandey, D. Byerlee and D. Dawe et al. (eds) *Rice in the Global Economy: Strategic Research and Policy Issues for Food Security*. Los Baños: International Rice Research Institute (IRRI), pp. 37–60.

Timmer, C. P. (2010c) 'Reflections on food crises past', Food Policy (35:1): 1–11.

Timmer, C. P., Block, S. and Dawe, D. (2010) 'Long-run dynamics of rice consumption, 1960–2050', in S. Pandey, D. Byerlee and D. Dawe et al. (eds) *Rice in the Global Economy: Strategic Research and Policy Issues for Food Security*. Los Baños: International Rice Research Institute (IRRI), pp. 139–174.

Traill, W. B. (2006) 'The rapid rise of supermarkets?', *Development Policy Review* 24(2):163–74

Trethewie, S. (2013) 'The ASEAN Plus Three Emergency Rice Reserve (APTERR): cooperation, commitment and contradictions', NTS Working Paper Series No. 8.

Trethewie, S. and Ewing, J. J. (2012) 'Build it and they will come: commitment to the association of Southeast Asian Nations' rice policy mechanisms', *TKN Perspectives* 1(1): 1–7.

Via Campesina. (2011) 'The international peasant's voice', 9 February; accessed at http://viacampesina.org/en/index.php/organisation-mainmenu-44, 31 October 2013.

Von Grebmer, K., Ruel, M. T. and Menon, P. et al. (2010) *Global Hunger Index – The Challenge of Hunger: Focus on the Crisis of Child Undernutrition*. Bonn, Washington, DC and Dublin: Deutsche Welthungerhilfe, International Food Policy Research Institute (IFPRI), Concern Worldwide.

Wailes, E. J. (2005) 'Rice: global trade, protectionist policies, and the impact of trade liberalization', in A. M. Ataman and John C. Beghin (eds) *Global*

Agricultural Trade and Developing Countries. Washington, DC: The World Bank, pp. 177–194.

Wilkinson, J. and Rocha, R. (2009) 'Agro-industry trends, patterns and development impacts', in C. A. da Silva, D. Baker, A. W. Shepherd, C. Jenane and S. Miranda-da-Cruz (eds) *Agro-Industries for Development.* New York: CABI, pp. 46–92.

World Food Summit (1996) *Rome Declaration on World Food Security.* Rome: UNFAO.

Wyatt, D. (1984) *Thailand: A Short History.* New Haven: Yale University Press.

Food security, the palm oil–land conflict nexus, and sustainability: a governance role for a private multi-stakeholder regime like the RSPO?

Helen E. S. Nesadurai

Abstract   This paper examines the nexus between food security and sustainability governance through a case study of palm oil. Palm oil's advocates claim that campaigns against palm oil and actions to halt its expansion due to sustainability concerns can undermine its food security role. However, palm oil expansion more directly undermines the food and livelihood security of rural and indigenous communities when land that rightfully belongs to, or has been used by, these communities is alienated to firms for oil palm cultivation with little or no consultation or compensation provided or alternatives considered. It is in this context that the paper examines whether the multi-stakeholder Roundtable on Sustainable Palm Oil (RSPO) is able to ensure that this commodity is cultivated in ways that minimise environmental damage and livelihood disruption, thereby safeguarding palm oil's contribution to food security. The findings are mixed. RSPO certification provides fairly comprehensive and progressive socio-environmental regulation that has enhanced sustainable production practises in this industry especially by the larger transnational plantation companies mindful of their global reputation. The RSPO is also far more responsive than governments have been to the land rights of rural and indigenous communities, providing *due process* for land claimants as well as recognising that these communities may have *legitimate* rights to land even if companies were awarded legal title by governments. However, multi-stakeholder regimes can be fragile, requiring a great deal of internal accommodation and trade-offs to work. Already, different interests in the RSPO are pulling in different directions while national certification systems have emerged that are less onerous compared to the RSPO even as the latter seeks to further enhance its sustainability credentials.

Introduction

> Palm oil has done more to enhance food security than any of the
> other vegetable oils and many other crops... Moreover, palm oil's
> clear and persistent price advantage makes it highly attractive for the
> many households in the developing world who rely on it as a food sta-
> ple. It makes no sense to willingly abandon these advantages. (World
> Growth 2010: 14)

Despite these claimed food and economic benefits of palm oil, this commodity is also heavily criticised. Large-scale oil palm cultivation, especially
through the conversion of forest and other types of land, is said to raise
greenhouse gas emissions (GHGs), undermine bio-diversity, and destroy
native habitats of endangered animal species while also displacing local
and indigenous communities from agricultural and customary lands. These
environmental and social effects of palm oil production have led to temporary suspension of financing for this industry, consumer boycotts and food
labelling initiatives that single out palm oil as an environmental hazard. By
threatening palm oil's market acceptability, palm oil's advocates claim
these actions also have the potential to undermine palm oil's substantial
contribution to food security. Palm oil production also creates food insecurities in a more direct way for local communities, usually rural and indigenous communities, whenever governments make over to plantation firms
the lands on which these communities depend for their food and broader
livelihood needs. Although the diversion of palm oil from food to bio-fuel
use undermines food security, this topic has already been addressed at
length elsewhere and will not be addressed in this paper, which focuses on
the food security implications of *how* palm oil is produced rather than the
end uses of the oil.[1] Nevertheless, land conversion for bio-fuel use can
affect food security when land is appropriated for oil palm cultivation. It is
clear that there must be changes to how this crop is produced if the direct
and indirect food security contributions of palm oil are to be maintained.
This takes us to the important question of how to govern its production.
Should governance towards enhancing palm oil's environmental and social
sustainability be primarily organised nationally within states, or is some
form of global governance more suited to the task?

One increasingly common global governance mechanism for securing
environmental and social sustainability for agricultural crops, fisheries and
commodities is private regulatory regimes such as [voluntary] certification;
the Forest Stewardship Council, the Roundtable on Sustainable Soy and
the Marine Stewardship Council are only three examples of the growing
multi-stakeholder phenomenon of which the FSC is the most studied. Palm
oil sustainability is currently certified by the Roundtable on Sustainable
Palm Oil (RSPO) established in 2004 under the Swiss Civil Code with a
secretariat and liaison office respectively located in Malaysia and

Indonesia, the world's largest producers of palm oil. For its advocates, a multi-stakeholder regulatory regime like the RSPO holds promise as the best available means of ensuring palm oil sustainability along multiple dimensions – economic, environmental and social.

However, the RSPO's potential as a sustainability regime for palm oil has been criticised on a number of grounds. A fundamental criticism is that the RSPO simply legitimizes what is at root an unsustainable agricultural model of large-scale monoculture plantation. Three other major criticisms are directed against the Roundtable's effectiveness. One is the enforcement criticism that the RSPO has been ineffective in enforcing its own sustainability criteria on its member firms while a second criticism is that RSPO principles, rules and procedures do not go far enough in addressing *climate change* concerns centred around greenhouse gas emissions (McLaughlin 2011; Richardson 2010; World Bank 2011: 134–135). Tying these two criticisms is the charge that the RSPO is dominated by industry with NGOs constituting a very small proportion of RSPO membership (Laurance et al. 2010). A fourth criticism is that RSPO certification does not do enough to safeguard the land rights of rural and indigenous communities while a fifth charge is that sustainability certification, which is expensive and onerous, can exclude smallholder producers of palm oil from the sustainable palm oil market, creating insecurities for these farmers (Colchester and Chao 2011). These latter two concerns tend to be less visible in public debates about palm oil and the RSPO that emphasize palm oil's environmental unsustainability but they are no less important for those whose livelihoods are undermined by oil palm cultivation. These types of criticisms, which are also levelled against other private or multi-stakeholder regulatory regimes like the FSC, raise the question of whether private regulation, which does not rely on the state to enforce but on voluntary actions by corporations offers any advantage over state-based national or international mechanisms in governing palm oil sustainability and by extension safeguarding food security.

In order to address this question, the paper begins by considering how land conversions for oil palm cultivation contributes to food insecurities, using cases from Southeast Asia to draw out the key problems that any governance regime must be able to address in order to be minimally effective. A regime is defined as a set of principles, rules, as well as monitoring, enforcement and decision-making procedures. While this paper does not offer a *comparative* analysis of private versus state-based governance regimes, the paper nonetheless highlights the prima facie advantages and pitfalls of the former relative to the latter in the light of these problems. A more detailed two-part analysis of the RSPO follows, drawing on two bodies of literature to examine regimes – institutional theory and critical international political economy (IPE). Institutional theory is useful in explaining how a governance regime, depending on a *specific* ensemble of principles, rules and procedures, is able to shape the behaviour of members and other actors outside the regime. Here, the paper examines the body of regulation developed by the RSPO in order to assess whether the Roundtable addresses some of the key sustainability and food security implications of oil palm cultivation identified in the paper.

But, there is another aspect to regimes beyond their design at a particular point in time, and this is the question of why a particular framework of principles, rules and procedures has emerged and how this design might evolve. To explore this dimension of the RSPO regime, the study draws on insights from critical IPE, specifically from Robert Cox's adaptation of Antonio's Gramsci's work on hegemony to explore the contested and thus dynamic nature of this regulatory regime. Far from being static, regimes are always in motion as different actors differently located within particular production and consumption structures compete to shape a regime's normative and regulative mechanisms as well as embed that regime as the dominant framework of governance for a particular issue area (see Cox 1996 [1981]: 99–100; Levy and Newell 2002). The dynamic nature of regimes means that regime effectiveness depends not only on the set of rules developed, it is also shaped by how these rules are set to change and the kinds of accommodations that have been reached amongst the various actors with the capacity to influence regime design (Levy and Egan 2003). Recognising the dynamic nature of regimes is important as it allows us to consider how robust or fragile the RSPO is – whether it is likely to be sustained, how it is challenged and by whom, and whether it will advance, or become irrelevant and stagnate or decay. Studies of the RSPO to date have not addressed this dimension, concentrating instead on its effectiveness by examining its rules and their enforcement. The paper concludes by drawing out the implications of the analysis for palm oil sustainability and the food and livelihood security of local and indigenous communities.

Palm oil and food security

Oil palm cultivation has seen a sharp spike worldwide in tropical zones from 1997 and more recently from 2007–2008, driven by rising global demand for edible oils and biofuel feedstock (Pye 2010; Laurance et al. 2010). Nevertheless, Indonesia and Malaysia still account for the bulk of oil palm plantings, respectively at 9.4 million and 4.6 million hectares (Colchester and Chao 2011: 5–7). These two countries also produce the bulk of palm oil, accounting for 85% of total palm oil production, which reached 50.3 million tonnes in 2010 (McLaughlin 2011: 1118). Palm oil accounts for 32% of the world's total consumption of vegetable oils compared to its nearest rival, soybean oil at 27.4% (Oil World, 2012 quoted in Adnan 2012a).

Palm oil's significant food security role, especially in the developing world cannot be denied given it is a cheap but nutritious food staple that is also the most efficient oil seed to date measured in terms of oil yield and land utilization (World Growth 2010; Teoh 2010). It currently accounts for only 14.4 million hectares or 0.3% of the 4.9 billion hectares of global agricultural land while soybean oil occupies 104 million hectares but produces far less edible oil (Basiron 2012). It is also a versatile commodity with vast industrial and consumer uses. Even its critics acknowledge that palm oil 'feeds millions, employs over a million and generates billions in dollar incomes' (FOE 2005: 9). However, when the environmental credentials of oil palm are challenged by key audiences, the crop's contribution to food security becomes indirectly threatened as well through calls to limit production.

Palm oil's claimed advantages are undermined by its role in deforestation, global warming, biodiversity loss, and social conflict despite assertions to the contrary by governments in producer countries (Laurance et al. 2010; FAO 2010). These concerns, previously linked to the tropical timber industry, were pushed to the front of civil society activism and public debate by the forest fires of 1997 (Teoh 2010: 17). The climate change impact of oil palm plantations is worsened when peat lands, which contain large amounts of carbon, are planted with oil palm.[2] It was these sorts of sustainability concerns in Indonesia and Malaysia that led the World Bank Group to suspend its long-standing financial support to the palm oil industry between 2009 and 2011. NGOs like Greenpeace continue to campaign for a global moratorium on converting forests and peat lands for oil palm cultivation while even entities outside the traditional NGO community such as Auckland Zoo and Melbourne Zoo have campaigned against palm oil and taken action to boycott products (like Cadbury's chocolate products) containing palm oil (*The Star*, 13 July 2009). Public campaigns to shun products containing palm oil have been growing in Europe, particularly in France although these have not been successful in changing official policy, for instance, to impose additional taxes on palm oil for its alleged adverse health and environment effects (Khor Reports 2013: 8). Another potential challenge to palm oil was the proposal in 2010 (later defeated) to introduce a food labelling bill in the Australian Senate that would require all food products containing palm oil (though not other vegetable oils) to specifically list it as an ingredient so that consumers moved by deforestation in Indonesia and Malaysia could make informed choices (Sheargold and Mitchell 2011).

Oil palm plantations do have more direct consequences for the food and livelihood security of rural and indigenous communities through the medium of land and rights to land. Food security considerations have led governments across the developing world to offer land to corporations for large-scale cultivation of a variety of food crops (Borras Jr and Franco 2011). But, far from involving the acquisition of *reserve* agricultural land or unused land, these new transnational land deals have been described as 'land grabs', involving land that is neither 'idle, marginal [nor] uninhabited' (ibid.: 11). Governments have used, or abused, their authority to categorize lands so that valuable lands currently in use or claimed by rural and indigenous communities are legally alienated by the state for development purposes, including to private corporations (De Schutter 2011). When state elites are directly involved as partners in these land deals, gains have accrued privately as well (Borras Jr and Franco 2011: 7–13). Consequently, rural and indigenous communities lose their ownership and/or use rights to land, often without sufficient compensation or consultation while the environmental consequences of these land conversions are also ignored (World Bank 2011: 141).

Critics and advocates of palm oil hold seemingly irreconcilable positions. In challenging palm oil's critics, its advocates point to the crop's positive socio-economic benefits for rural communities, many of which are keen to be part of the palm oil boom (see Rist et al. 2010). Oil palm cultivation's poverty reduction effects as experienced in Indonesia and Malaysia confirm for these and other developing country governments the value of this crop, a position that aligns nicely with corporate interest in a commodity that has witnessed rising average prices over the last decade. But, it is precisely the national and corporate passion driving land conversion for oil palm cultivation that is at the root of conflicts over land. Plantations prefer large contiguous tracts of land to maximise returns. As already noted, the lands acquired are often forested lands, forest dwellings or lands that are lived on and farmed by local communities, often productively and sometimes for generations (Pye 2010: 855; Borras Jr and Franco 2011: 11; Colchester and Chao 2011). In many instances, indigenous land rights are usurped. Unsurprisingly then, palm oil production is accompanied by local land conflicts.

Palm oil and land conflicts in Southeast Asia

In Southeast Asia, oil palm-related land conflicts have been most pronounced in the traditional oil palm growing countries of Malaysia and Indonesia but recent country studies reveal similar conflicts in other Southeast Asian countries witnessing expansion in oil palm cultivation such as Cambodia and the Philippines (Borras Jr and Franco 2011; Colchester and Chao 2011).[3] The Indonesian national land agency has confirmed 3,500 land conflicts linked to palm oil across the country (Aliansi Maasyarakat Adat Nusantara et al. 2010). In Malaysia, land conflicts involving oil palm plantations are mostly found in the East Malaysian states of Sabah and Sarawak located on the island of Borneo. Notwithstanding the different settings in which oil palm-related land conflicts occur, one common feature is the complicity of the state in these conflicts. Vast disparities in power between governments and rural/indigenous communities mean that the former has been able to use policy and especially the law to alienate community lands to private or state-owned firms for large-scale plantations (see Hamilton-Hart 2013). States also use their powers to *categorize* lands to facilitate land alienation to private firms.

In Cambodia, for instance, lands used by local and indigenous communities for growing crops have been categorized by the state as unproductive or marginal so that these lands can be legally alienated to private companies for large-scale agricultural development, including oil palm cultivation. In some cases, political elites have interests in the companies involved, leading a senior UN official on Cambodia's human rights to criticise the country's land concession programme for depriving local communities of their livelihoods while enhancing the wealth of those with influence (Sokhannaro 2011). In the Philippines, oil palm development in some parts of the country has taken place on existing agricultural and customary lands once the government classified these as unused lands (Villanueva 2011: 164). Although Vietnam does not as yet have any major oil palm cultivation, the government's bio-fuels programme coupled with the insecure land rights accorded to rural communities, especially ethnic minorities, suggests the potential for similar conflicts (Vo 2011). Already, land conflicts top the list of major grievances cited by the Vietnamese people against officials and the government, accounting for 70% of all complaints filed across the country (Hiebert and Nguyen 2012).

The Indonesian experience demonstrates how over 25 years oil palm cultivation has turned from what was once 'a comparatively pro-poor and pro-smallholder' approach to one where local and indigenous landowner rights have been undermined by a steady stream of national laws that accord centrality to the large-scale corporate plantation model (Gillespie 2012: 260). Only 40% of land holdings are titled while between 60 and 110 million rural Indonesians who are categorised as 'indigenous' hold lands by custom (Colchester 2010: 8). Although customary rights to land are recognised by the revised Indonesian Constitution, the latter accords control over natural resources to the state, which has used these powers to either ignore or terminate land rights (Borras Jr and Franco 2011).

State land development projects that make over lands to plantation companies do not always ignore local communities; many of these projects clearly have poverty reduction, rural development, and rural employment goals while many local communities see palm oil as providing the best option for meeting their financial needs compared to other types of rural economic activities (see Rist et al. 2010). However, the design of such schemes can impoverish local communities. For instance, changes have occurred to the nucleus estate scheme (*inti-plasma* scheme) in Indonesia, which had once created economic opportunities for local communities within large plantations by allowing them to retain their title to smallholdings on which they can grow oil palm. However, the portion of public land alienated by the authorities to the nucleus plantation has become progressively larger over the years and that allotted to the smallholding lower. Indonesia's decentralization drive that devolved power over economic affairs to districts has compounded the situation as local authorities compete to attract plantation firms to their districts by offering them the one item they have in abundant supply – land (Gillespie 2012: 261). Increasingly, smallholding communities become indebted to the plantation company, which effectively holds the land titles as debt collateral for the oil palm plantings and other improvements it provides for these smallholdings (Pye 2010: 855). First person testimonies reveal other problems – debts that are manipulated, unfair allocation of smallholdings, non-transparent land titling – that make the livelihoods of rural communities insecure in the cycle of landlessness, debt and poverty thus created (Colchester 2010: 12). The competition to attract plantations to drive the local economy compounded by corruption of officials means that any challenge from smallholders or legitimate claimants of land is either ignored or put down, sometimes violently, by the authorities. When land is already privately owned, whether local landowners gain from leasing their land to plantation companies depends on the fairness of the contracts, and whether local officials administer impartially these land contracts, including providing advice to local land owners (Rist et al. 2010).

Similar livelihood insecurities are evident in the Malaysian state of Sarawak, which in the mid 1990s focused on the palm oil industry as a key route to development in the state. It has also seen the largest number of land conflicts linked to oil palm cultivation in the past decade (Cramb 2007; Colchester et al. 2007; Colchester 2010). The *New Concept of NCR Land Development* adopted by the state government in 1994 centres on the use of indigenous lands for oil palm expansion through the formation of joint venture companies between indigenous land owners and private plantation companies.[4] However, indigenous communities have had to *surrender* their native customary rights (NCR) lands to a land bank managed by the state, which then leases the land to the joint venture corporation for 60 years to develop oil palm plantations. Although these communities receive 30% equity in this joint venture company, with the private oil palm plantation company owning 60% and the government 10%, the dividends from these deals have been minuscule and far below what the government had indicated when advocating this particular development project (Cramb 2007: 270; Tawie 2009, 2011). Lack of transparency over how dividend payments are calculated and distributed has been an added concern (Brimas 2009). The employment promised to indigenous communities on the plantations rarely materializes, while the wages paid are too low to support a family (Tawie 2009). Where previously these communities had access to land for their subsistence needs, those who lose their jobs on the plantations or fail to find suitable work have no social safety net offered by subsistence farming because their land has been turned over to oil palm plantations (Majid Cooke 2006; Cramb 2007; Colchester et al. 2007).

Although native customary rights to land are recognised by law in Malaysia,[5] the law in Sarawak became the instrument through which a powerful state appropriated native lands for oil palm development (Majid Cooke 2006: 36–38). The Taib Mahmud government, in power since 1981 and supported by a major indigenous political party from the late 1980s, was able to amend Sarawak state laws at will towards this end (Cramb 2007). Forestry laws were amended to allow conversion of forests into oil palm and other planted tree plantations with the state pledging 'to protect or safeguard the interests of those who are prepared to invest in tree plantations in the State' (Forest Department Sarawak 1997). Clearly, the state has bound itself by law to protect the interests of private firms against any resistance by local communities or NGOs. This pledge has been supported by laws making direct action protests such as blockades a criminal offence. In 1994, 1996, 1998 and 2000, the *1958 Sarawak Land Code* was amended so that the state could extinguish customary rights to land for virtually *any* purpose, decide on the quantum of compensation to be paid, placed the onus on the indigenous claimant to prove that (s)he held customary rights to land, which was therefore presumed to be unencumbered state land, and removed previously granted rights to the uncultivated lands and virgin territory surrounding native farmed areas and longhouses (Cramb 2007; Bulan 2006). The state also revised the *Land Surveyors Ordinance 2001* to make community mapping of customary lands by indigenous communities illegal. This move immediately followed a High Court decision in May 2001 that used evidence from community mapping to rule in favour of the indigenous claimants to land that the state had alienated to a private firm (Bujang 2004: 6).

In Sarawak, indigenous communities have increasingly turned to the civil courts to rule on their land claims.[6] Even though legislative changes have narrowed the definition and operation of customary law, state and federal courts in Malaysia have in various judgments upheld customary rights to lands. However, the Sarawak state government continues to ignore such judgments, thus prolonging the uncertainty and insecurities faced by the indigenous land claimants (Bian 2009, 2012). In Indonesia, courts do not usually rule in favour of local communities partly due to corruption and partly due to weak land laws (Colchester 2010: 13). But, having progressive indigenous rights laws such as in the Philippines does not also guarantee that these rights will be translated on the ground into effective tenure and ownership rights to ancestral lands (Colchester and Chao 2011: 15).

Food security and the governance of palm oil sustainability

The preceding discussion highlights three key points that must be taken into account when considering governance mechanisms aimed at ensuring palm oil's environmental and social sustainability. One, land conflicts involving rural and indigenous communities are a near universal phenomenon wherever oil palm is cultivated, featuring not only in Southeast Asia but elsewhere in Africa and Latin America as well (Pye 2010). Oil palm-related land conflicts have become globalized, reflecting the global nature of this industry and the continuing transnationalization of oil palm plantation firms and groups. Established plantation firms are venturing to other Southeast Asian locations beyond Indonesia and Malaysia as well as to non-traditional sites in Central and Eastern Africa where governments are supporting large-scale plantation agriculture for development and food security purposes (Borras Jr and Franco 2011; Adnan 2012b). The strong demand for this commodity coupled with its high profitability has also sparked interest amongst firms new to the business from palm oil consuming countries like China, India and the Gulf states; these firms are acquiring land for oil palm cultivation in Southeast Asia and Africa. A governance mechanism for this industry must therefore be global in scope and reach.

The second point to note in considering the future of palm oil is that a balance needs to be reached between global/national food security on the one hand and the food and livelihood security of local, including indigenous communities on the other hand. Palm oil's extensive and varied use in both food and non-food use mean that calls to halt oil palm expansion is impractical and unlikely to work. The large-scale agri-business model is here to stay, at least for the foreseeable future. Mixed development involving both large-scale plantations and smallholdings has been suggested as a workable option, able to enhance the livelihoods of farmers provided their right to land is secured by law (De Schutter 2011).

This leads to the third observation that governance solutions for this industry that require the *state* to adopt, implement and enforce regulation may not work well because the state is deeply implicated in most oil-palm related land conflicts. Although global and/or regional codes and guidelines such as the *World Bank's Principles of Responsible Agricultural Investment* (World Bank 2011) or the *Bali Declaration on Human Rights and Agribusiness in Southeast Asia* (Bali Declaration 2011) are valuable normative frameworks that can guide the way states and firms deal with land issues, these guidelines will remain limited instruments unless they become binding on states and enforceable. But, with the state deeply implicated in land conflicts, relying on these same actors to adopt and enforce principles, laws and policies that safeguard local communities' rights to land will probably not get us very far. Court rulings and advocacy by human rights groups have not always produced outcomes favourable to rural and indigenous communities although judicial activism by the Sarawak courts in favour of indigenous land claimants is a positive development.

While political reform may alter state behaviour, democratization does not always guarantee that community land rights or subsistence interests will be secured. Oil palm development has come to be seen as a valuable route to economic growth and rural development by many developing country governments. In democratic Philippines and despite democratic reform in Indonesia, community land claims are routinely ignored by forestry authorities and regional (local) governments in the interests of revenue-generating big-firm investments (Villanueva 2010; Rist et al. 2010; Bartley 2011). The continuation of patronage politics in post-Suharto Indonesia, albeit one dominated by local business oligarchs rather than bureaucrats as in the past, suggests that private interests will be privileged for now (Fukuoka 2012). Similarly, democratisation in the Philippines did not alter the dominance of the powerful landed oligarchs who ended up controlling democratic political processes and a weak state (Manacsa and Tan 2012).

In the light of these realities, private regulation such as sustainability certification that operates through market incentives on businesses concerned about their 'sustainability credentials' could be a workable option if such a mechanism directs business behaviour towards a more sustainable direction. However, market-based governance regimes are not without their limitations. Private regulatory regimes have been criticised as 'soft law' mechanisms dependent on voluntary actions by firms or worse, as shams or 'greenwash' (Perez 2011: 543). These regimes work only if key audiences – consumers and clients – see the value of sustainability and demand the firm acts accordingly. However, eco-consumerism works only slowly and in incremental steps in improving sustainability (Dauvergne and Lister 2010). Moreover, 'green' markets are not yet a global phenomenon and are mostly confined to the western world of Europe, North America and the Australia–New Zealand region. Yet, I argue that it is worth exploring the role of private sustainability regimes in the face of state complicity in land conflicts.

In the rest of this paper, I analyse how the RSPO measures up to the task of ensuring the sustainable production of palm oil in the light of these limitations and the more specific criticisms that have been levelled at the RSPO. I am especially concerned with how the RSPO has responded to the question of local land rights.

The Roundtable on Sustainable Palm Oil (RSPO): a solution to the sustainability problem?

In 2002, palm oil plantation firms such as Golden Hope and IOI, plantation industry groups such as the Malaysian Palm Oil Association, end-use manufacturers such as Unilever, retailers such as Sainsbury's and the Worldwide Fund for Nature (WWF), an NGO, mooted the idea of the RSPO as a certification body to ensure that palm oil would be sustainably produced (RSPO 2004). The palm oil industry had, by this time, become concerned by growing consumer boycotts against this edible oil. Since its official formation in 2004, RSPO membership has grown significantly, with 383 members in 2010, 637 by May 2012 and 828 in April 2013. Aside from government bodies that are not permitted to become members, the RSPO brings together the following seven stakeholder groups (membership numbers/as a proportion of total membership as at April 2013 in parentheses) (see RSPO nd):

- palm oil processors or traders (307/37%);
- manufacturers of consumer goods using palm oil as an ingredient (305/36.8%);
- oil palm growers and millers producing crude palm oil (124/15.1%);
- retailers that sell products containing palm oil to final consumers (49/5.9%);
- banks and investors that fund any aspect of the industry (11/1.3%);
- environmental or conservation NGOs concerned about the ecological aspects of the industry (22/2.7%); and
- social NGOs or development organizations concerned with palm oil production's social impact (10/1.2%).

The RSPO's rules: sustainability and land rights concerns

If the RSPO is to function as a credible sustainability regime for palm oil, then its rules[7] should create binding obligations for industry players, these obligations must also be precisely outlined and they must be effectively enforced.[8] On the first two counts, the RSPO performs fairly well with some limitations. It has a Code of Conduct for its members and an extensive set of certification rules (comprising eight Principles, 39 Criteria and 112 Indicators) that are also clearly defined for the most part (RSPO 2007a, b). Audited conformity to these rules allows the company to claim that it produces certified sustainable palm oil (CSPO). Moreover, despite being *voluntary,* the regime becomes binding once membership is accepted (RSPO 2004). However, the company can select from its entire operations which particular palm oil mill or mills (and their respective supplier estates) to submit for assessment; thus, a plantation company can enjoy certified status whilst still continuing unsustainable practices in its uncertified operations. Although RSPO standards require the company to submit *all* its remaining operations for assessment within a self-specified time period once even one operation has been certified (RSPO, 2007b), the deadline for complete certification is left to the company to determine. Consequently, despite an increase in the number of certified palm oil producers from four (and 17 certified mills) operating in Malaysia and Papua New Guinea in 2008 to 29 certified producers (and 135 certified mills) operating in six countries (Brazil, Colombia, Indonesia, Malaysia, Papua New Guinea and the Solomon Islands) in 2011, only 11% of total annual global palm oil production was certified (RSPO 2011: 3). In 2012, 15% or 8.2 million tonnes of total annual global production of palm oil was certified (RSPO 2013).

Notwithstanding these limitations, an important achievement for the RSPO is the inclusion of land rights criteria in its Principles and Criteria

(P&C) considering that only seven participants, essentially NGOs, out of about 200 participants at the inaugural Roundtable Meeting in 2003 voted to establish a working group to develop rules and standards on land rights (FOE 2005: 10–11). Ten out of the 39 RSPO criteria directly pertain to the land rights of local and indigenous communities.[9] Despite initial resistance, Indonesian and Malaysian oil palm plantation companies, which dominated the industry, had been prepared to work towards compliance. Under RSPO regulation on land rights, indigenous (and local) communities must be consulted, their consent given freely before planting or expansion can start, and consent must have been the result of open communication and exchange of information between the plantation and the community to allow well-informed decision-making by claimants having legitimate rights to the land. The ten rules thus accord local and indigenous communities a set of valuable participatory rights that these communities have been denied in Indonesia, Sarawak and other locales, both by authorities and by oil palm plantations. In addition, the RSPO set up a fund to finance small-holder certification (RSPO 2012a). This is an important development as smallholdings are not an insignificant part of this industry, accounting for about 40% and 35% respectively of planted oil palm in Malaysia and Indonesia (Tan 2011: 22). About 200,000 hectares of smallholdings have already been certified (RSPO 2011).

Where the RSPO faces the most criticism is in enforcement of its regulation, with the charge that no plantation firm has had its membership or certified status revoked despite violating RSPO rules (see Richardson 2010: 48–49). There are two parts to this criticism, one relating to the quality of auditing and the second the absence of any form of sanctioning of offenders. Although the RSPO imposes strict accreditation requirements for the third-party accreditation bodies that conduct the certification, concerns have been raised about the 'varying degree of thoroughness, being applied by different auditors (RFA 2010: 37). Part of the problem is with the RSPO standards. Although these standards are, for the most part, clearly defined, those addressing land rights issues often require subjective judgment, which can lead to charges of compromised certification. Assessing 'free, prior and informed consent' is especially difficult when plantations come under new ownership, when local communities are divided over the matter or when local communities regret having accepted earlier land deals involving lower compensation because palm oil prices were then lower. Moreover, certification is not usually denied even if land conflicts or adverse impacts on local/indigenous communities are present provided the plantation company has put in place a consultative or conflict mediation process acceptable to all stakeholders to address these issues. This is why despite disputes with local communities and despite heavy criticism by NGOs, Indonesian plantation company *PT Musim Mas* received RSPO certification and Malaysian company, IOI Corporation continues to maintain its certified status (RSPO 2008: 22–23; RSPO 2012b). The IOI case involving conflict over land claimed by the *Long Teran Kanan* indigenous community in Sarawak reveals how an emphasis on 'process' rather than outcome can prolong conflict between the plantation and land claimants (see RSPO 2012b). Nevertheless, the option of using mediation through the RSPO Grievance Process and Dispute Settlement Facility offers local communities the opportunity of having their grievances heard and a chance at gaining redress, something that had previously been denied to local land claimants by state authorities or the plantation company concerned. However, plantations not currently members of the RSPO are not bound to engage with local communities over land rights claims.

Another rule that benefits local and indigenous communities is the requirement for auditors to consult directly with them when assessing plantation operations to confirm that any land transfer and land use agreements possessed by the company have been obtained with the free, prior, and informed consent of these communities (RSPO 2007c: 14). The RSPO is acknowledging that although a company may possess all land transfer and land use agreements in full accordance with the relevant local law, these may have been obtained against the wishes or prior knowledge of indigenous or local communities, in effect recognising that these communities may have a *legitimate* (even if not a legal) claim to the land. This condition directly speaks to situations common in Southeast Asia where states devise or alter land laws to appropriate lands belonging to or claimed by rural and indigenous communities.

Although intended to be thorough and independent, certification audits can sometimes miss violations, especially when large plantations are being audited while there may be instances of biased audits. In fact, the RSPO functions less as an enforcement mechanism and more as a compliance regime where its rules and standards are set out for members to comply with. This is where the public monitoring processes formally and informally linked to the RSPO Grievance Process becomes important as these processes allow complaints to be lodged against any member violating the RSPO Codes and its body of regulation. Most complaints to the RSPO have been lodged by NGOs (RSPO 2009). The RSPO's Grievance Procedure also mandates a response and corrective action from the 'defendant' company if the complaint is judged to have validity. Because complaints can be received from any NGO and not just NGOs that are RSPO members, the monitoring scope of the RSPO goes beyond its institutional structure. In effect, the RSPO should be seen as part of what I term an 'extended governance complex' for palm oil in which NGOs, particularly well-organized ones, function as public watchdogs for the RSPO and the industry more generally. In short, NGOs have disproportionately more voice in the RSPO than their low numbers suggest (4% of membership in 2013, between 6–8% in previous years).

The public monitoring route provides a valuable avenue through which the sustainability practices of plantations *and* the quality and reliability of the audit process is monitored and improved. It is true that many egregious environmental practices and land appropriations have been committed by RSPO members but the more globally-oriented plantation firms are changing their practices to comply with RSPO sustainability criteria (Richardson 2010; Khor 2013). The Wilmar plantation group of Singapore ceased planting on disputed lands in Indonesia acknowledging that it had received an 'irregularly issued IUP (plantation operation certificate)' from the Indonesian authorities (Wilmar 2008). In March 2011, Indonesian company *PT Agro Wiratama* returned to the landowners 1000 hectares of a 9000 hectare concession it had been granted by the local government. Because the RSPO's 'New plantings procedure' requires public notification (also reported on the RSPO website) of planned expansions, NGOs had been able to alert affected local communities before operations started. Previous critics of the RSPO are beginning to recognise that the alternative – state-based regulation and enforcement – is not always likely to deliver justice to indigenous and rural land claimants. Norman Jiwan of the oil palm monitoring NGO, SawitWatch who is also an alternate member of the RSPO Executive Board, underlined the value of 'voluntary standards to get peoples' basic rights respected' because state authorities fail to respect land rights (SawitWatch 2011). In fact, plantation companies consider the RSPO's land rights criteria to be the key constraint to their operations although, as discussed below, more stringent environmental criteria are beginning to impede the operations of a number of plantation companies, including the bigger players (Khor 2013: 7). The larger plantation companies with transnational operations have started cutting back on previously announced oil palm expansion plans in anticipation of strict GHG emission criteria in the RSPO that would further raise production costs amidst softening prices for crude palm oil (Khor 2013).

The above analysis shows that the RSPO has in place fairly comprehensive environmental and social sustainability regulation where nothing comparable existed before, and because of the progressive changes in the behaviour of oil palm growers, especially the bigger plantations, it has become a valuable governance regime for palm oil sustainability, notwithstanding the deficiencies described above. However, the future of the RSPO also depends on how robust the regime is, whether it can continue to sustain sufficient internal consensus amongst quite diverse parties even as it responds to changing external pressures. Since 2009, a number of serious conflicts have emerged that signal a potential breakdown of the multi-stakeholder consensus that had prevailed since 2003 (Khor 2009).

How robust is the RSPO? Realignment of social forces in the Roundtable

Two key issues currently plague the RSPO; these emerged at the seventh RSPO Roundtable (RT 7) held in November 2009. One item of contention centred on proposed mandatory rules and targets for greenhouse gas (GHG) reduction. Following the adoption of the European Union's Renewable Energy Directive in 2009, NGOs and downstream firms (such as consumer manufacturers or retailers) in the RSPO proposed including similar GHG emission criteria and targets in the RSPO. Although RSPO rules already included emissions reductions, the relevant Criterion (#5.6) had been vaguely worded. The second contentious issue centres on the low uptake of certified sustainable palm oil (CSPO) by downstream manufacturers and their unwillingness to pay a premium price for CSPO, thus placing all the burden of enhancing palm oil's sustainability on oil palm producers (Khor 2009). These issues have divided the key social forces – stakeholders – underpinning the RSPO. The divide over the GHG issue pits oil palm producers, particularly from Indonesia and Malaysia, against NGOs and downstream corporations that use palm oil in their operations. The second divide over the CSPO issue sees oil palm producers (upstream sector) and NGOs facing off downstream corporate users of palm oil.

NGOs essentially took the lead in shaping the RSPO's rules on environmental and social sustainability despite their low numbers in the RSPO. Their strength lies in their superior organizational capacity and the very effective strategies they use to get their message across, including in-depth field research, photographic and interview evidence of unsustainable practices, and direct lobbying of firms and governments, especially European governments, and RSPO member firms such as Unilever. Having Jan Kees Vis, who is also Global Director of Sustainable Sourcing Development for Unilever as RSPO President aided the NGO cause to embed strong green and social credentials within the RSPO. But, the material dangers to the industry posed by sustainability concerns, principally through boycott of palm oil, had also led firms in the industry, including plantation firms, to work with NGOs on developing the current body of RSPO regulation (Khor 2009).

However, the early broad-based, if at times uneasy, consensus between different stakeholders that had stabilized the regime since its establishment in 2004 may be at risk as NGOs and downstream corporations push the RSPO to specify clearer targets on GHG emission reduction. The initial NGO suggestion to adopt mandatory rules and targets on GHG emissions had been rejected by Malaysian and Indonesian plantation firms, which hold substantial peat lands in their land banks (Khor 2009: 4). Rules on GHG emission reduction would have severely restricted conversion of peat lands for oil palm cultivation. Some firms threatened to leave the RSPO if GHG reduction rules are made mandatory (*The Star*, 21 November 2009). In fact, the Indonesian Palm Oil Producers' Association (GAPKI) withdrew from the RSPO in 2011 due to unhappiness with the growing stringency of RSPO rules (*Jakarta Post*, 16 April 2012). However, downstream businesses such as manufacturers using palm oil in their products and retailers selling final goods incorporating palm oil were more inclined to side with proponents of GHG criteria in the RSPO. Many of these firms are European firms, including Unilever, Sainsbury, and Neste Oil, all with an eye not only on the European market but also sensitive to European public opinion, which demands European firms take responsibility for addressing climate change (European Commission 2011). Thus, deeming the RSPO to be 'industry-dominated' by counting the proportion of firms versus NGOs as RSPO critics do is simplistic. For one, NGOs have disproportionate voice in the RSPO as already noted. Second, firms in the RSPO are not always aligned on the same side because they are differently located within the palm oil supply chain, which consequently gives rise to divergent preferences amongst these firms with regard to sustainability regulation.

When RSPO principles and criteria were revised in 2012 following extensive public consultations, they stipulated targets for GHG emissions from new oil palm plantings. However, negotiations amongst all RSPO stakeholders on these new rules ended with a final set of revised P&C that did not include clear, stringent standards on GHG emission reductions nor impose a moratorium on the use of peat lands, among other gaps (WWF 2013). The final version of the revised rules, voted in by 213 members (six against and three spoilt votes) at an RSPO extraordinary general assembly (EGA) in Kuala Lumpur on 25 April 2013, nevertheless contain new rules on reducing GHG emissions from new plantings and reporting on the reductions, ethical business practices as well as human rights considerations in relation to forced migrant labour (RSPO 2013; Adnan 2013). Yet, many NGOs and activists were disappointed that these rules do not go far enough on GHG emissions. The WWF, a founding member and long-standing supporter of the RSPO had issued a statement just before the April 2013 EGA that acknowledged these shortfalls in the revised RSPO regime and called on 'progressive companies' to go beyond these rules and for investors and retailers to 'make parallel commitments to only do business with growers that take... extra actions' that address more comprehensively palm oil sustainability (WWF 2013). Through this statement, the WWF was signalling that the RSPO could not now be used as a benchmark standard on GHG emissions. Palm oil growers, on the other hand, were reportedly unhappy that the overwhelming focus on enhancing environmental and social sustainability was once again burdening growers while ignoring the socio-economic and developmental benefits of palm oil cultivation (Adnan 2013). While the larger plantation firms seem prepared to accede to new more stringent RSPO rules (see Khor 2013), other medium-sized growers see the revised rules on GHG emissions, even though watered down from the original, as an unfair burden borne primarily by one stakeholder group, namely the growers (*Borneo Post*, 18 April 2013).

These tensions in the RSPO have been exacerbated by the unwillingness of downstream manufacturers and retailers to pay a premium for CSPO and indeed to increase the use of CSPO in their products and operations, leaving a large stock of unsold CSPO. Market uptake at the end of 2010 was 45% of total CSPO produced, mostly by European purchasers (RSPO 2011: 13). Although European firms using palm oil had committed to using CSPO for their European products, the amounts pledged were a low 2 million tonnes by 2015 according to WWF estimates (Khor 2009). The limited demand for CSPO and the reluctance to pay a 'sustainability premium' has divided the industry between upstream plantation firms and downstream users. The Malaysian Palm Oil Association (MPOA) proposed, unsuccessfully, in November 2011 a moratorium on further certification exercises until 2015 to clear unsold CSPO stocks and wait for pledged CSPO purchases to take effect (Adnan 2011a). With only the European market interested in sustainable palm oil to date and no firm commitment to CSPO in the fastest growing markets of China, South Asia and the Middle East, there is little incentive for producers beyond the largest plantation groups to commit to certification. The RSPO has now begun lobbying governments in new markets to support the use of CSPO (Adnan 2011b).

The RSPO is clearly at a cross-road. The regime is somewhat fragile given the fractures and realignments in the coalitions that had once underpinned the RSPO's multi-stakeholder consensus. NGOs are insisting that producers conform to an expanded range of environmental and social sustainability criteria beyond existing RSPO rules, including the incorporation of global human rights principles to govern the treatment of workers, address human trafficking concerns in relation to migrant workers and restore land rights to rural and indigenous communities (RSPO 2012b). In contrast, the Malaysian and Indonesian governments and their respective producer groups are calling for equal emphasis on the profitability of the palm oil industry to balance what they consider an already adequate set of environmental and social sustainability criteria (*The Star*, 21 November 2009). These two countries have developed national sustainability certification schemes as a preferable alternative to what they see as the RSPO's NGO-dominated agenda and its increasingly burdensome sustainability rules (Adnan 2011a; *Jakarta Post*, 16 April 2012). However, these national certification schemes may not go as far as the RSPO in safeguarding land rights for rural and indigenous communities given these governments' poor track record in this regard, weak land laws and the close patronage relations between plantation firms and governments in these countries.[10] It is also unclear if these national systems will apply to the transnational operations of Malaysian and Indonesian firms outside their home countries. If the RSPO unravels or faces serious competition from these national schemes, the losers will be the indigenous and rural communities who have been accorded participatory rights by the RSPO, rights not normally accorded them in these countries.

Conclusion

This paper examined the nexus between food security, land issues and sustainability governance through a case study of palm oil. It identified two ways in which palm oil's contribution to food security may be undermined. One, if limits are imposed on palm oil expansion because of its poor sustainability record, then its contribution to food security, particularly in the developing world more generally, will be undermined, especially as it is a cheap but nutritious food staple that is also the most efficient oilseed to date. Two, oil palm expansion directly undermines the food security of rural, including indigenous communities when these communities are dispossessed of the land that sustains their livelihood, with inadequate compensation provided and/or no other realistic livelihood options available to them. Because of state complicity in the environmental damage and land dispossession associated especially with large-scale oil palm plantations, the paper considered a non-state governance regime as a potential alternative governance mechanism that would minimise both the environmental damage and livelihood disruption associated with oil palm cultivation.

The paper's findings indicate that the RSPO's present certification regime provides fairly comprehensive and progressive socio-environmental regulation for the palm oil industry although there are weaknesses, especially in enforcement. Importantly, oil palm growers, particularly the larger plantation firms mindful of their international reputation and market acceptability, are embracing far more sustainable production practices as a result of their membership of the RSPO. As for the food and livelihood insecurities that result from land conflicts, the paper finds the RSPO to be a valuable governance alternative to state-based mechanisms. With states often complicit in land grabs, it is unlikely that state-based governance or global guiding principles that depend on states to adopt and enforce will be up to the task. In particular, the emphasis in the RSPO on ensuring *due process* for land claimants is an advance on the usual practice by states and firms of silencing these groups while RSPO rules also recognize that these communities may have *legitimate* rights to land even if companies hold legal title, in effect acknowledging how national land laws are used in land grabs.

While multi-stakeholder regulation clearly has a role to play in enhancing palm oil sustainability and food security, multi-stakeholder regimes can be fragile, requiring a great deal of internal accommodation and trade-offs to work. Already, different interests in the RSPO are pulling in different directions. Fragmentation in the governance of palm oil sustainability is already evident with the development of national certification regimes in Indonesia and Malaysia that are expected to be less onerous, and thus more attractive to, growers less concerned about their reputation in western markets. These national certification schemes could also become acceptable in fast growing palm oil markets in China, India and the

Middle East not yet strong demanders of *sustainable* palm oil. However, these national regimes are unlikely to address land rights issues to the extent the RSPO does. Until governments become more responsive to their needs and interests, rural and indigenous land claimants are, therefore, more likely to gain through the RSPO system.

Acknowledgements

Research for this paper was supported by a research grant from the East Asian Development Network (EADN).

Notes

1 There is now a substantial literature on the food security implications of the turn to bio-fuels. A good collection is Matondi et al. (2011).
2 Tropical peat lands contain up to 90 gigatons of carbon that can be released when these lands are drained for cultivation (Miettinen et al. 2012).
3 Statistics on land-related conflicts linked to oil palm cultivation are hard to come by, but NGOs have documented case studies of such conflicts. This paper draws on these studies.
4 Of Sarawak's population of 2.5 million people, at least 65% are classified as indigenous (UNHCR 2008).
5 There are exceptions. Customary rights to land of the Orang Asli of peninsular Malaysia are not recognized by law; neither are those of the Penans of Sarawak (Brosius 1997: 476; Suhakam 2007: 3).
6 Of the 200 cases pending in the courts, 25% are oil palm-related land conflicts (Colchester 2010).
7 The RSPO's body of certification regulation is best deemed to be a combination of rules and standards, with the former specifying in advance precisely what conduct is permissible (example: do not drive above 80 kph on the highway) while the latter offers more discretion by outlining particular forms of desirable behavior (example: do not drive at excessive speed on the highway). See Kaplow (1992) on the distinction between rules and standards and from which comes the example cited.
8 These criteria are drawn from the definition of hard law outlined by Abbott and Snidal (2000).
9 The 10 criteria are #1.1, 2.1–2.3, 6.1–6.4, 7.5 and 7.6. See RSPO (2007c, 2008).
10 On patronage relationships in the palm oil industry in Indonesia and Malaysia, see Varkkey (2013).

References

Abbot, K. W. and Snidal, D. (2000) 'Hard and soft law in international governance', *International Organization* 54(3): 421–456.
Adnan, H. (2011a) 'RSPO meets amid brewing tension', *The Star*, 22 November.
Adnan, H. (2011b) 'RSPO chief: be committed', *The Star*, 23 November.
Adnan, H. (2012a) 'New frontiers', *The Star*, 12 May.
Adnan, H. (2012b) 'Malaysia's oil palm land depleting fast', *The Star*, 24 May.
Adnan, H. (2013) 'Oil palm growers fail to block adoption of new RSPO principles', *The Star*, 26 April.

Aliansi Masyarakat Adat Nusantara, SawitWatch, HuMA and Forest Peoples' Programme (2010) 'Indonesia: palm oil development on indigenous peoples' lands', *Case on Land Rights and the Right to Food*, January.

Bali Declaration (2011) *Bali Declaration on Human Rights and Agribusiness in Southeast Asia*. 1 December; accessed at http://www.forestpeoples.org/sites/fpp/files/publication/2011/12/final-bali-declaration-adopted-1-dec-2011.pdf, 9 June 2012.

Bartley, T. (2011) 'Transnational governance as the layering of rules: intersections of public and private standards', *Theoretical Inquiries in Law* 12(2): 517–542.

Basiron, Y. (2012) 'Sustainable palm oil from the Malaysian perspective', presentation by Dr Yusof Basiron, CEO of Malaysian Palm Oil Council (MPOC) at the Third International Exhibition and Conference for Palm Oil, 9 May, 2012, Jakarta, Indonesia.

Bian, B. (2009) Press release on 20 June 2009; accessed at http://hornbillunleashed. wordpress.com/2009/06/22/1989/, 12 January 2010.

Bian, B. (2012) 'Press statement: court declares "Konsep Baru" to develop NCR land a nullity', press statement released by Baru Bian, Advocates and Solicitors for the Plaintiffs, 2 May; accessed at http://www.barubian.net/2012/05/press-statement-court-declares-konsep.html, 25 may 2012.

Borneo Post (2013) 'Association dissatisfied with upcoming EGM', *Borneo Post*, April 18.

Borras Jr, S. M. and Franco, J. C. (2011) *Political Dynamics of Land Grabbing in Southeast Asia: Understanding Europe's Role*. Amsterdam: The Transnational Institute; accessed at http://www.tni.org/report/political-dynamics-land-grabbing-southeast-asia-understanding-europes-role, 1 May 2012.

Brimas (2009) 'Suai NCR land owners want out of oil palm joint venture'. Miri: Borneo Resources Institute, Malaysia; accessed at www.rengah.c2o.org/news/article.php?identifier=de0680t, 11 December 2009.

Brosius, P. J. (1997) 'Prior transcripts, divergent paths: resistance and acquiescence to logging in Sarawak, East Malaysia', *Comparative Studies in Society and History* 39(3): 468–510.

Bujang, M. (2004) 'A community initiative: mapping Dayak's customary lands in Sarawak', paper presented at the Regional Community Mapping Network Workshop, 8–10 November, Diliman, Quezon City, Philippines.

Bulan, R. (2006) 'Native customary land: the trust as device for land development in Sarawak', in F. Majid Cooke (ed.) *State, Communities and Forests in Contemporary Borneo*. Canberra: ANU-EPress, pp. 45–64.

Colchester, M. (2010) *Palm Oil and Indigenous Peoples in Southeast Asia: Land Acquisition, Human Rights Violations and Indigenous Peoples on the Palm Oil Frontier*. Moreton-in-Marsh and Rome: Forest Peoples Programme and International Land Coalition.

Colchester, M. and Chao, S. (2011) 'Oil palm expansion in Southeast Asia: an overview', in M. Colchester and S. Chao (eds) *Oil Palm Expansion in Southeast Asia: Trends and Implications for Local Communities and Indigenous Peoples*. Moreton-in-Marsh: Forest Peoples Programme, pp. 1–23.

Colchester, M., Wee, A. P., Wong, M. C. and Jalong, T. (2007) *Land is Life: Land Rights and Oil Palm Development in Sarawak*. Moreton-in-Marsh, England and Bogor, Indonesia: Forest Peoples Programme and Perkumpulan Sawit Watch.

Cox, R. W. (1996 [1981]) 'Social forces, states and world orders: beyond international relations theory', in R. W. Cox with T. J. Sinclair (eds) *Approaches to World Order*. Cambridge: Cambridge University Press, pp. 85–123.

Cramb, R. A. (2007) *Land and Longhouse: Agrarian Transformation in the Uplands of Sarawak*. Netherlands: NIAS Press.

De Schutter, O. (2011) 'How not to think of land-grabbing: three critiques of large-scale investments in farmland', *The Journal of Peasant Studies* 38(2): 249–279.

Dauvergne, P. and Lister, J. (2010) 'The prospects and limits of eco-consumerism: shopping our way to less deforestation', *Organization and Environment* 23(2): 132–154.

European Commission (2011) *Climate Change Report*. Special Eurobarometer 372, Brussels: European Commission, October; accessed at http://ec.europa.eu/public_opinion/archives/ebs/ebs_372_en.pdf, 30 August 2012.

FAO (2010) *Global Forests Resources Assessments: Key Findings*. Rome: Food and Agricultural Organization.

FOE (2005) *Greasy Palms: The Social and Ecological Impacts of Large-Scale Oil Palm Plantation Development in Southeast Asia*. England, Wales and Northern Ireland: Friends of the Earth; accessed at www.foe.co.uk/resource/reports/greasy_palms_impacts.pdf, 29 September 2010.

Forest Department Sarawak (1997) *The Forests Ordinance: The Forests (Planted Forests) Rules 1997*. Kuching: Forest Department Sarawak.

Fukuoka, Y. (2012) 'Politics, business and the state in post-Suharto Indonesia', *Contemporary Southeast Asia* 34(1): 80–100.

Gillespie, P. (2012) 'The challenges of corporate governance in Indonesian oil palm: opportunities to move beyond legalism?', *Asian Studies Review* 36(2): 247–269.

Hamilton-Hart, N. (2013) 'The costs of coercion: modern Southeast Asia in comparative perspective', *The Pacific Review* 26(1): 65–87.

Hiebert, M. and Nguyen, P. (2012) 'Land disputes stir political debates in Vietnam', *Critical Questions*, 24 July, Washington DC: Center for Strategic and International Studies; accessed at http://csis.org/print/38524, 22 April 2013.

Jakarta Post (2012) 'Indonesia develops rival sustainable palm oil scheme', *Jakarta Post*, 16 April.

Kaplow, L. (1992) 'Rules versus standards: an economic analysis', *Duke Law Journal* 42(2): 557–629.

Khor Reports (2013) *Palm Oil*, Issue 1, March/April.

Khor, Y. (2009) *Roundtable 7: Notes and Analysis on the Sessions and General Assembly from an Upstream Corporate Perspective*. Kuala Lumpur: Acacia Services Pte Ltd, 16 November 2009, unpublished report.

Khor, Y. (2013) 'Struggle for sustainability in palm oil industry shows results', *ISEAS Perspective #18/2013*, Singapore: ISEAS.

Laurance, W. F., Koh, L. P., Butler, R., Sodhi, N. S., Bradshaw, C. J. A., Neidel, J. D., Consunji, H. and Vega, J. M. (2010) 'Improving the performance of the roundtable on sustainable palm oil for nature conservation', *Conservation Biology* 24(2): 377–381.

Levy, D. and Newell, P. (2002) 'Business Strategy and international environmental governance: towards a neo-Gramscian synthesis', *Global Environmental Politics* 2(4): 84–101.

Levy, D. and Egan, D. (2003) 'A new Gramscian approach to corporate political strategy: conflict and accommodation in the climate change negotiations', *Journal of Management Studies* 40(4): 803–829.

Majid Cooke, F. (2006) 'Expanding state spaces using "idle" native customary land in Sarawak', in F. Majid Cooke (ed.) *State, Communities and Forests in Contemporary Borneo*. Canberra: ANU-EPress, pp. 25–44.

Manacsa, R. C. and Tan, A. C. (2012) '"Strong republic" sidetracked: oligarchic dynamics, democratization and economic development in the Philippines', *Korea Observer* 43(1): 47–87.

Matondi, P. B., Havenevik, K. and Beyene, A. (2011) *Biofuels, Land Grabbing and Food Security in Africa*. London: Zed Books.

McLaughlin, D. W. (2011) 'Land, food and biodiversity', *Conservation Biology* 25(6): 1117–1120.

Miettinen, J., Chi, S., and Soo, C. L. (2012) 'Two decades of destruction in Southeast Asia's Peat Swamp Forest', *Frontiers in Ecology and the Environment* 10(3): 124–128.

Perez, O. (2011) 'Private environmental governance as ensemble regulation: a critical exploration of sustainability indexes and the new ensemble politics', *Theoretical Inquiries in Law*, 12(2): 543–579.

Pye, O. (2010) 'The bio-fuel connection – transnational activism and the palm oil boom', *Journal of Peasant Studies* 37(4): 851–874.

Richardson, C. L. (2010) 'Deforestation due to palm oil plantations in Indonesia: towards the sustainable production of palm oil', *Research Report of the Palm Oil Action Group*; accessed at http://www.palmoilaction.org.au/downloads/palm-oil-research-project.pdf, 3 September 2012.

Rist, L., Feintrenie, L. and Levang, P. (2010) 'The livelihood impacts of oil palm: smallholders in Indonesia', *Biodiversity and Conservation* 19(4): 1009–1024.

RFA (2010) *Palm Oil Cultivation in Malaysia: Case Study*. United Kingdom: Renewable Fuels Agency; accessed at www.renewablefuelsagency.gov.uk/_db/_documents/RFA_Year_One_palm_case_study.pdf, 26 February 2010.

RSPO (2004) *Code of Conduct for Members of the Roundtable on Sustainable Palm Oil*. Kuala Lumpur: Roundtable on Sustainable Palm Oil, April; accessed at www.rspo.org/files/resource_centre/CoC.pdf, 15 August 2008.

RSPO (2007a) *RSPO Principles and Criteria for Sustainable Palm Oil Production*. Kuala Lumpur: Roundtable on Sustainable Palm Oil, October; accessed at www.rspo.org/files/resource_centre/RSPO%20Principles%20&%20Criteria%20Document.pdf, 28 August 2009.

RSPO (2007b) *FAQ on the Roundtable on Sustainable Palm Oil*. Kuala Lumpur: Roundtable on Sustainable Palm Oil, 7 November; accessed at www.rspo.org/resource_centre/FAQ%20on%20the%20Roundtable%20on%20Sustainable%20Palm%20Oil.pdf, 31 August 2009.

RSPO (2007c) *RSPO Certification Systems*. Kuala Lumpur: Roundtable on Sustainable Palm Oil, 26 June; accessed at www.rspo.org/files/resource_centre/RSPO%20certification%20systems_1.pdf, December 2009.

RSPO (2008), *RSPO Assessment Report (Public Summary): Musim Mas, Riau, Sumatra*. Kuala Lumpur: Roundtable on Sustainable Palm Oil, 10 July; accessed at www.rspo.org/resource_centre/Musim_Mas_RSPO_ASSESS_08_1_ENG.pdf, 29 August 2009.

RSPO (2009) *Consultation on RSPO Dispute Settlement Facility (DSF): Rationale, Objectives, Terms of Reference, Protocol and Request for Comments*. Kuala Lumpur: RSPO Dispute Settlement Facility Working Group, September; accessed at ww.rspo.org/resource_centre/RSPO%20Grievance%20Procedure.pdf, 15 November 2009.

RSPO (2011) *RSPO CSPO Growth Interpretation Narrative 2011*. Kuala Lumpur: Roundtable on Sustainable Palm Oil.

RSPO (2012a) *One of the World's Largest Scheme Smallholders in Indonesia to be RSPO Certified*. Kuala Lumpur: Roundtable on Sustainable Palm Oil, 7 September; accessed at http://www.rspo.org/news_details.php?nid=119, 15 September 2012.

RSPO (2012b) *Letter from RSPO to IOI Corporation and the Long Teran Kanan Community in Sarawak*. Kuala Lumpur: Roundtable on Sustainable Palm

Oil, 3 May; accessed at http://www.rspo.org/file/RSPO%20letter%20to%20IOI%20LTK%20sNGO%2020120503.pdf, 10 June 2012.

RSPO (2012c) *RSPO Principles and Criteria Review: Phase 1 Public Consultations/ Overall General Comments by Stakeholder*. Kuala Lumpur: Roundtable on Sustainable Palm Oil; accessed at http://www.rspo.org/en/principles_and_criteria_review, 21 July 2012.

RSPO (2013) *RSPO Extraordinary General Assembly Concludes with Revised Principles and Criteria adopted*. Kuala Lumpur: Roundtable on Sustainable Palm Oil, 25 April; accessed at http://www.rspo.org/news_details.php?nid=155&lang=1, 27 April 2013.

RSPO (nd) 'Membership key statistics'; accessed at http://www.rspo.org/en/membership_key_statistics, 25 May 2012.

SawitWatch (2011) 'Precedent-setting land deal in palm oil expansion zone in Borneo', 22 March; accessed at http://indigenouspeoplesissues.com/index.php?option=com_content&view=article&id=9534:malaysia-precedent-setting-land-deal-in-palm-oil-expansion-zone-in-borneo&catid=32:southeast-asia-indigenous-peoples&Itemid=65.

Sheargold, E. and Mitchell, A. D. (2011) 'Oils ain't oils: product labelling, palm oil and the WTO', *Melbourne Journal of International Law* 12(2): 396–418.

Sokhannaro, H. E. P. (2011) 'Oil palm development in Cambodia', in M. Colchester and S. Chao (eds) *Oil Palm Expansion in Southeast Asia: Trends and Implications for Local Communities and Indigenous Peoples*. Moreton-in-Marsh: Forest Peoples Programme, pp. 52–78.

SUHAKAM (2007) *Penan in Ulu Belaga: Right to Land and Socio-Economic Development'*. Kuala Lumpur: Human Rights Commission of Malaysia.

Tan, J. (2011) 'Fronds of a dilemma', *Green Purchasing Asia* 4 (September): 22–24.

Tawie, J. (2009) 'NCR landowners being exploited – DAP', *Malaysian Mirror*, 17 November; accessed at www.malaysianmirror.com/homedetail/12-sabahsarawak/19245-ncr-landowners-being-exploited-dap, 27 November 2009.

Tawie, J. (2011) 'Pittance for native landowners in joint ventures', 29 August; accessed at http://www.freemalaysiatoday.com/category/nation/2011/08/29/pittance-for-native-landowners-in-joint-ventures/, 25 May 2012.

Teoh, C.-H. (2010) *Key Sustainability Issues in the Palm Oil Sector*. Washington, DC: The World Bank.

The Star (2009a) 'Zoo withdraws chocolate products over palm oil ingredients', *The Star*, July 13.

The Star (2009b) 'RSPO still intact despite greenhouse gas contention', *The Star*, November 21.

UNHCR (2008) 'World directory of minorities and indigenous peoples – Malaysia: indigenous peoples and ethnic minorities in Sarawak'; accessed at http://www.unhcr.org/refworld/topic,463af2212,49709cbd260,49749ce83a,0,,,.html, 25 May 2012.

USDA (2013) 'Palm oil world supply and distribution', Foreign Agricultural Service Statistics, United States Department of Agriculture, 10 April; accessed at http://www.fas.usda.gov/psdonline/psdreport.aspx?hidReportRetrievalName=BVS&hidReportRetrievalID=710&hidReportRetrievalTemplateID=8, 23 April 2013.

Varkkey, H. (2013) 'Patronage politics, plantations fires and transboundary haze', *Environmental Hazards*, DOI: 10.1080/17477891.2012.759524.

Villanueva, J. (2011) 'Oil palm expansion in the Philippines: analysis of land rights, environment and food security issues', in M. Colchester and S. Chao (eds) *Oil Palm Expansion in Southeast Asia: Trends and Implications for Local*

Communities and Indigenous Peoples. Moreton-in-Marsh: Forest Peoples Programme, pp. 110–216.

Vo, T. D. (2011) 'Oil palm development in Vietnam', in M. Colchester and S. Chao (eds) *Oil Palm Expansion in Southeast Asia: Trends and Implications for Local Communities and Indigenous Peoples*. Moreton-in-Marsh: Forest Peoples Programme, pp. 79–109.

Wilmar (2008) 'Wilmar reaches resolution with RSPO', press release issued by Wilmar International, 4 February; accessed at http://www.wilmar-international.com/news/press_releases/Wilmar%20Reaches%20Resolution%20With%20RSPO.pdf, 10 June 2012.

World Bank (2011) *Rising Global Interest in Farmland: Can it Yield Sustainable and Equitable Benefits?*, Washington, DC: The World Bank.

World Growth (2010) *Palm Oil and Food Security: The Impediment of Land Supply*. Arlington, VA: World Growth.

WWF (2013) *WWF Statement on the Review of the RSPO Principles & Criteria*. April 18; accessed at http://awsassets.panda.org/downloads/wwf_statement_revised_rspo_principlescriteria_april_2013.pdf, 24 April 2013.

Going out: China's food security from Southeast Asia

Nicholas Thomas

Abstract China's new five-year plan recognised the looming insecurity in its agricultural sector. On the one hand, the country faces a diminishing arable land supply; on the other, a large population with rapidly increasing diets. Although large-scale trade and investment in this sector has been developing since the mid 1990s between China and a variety of African states, it is a relatively new addition to the more established China-Southeast Asian economic relationship. This article seeks to explore the impact that China's agricultural investments are having on two Southeast Asian countries – Indonesia and the Philippines – where there has been a marked increase in activities by Chinese firms in agricultural produce. The findings from these two case studies – and a series of smaller studies of the situation in other regional states – are used as a benchmark to clarify some of the consequences of China's agricultural investment from Southeast Asia for regional food security.

Introduction

> Only when the Chinese people are free from food availability and stability of food supply worries can they concentrate on and support the current reform, thus ensuring a sustained, rapid and healthy development of the economy.
> (State Council 1996)

China's rapid rise has had negative consequences for its capacity to ensure its own food security. As China has modernised, the population have moved from the countryside to the cities, with a concomitant expansion of urban spaces and a loss of arable land. At the same time, industrial pollution and waste has rendered land unviable for agricultural production, while deforestation and the loss of topsoil has further reduced land supply. Estimates suggest that approximately 8.3 million hectares of arable land have been lost since the mid 1990s (an area roughly twice the size of

Switzerland). This presents the Chinese leadership with a critical challenge, namely how to guarantee food security without disrupting the on-going economic development of the state and society.

In 2011, in a bid to resolve this challenge, China announced the need to maintain a strategic reserve of 1.8 billion mu (120 million hectares) of arable land (China Daily 2011). With this land, China intends to protect its base for feeding its citizens; yet population pressures and water resource scarcity already makes this a marginal proposition. As a USDA study noted, China – with roughly 20% of the world's population – is trying to feed its people with only 10% of arable land supplies and only 6% of fresh water supplies, while still maintaining an overseas trade in agricultural produce that brings in much needed foreign revenue. Already 'China's current exploitation of land and water resources is either at or beyond sustainable levels' (Lohmar and Gale 2008). At the same time, Chinese food preferences are changing away from rice to diets dominated by wheat and proteins, requiring more resource-intensive forms of farming and animal husbandry (Asia Pulse 2011).[1] Thus, the plan by China to safeguard its food security only reveals a further challenge, the need to guarantee sufficient arable land for an increasing population; one whose changing patterns of food consumption require ever more intensive land use activities.

To address both of these challenges China has grafted its agricultural development policy onto its 'going out' strategy (Zha and Zhang 2013). In essence, if the developmental problems caused by China's rapid rise are likely to continue – and if there is insufficient land within the country to ensure food security – then China needs to identify land investment opportunities overseas to supplement domestic food production capacity. The purpose of this article is to provide an initial exploration of China's overseas agricultural investment practices in Southeast Asian countries; where Chinese companies have become increasingly active in the acquisition of arable land. This paper begins with a review of the development of domestic drivers behind China's overseas investments in the agricultural sector – looking particularly at the physical constraints faced by China in terms of land utilisation as well as some of the macro-level policies that have been emplaced to address the implications of these constraints. The actualisation of these policies is then placed within the context of deepening economic and investment ties between China and Southeast Asia. Indonesia and the Philippines – which have the highest value of Chinese AODI in the region – together compromise the two main case studies. Other states – Cambodia, Laos, Myanmar and Vietnam – that have experienced increased Chinese AODI are then reviewed. The implications of these findings for China's food security being derived from Southeast Asia are then considered, before concluding.

China's food insecurity: domestic drivers and policy responses

With grain in our hands, there is no panic in our hearts.
(Mao)

China's food sector is naturally insecure. China's arable land holdings are small, relative to other states, their populations and available water supplies. Yet, with the exception of events such as the Great Leap Forward, China has not only managed to grow enough produce to feed its population but also to maintain agricultural exports to other nations. However, the opening up of China from the late 1970s onwards and the resulting economic development of China's coastal regions and municipalities also had a spill-over effect into China's overall food security with changing patterns of consumption, land and water use, and crop production.

While most apparent in its changing urban landscapes, China's modernisation has had no less a profound effect on the types of food Chinese people consume. 'In recent times, both consumption and production of meat, milk and eggs have increased in China at rates well-above those for the developing world in general, and even faster if compared with developed countries' (Rae 2008: 283). However, these new types of consumption are not standard across the country. As Ma et al note with respect to China's cities, 'grain consumption has fallen precipitously in urban areas, while the consumption of animal products has risen' (Ma et al. 2006: 102; see also Hovhannisyan and Gould 2011). But in the rural areas, grain-centric diets remain the nutritional standard. Nonetheless, as more Chinese people now live in urban areas – a trend unlikely to be reversed – this dietary shift will only become more entrenched. These changing patterns of consumption have had knock-on effects as to the types of foodstuffs and livestock produced in China, with corollary impacts on other areas important to domestic food production; such as competing farming demands on the same land, and competing water usage. Of course, the changes in dietary preferences are not unique to China. As Freedman (2013) noted, this is also a challenge to food security in Southeast Asia; further complicating that region's ability to manage increasing demands from external agricultural powers.

Meeting the challenges of shifting patterns of consumption against reduced agricultural resources is further complicated by an overall reduction in available land, as a result of unchecked urbanisation and climate shifts. As Zhu (2011: 44) observed with respect to grain-type crops, 'agricultural resources are becoming scarce, which makes it difficult to promote further growth of grain production... In 2009, China's arable land area was roughly 121.73 million hectares, a decrease of 7.47 million hectares since 1999'. Yet, as a study by the Chinese Academy of Agricultural Sciences concluded in 1992, the 'national actual cultivated surface is 1,987,792,900 mu [132,519,527 ha]' (CAAS 1992, as cited in Christiansen 2009). This would suggest that between 1992 and 2009, China lost over 10.8 million hectares of land. Given that this loss has occurred during an economic boom period (which is still continuing), there is little evidence to suggest that the fall in land supply has been significantly slowed, arrested or reversed.

Extrapolating this data even in a rough linear manner forward to 2012–2013, suggests that China's arable land has already dropped below the policy redline of 120 million hectares. Even factoring in land reclamation efforts and changing patterns of land use for farming, there is the known fact that in the same period urbanisation of the Chinese landscape has only accelerated, as has illegal use of arable land by provincial and municipal governments for pet projects such as housing estates, golf courses or industrial parks. Indeed, as early as 2007, analysts in China were warning that unless the decline in arable land stocks was halted then China would fall below the threshold within six years (2013) (Asia Times 2007).

Tacit recognition of this shortfall was the recent statement by the Chinese Minister of Land and Resources Xu Shaoshi, who declared that 'China is "very confident" of guaranteeing its bottom line of 120 million hectares of farmland to ensure the nation's food security' (China Daily 2012).[2] This conclusion is supported by a Bank of America report that found China's supply of arable land has already fallen below 120 million hectares and could go as low as 117 million hectares by 2015 (Thompson 2012).

China's food insecurity has also become an economic challenge as well. This negative spillover is being driven by domestic demand factors as much as international supply issues. In agricultural terms, China has been a global actor since the founding of the PRC (Mah 1971). However, while its agricultural trade has usually supported foreign currency reserves, China has – since the early 1990s – become a net importer of grains. Although these imports spiked in the mid 1990s, increases in domestic production allowed these imports to be reduced to minimal levels by 1997 (Lohmar 2004: 7). However, since 2003, domestic prices have been rising, with a parallel increase in the costs of imported agricultural produce. As a report from the Food Security Portal observed:

> ... food prices registered relatively slow increase in 2005 (by 2.9 percent) and 2006 (by 2.3 percent), before suddenly shooting up to an annual jump of 12.3 percent in 2007. Meanwhile, rural areas reported even bigger food price rise (11.7 percent in cities and 13.6 percent in the countryside).
>
> ('China: country resources', undated)

Up until the end of 2008, pricing policies in China helped to contain the impact of higher food prices from the global market (Yang et al. 2008). Over the next three years, food prices (which comprise approximately one-third of China's CPI) increased significantly; causing economic stress which fed social and political unrest. Between 2009–2010, food prices increased by 9.6% (Xinhua 2011). Between 2011–2012, prices of rice and wheat flour (key components of the Chinese diet) surged by 5% (GIEWS 2012). According to the New York Times, 'food prices alone rose 11% in February. The government also said that the producer price index, a measure of inflation at the wholesale level, rose 7.2 percent in February, the biggest increase since October 2008' (Barboza 2011).

Moreover, as information from the Ministry of Agriculture showed, 'China's total import of agricultural products reached 94.87 billion dollars in 2011, up 30.8% from 2010. As for the three major grains, wheat import was 1.258 million tons, up 2.2%; corn import 1.754 million tons, up 11.5%; rice import 59.8 thousand tons, up 54.0%' (Chi-agri.com 2012), while cereal imports nearly doubled between 2010/2011–2011/2012 from 4,767,000 tonnes to 9,117,000 tonnes (GIEWS 2012). In sum, 'China's agricultural imports rose by nearly 30 per cent last year and it expects to become the world's biggest importer of agricultural produce within two to three years' (Songwanich 2012). These price rises and increased food imports, although partly due to domestic factors that the government addressed through macro-economic policies (The Economist 2010), were a spill-over of the upwards trend in global food prices. As of mid 2012, the World Bank noted that global food prices for major staple crops were again on the increase (World Bank 2012); further forcing the Chinese government to support the domestic markets, even as they seek alternative sources of supply elsewhere.

Hence, on the one hand, China's leaders are faced with a declining supply of arable land, the usage patterns of which are becoming more intense – especially with the shift towards the supply of livestock and population pressures – bringing the land closer to its maximum ecological output (Mold 2011). On the other hand, China needs to feed its people without jeopardising its domestic economic development and its international trading relationships. The most recent attempt to balance these competing demands can be seen in the 2011–2016 Five Year Plan (hereafter 2011 FYP).

Within the 2011 FYP, food security was given policy primacy. As the Plan stated, 'National food security is the first goal, we should speed up to transform the agriculture development style, enhance the capacities on agriculture integrated production, risk resistance, and market competence'. Although domestically focused, this policy was tied to China's going out strategy, particularly those aspects that related to 'expanding agricultural international cooperation, develop overseas projects and labor cooperation. [Be] active in improving cooperation projects which benefit to local people's livelihood' (*Zakendoen in China*, undated). Indeed, as Chang et al. (2013: 19) have observed, 'China has actively sealed quite some agricultural cooperation deals with developing countries for overseas farming'.

In conjunction with the 2011 FYP, the National Development and Reform Commission (NDRC) released the Strategic Research Plan for Agricultural 'Going Out' in early 2012. This built on the agricultural emphasis in the 2011 FYP to more explicitly establish how Chinese AODI was going to expand. Structurally, this expansion will be underwritten by an RMB30 million reserve to support overseas investments or acquisitions in agriculture, forestry, and fishing enterprises (Jiang 2012). This strategy had already been publically floated as early as May 2011, when a consultant's report to the Ministry of Agriculture publically concluded that China needed to develop overseas production bases for key crops, in order to help support domestic food security (Chen 2011). However, data on Chinese outbound investments shows that – from 2003 to 2009 – the agricultural sector only accounted for 2% of all merger and acquisition activities, which was valued at less than 1% of all mergers and acquisitions (Deloitte 2009). This would suggest that the shift in resources investments to encompass soft resources (such as agricultural produce) is just beginning, even as the domestic motivations increase.[3]

When reviewing the Chinese language discourse on the state of China's food security, it is apparent that China – by any measure – is becoming more insecure. This is not due to a failure of the agricultural sector. Indeed, purely from the perspective of this sector, China could be considered a success story. With its imbalanced population size to land and water ratio, the Chinese state could still manage to produce enough to feed its population and generate export surpluses from sales on the global market. However, the physical and nutritional changes arising from its four decades of modernisation means that not only is the supply of arable land shrinking below the redline of 120 million hectare, but that the demands on the remaining land are becoming more intense. As these factors seem to be outside of the central government's ability to manage – except in the broadest sense – then China must become even more dependent on foreign sources for its food supply.

If Mao's axiom still holds true, then there is both an ideological as well as a national security rationale for ensuring that these foreign production bases are oriented to the Chinese domestic market. In this regard, the increasing volume of investments by Chinese companies raises the twinned questions as to what extent they are aligned with central policies and to what extent they are driven by market forces. In trying to answer these questions, this paper now explores different examples of Chinese agricultural investments in Southeast Asia.

Food security from Southeast Asia

While Sino–ASEAN economic and trade ties had been gradually developing since the late 1970s, the 1997 financial crisis provided a window of opportunity for realising their potential. In the two decades since, two-way trade has increased from US$22.6 billion in 1997 to $223 billion by 2008 (Tang and Wang 2006; Tong and Chong 2010). By the end of 2011 two-way trade reached US$362.3billion, an increase of 24% over the previous year, indicating that bilateral trade continued to grow even as the developed economies struggled with the fallout from the global financial crisis (Bao 2012). Within the period from 2003 to mid 2011, bilateral investment also grew from just over US$3.1 billion to in excess of US$80 billion (China

Daily 2011b); although just US$13 billion of that total was from China ('Chinese commerce minister calls for expanding economic co-op between China, ASEAN' 2011). Indeed, at the end of the first decade of the twenty-first century, China was the largest trading partner of all states in Southeast Asia, while ASEAN – as a group – was the third largest trading partner of China. This expansion of ties reflects the economically complementarity nature of the relationship where Southeast Asia generally takes the role of supplying primary resources (particularly farm produce and maritime products) and machinery parts and China provides these as well as more developed products in return (Hong Kong Trade and Development Council 2010).

Bilateral trade received a boost with the signing of the China–ASEAN Free Trade Agreement (CAFTA) in 2002 and the implementation of the early harvest programme for the Southeast Asian economies in 2005. The operationalisation of CAFTA in January 2010 further reduced or elimi-nated tariffs on most goods and products within the 11-member agreement. Given the importance of the agricultural sector to individual national econ-omies, where most populations are still predominantly rural, the issue of new trade and investment opportunities provided by the liberalisation of this market sector was particularly sensitive in terms of who would benefit, and would there be losers.

As Qiu et al. (2007) note, there is no clear consensus on the impact of CAFTA on the regional agricultural market. Some studies suggest that the trade is largely complementary, so all members will benefit to a greater or lesser extent (Lu 2006). Other studies (such as Rong and Yang 2006) argue that the trade is competitive with clear winners and losers. Given the size and geographical diversity of the Chinese agricultural sector in contrast to the ten national markets in Southeast Asia, Rong and Yang's conclusion would suggest that China's food security will be bought at Southeast Asia's expense. Qiu et al.'s simulation of the impact of CAFTA for the agricul-tural sector concludes that a complementary model is more feasible with both sides benefiting from the economic stimulus, but that within China the northern regions will benefit slightly more than their southern counter-parts where the produce is similar to that produced in Southeast Asia (2007: 89).

However, the problem with these studies is that agriculture is not a major focus of Chinese investment in Southeast Asia, yet it is a critical component of the regional economies. In 2011–2012, China's top invest-ment destinations were Indonesia, Vietnam, the Philippines, Malaysia, Singapore, and Thailand. Within this set of investments agriculture was not a major focus – with 'textiles, electrics, steel, shipbuilding, chemical and IT popular investment themes' (Hodal 2012). Nonetheless, as domestic demand for agricultural products increases, the geographic proximity of Southeast Asia coupled with the deep economic relationship between China and the ten members of ASEAN, provides a natural symmetry for the development of offshore supply sites; one where the established trade and investment agreements and commercial flows provide an initial framework for investment choices. At present, agricultural investment by Chinese companies in Southeast Asia takes a variety of forms: from direct purchases of arable land to development of agricultural products for biofuels to investments in crop production.

Agricultural overseas direct investments in Southeast Asia[4]

The two most significant Southeast Asian destinations for direct Chinese investments in agriculture are the Philippines and Indonesia. However, the responses from these countries to these activities have been starkly different. In the case of the Philippines, there has been sustained resistance to Chinese AODI; while, in Indonesia, the response has been more benign. These differences are, in part, due to the different domestic investment climates, different perceptions of elite-mass interests, as well as the evolution of the general bilateral strategic relationship between China and the two countries. Similar issues also emerge when considering Chinese AODI in other regional states, allowing for the two case studies to be viewed as possible templates for understanding how China seeks to ensure its food security from the agricultural sector in Southeast Asia.

The Philippines

The agricultural sector in the Philippines is a major, albeit uneven, contributor to employment and domestic revenue. According to World Bank data approximately 37–40% of the country (up to 2009) can be considered as agricultural land, with arable land account for between 16–18% of the total area (World Bank data 2012). It is estimated that agriculture employs approximately one-third of the population (Department of Primary Industries 2010), yet the economic contribution from the sector has been steadily falling: from 23% of GDP in 1982 to 15% in 2010 (dela Cruz 2010: 1). Moreover, according to the Bureau for Agricultural Statistics (BAS) the overall value of the sector – in terms of imports and exports – is in deficit. The latest data shows that for the first half of 2012, the agricultural trade deficit was US$1.428 million, an increase over the same period in 2011 of 9.48% when the shortfall was US$1.305 million (BAS 2012: 2).

Part of the reason for this decline in this sector is that it is dominated by small and medium size farms. This provides an economic space where large scale operators can realise greater financial returns through operational efficiencies in production and processing placing pressure on the smaller operators. At the same time, numerous studies have shown that the poor governance of the agricultural sector has led to misallocations of resources and poor investments in infrastructure (David 1995; David et al. 1992;

Tiongco and Francisco 2011; Habito and Briones 2005). The importance and potential of the agricultural sector to the Philippines, restricted by the dominance of small and medium size operations and the poor state policy choices, makes investments in the sector commercially attractive for foreign companies able to create the own infrastructure.[5] With both governments seeking options to redress the trade imbalance as well as China's needs to improve its food security, it is not surprising that agriculture has been identified as one sector where increased Chinese AODI could benefit all parties.

Despite the attractiveness of the Philippines as a destination for Chinese AODI, the overall economic relationship has been problematic. It is only since 2006–2007 that significant efforts have been made to upgrade the value of the relationship. However, many of those initial agreements have floundered in the face of domestic opposition to Chinese investments. In addition, since 2009 bilateral trade volume has been falling year-on-year, while 'investments from the Philippines into China significantly outstripped the reverse with Chinese investment reaching US$42.68 million versus Philippines-based investments in China worth US$110 million' (MOFCOM 2010). By mid 2012 the Philippines had slipped from once being a possible favoured destination for Chinese investment to rank sixth out of the ten ASEAN states for trade with China. Moreover, strategic complications such as the Scarborough Reef stand-off and closer ties with the United States have had further negative consequences for the economic relationship (The SunStar Manila 2012). For instance, China's National Tourism Administration recommended travellers avoid the Philippines, while China's General Administration of Quality Supervision, Inspection and Quarantine has imposed stricter inspections on produce from the Philippines (Li 2012).[6]

Within this bilateral context, 2007 was a high point in agricultural ties; although the aftermath of this period has raised further questions as the future of Chinese agro-business investments within the overall relationship. Early 2007 saw 18 separate agreements signed covering Chinese investment in local fishing and agricultural research.[7] Almost immediately, however, there was a significant backlash against the largest agreement for cooperation in genetically modified grains (corn, rice and sorghum) for biofuels and food produce between the Philippines Department of Agriculture, Department of Agrarian Reform, and Department of Environment and Natural Resources – on the one side – and the Jilin provincial government, the China Development Bank, and the Jilin Fuhua Agricultural Science and Technology Development company, on the other side. This backlash from a variety of stakeholders focused on different aspects of the agreement. Within the rural communities, possibly the biggest issue was the size of the land concession given to Fuhua. With an initial provision of 50,000 hectares, the agreement was to cover one million hectares – approximately 10% of all agricultural land in the Philippines. This was a significantly larger land concession than any other that had previously been granted to either private or state-linked companies.[8] Other MoUs signed in this tranche were also problematic, just not to the same extent as the Fuhua agreement. The agreement between the Philippines Department of Agriculture and the privately-owned Guangzhou Zongbao Fiber Product company was of concern as it was intended to develop agricultural products for export to China rather than solely for the domestic market or, at least, for the domestic/international markets (san Juan 2007).

However, the size of the agreement and the way it was negotiated caused a social and legal backlash against Chinese investments and the Philippines' state that still continues. Often characterised in the popular media as an example of a 'land-grab' because of perceptions of corrupt practices as well as the impact on rural people's livelihoods, this agreement became the focus for legal challenge (Supreme Court 2008). Although this challenge centred on the constitutionality of transferring such a significant amount of land to long-term foreign control, the protests also showed a number of questionable business practices on the part of the Philippines' companies. In particular, research by the NGOs supporting the protest showed how a number of the companies had only been registered immediately prior to the agreements being signed, while a number had not been formally registered (Filipinosocialism 2007). Other issues – such as the links between state elites and these new companies – were also raised. Even though the questions of corrupt practices have not been substantiated, the suspension of the project was made all but inevitable once the scandal involving managers from the Chinese company ZTE bribing local officials involved in the national broadband project became public. The political fallout from this case saw a number of other large-scale Chinese investments halted, including the Bauang irrigation project, the General Santos Fish Port complex development, and the Northrail Project. In assessing the situation, the Chair of the Senate Foreign Relations Committee, Miriam Santiago, declared that 'the Chinese had invented corruption for all human civilization' (US State Department 2008).

In 2011 both sides tried to reboot the investment relationship. A large delegation of business representative and officials – led by President Aquino – visited China in August in an effort to increase Chinese levels of investment in the Philippines. Despite announcing US$13 billion in new investments, the value of the confirmed investments was only US$1.3 billion (Tubeza 2011), none of which was in agriculture. However, in September 2011, a delegation from Jilin province visited Manila, led by former Chinese Minister for Agriculture Sun Zhengcai. The provincial delegation committed to increasing investment and cooperation ties in agriculture and fisheries (Department of Agriculture 2011). During the delegation's visit a total of US$721 million in new agreements were signed, including a:

... 3000-hectare hybrid maize project signed between Jilin Fuhua Agricultural Science and Technology Development Co. Ltd. and Philippines Xiling Agricultural Science and Technology Co., Ltd... and a 300,000-ton grain deep processing project signed between Yushu City Government and Philippines Jielongfa Group.
(Jilin Daily 2011)

Given the role of Jilin-based government departments and companies in the 2007 tranche of agreements, it may signal that China is using its subnational actors to develop targeted foreign economic relations, while still allowing other, more prominent SOEs to play a role as desired.

Given that the legal challenge to the 2007 Jilin Fuhua investment is (as of the end of 2012) still on-going, other large-scale investments by Jilin provincial or municipal authorities and/or companies are unlikely to proceed until the legal basis for such investments is clarified. Nonetheless, in the intervening period since the Jilin Fuhua investment was challenged, the Philippines and local companies have signed agreements with other governments and private companies for the large transfer of land for commercial purposes. For example, the following year the San Miguel Corporation signed an agreement with the Kwok Group (Malaysia) for the:

... development of green areas into food production areas along with the establishment of logistics, post-harvest and processing facilities for the raw crop produce... The deal envisages the use of 1 million hectares of government land under supply and purchase, corporate farming, lease and co-management agreement.
(Dela Cruz 2011)

In 2010, the government and the Itochu corporation (Japan) signed an agreement for an 11,000 hectare bioethanol operation in San Marino, Isabela (Sisante 2010). Although there was local opposition to the operation (Philippine Revolution Web Central 2012), there was also local support due to the economic benefits the plant is expected to bring to the local community (Manila Bulletin 2011). Despite a municipal investigation into the agreement and questions of environmental approval, the plant came online in November 2012.[9] The lack of significant legal challenges to suspend these operations could be a signal that the investment climate in the Philippines for large-scale foreign agri-business has changed since 2007. It could equally be a reflection that the Philippines' bilateral political relationships with Malaysia and Japan are deeper, even as its trading relationship is stronger with China. On such issues as trust and a bifurcation between foreign political and economic relations, the Philippines presents a similar (albeit not identical) case to that of Indonesia, which is the second main case study of this paper.

Indonesia

Despite its burgeoning cityscapes, Indonesia retains large agricultural tracts of land. At slightly more than 202.7 million hectares for the country, 54 million hectares are labeled as agricultural areas. However, only 44% (23.76 million hectares) of these areas are classified as arable land, with another 17% (9.18 million hectares) defined as irrigated land. In terms of food security, Indonesia remains heavily dependent on imports of key produce such as sugar, soya beans and beef, as well as – to a lesser extent – on rice. Yet, the agricultural sector remains inefficient and heavily protected. A 2012 OECD report argued that a greater exposure for the sector to international trade as well as greater infrastructure support would do much to help the country achieve greater self-sufficiency (OECD 2012). Although these conclusions were not new, Indonesia has not managed to attract agriculturally-focused FDI in significant amounts. Indeed, between 1999–2010, only 3% of all FDI went to this sector – with most of this investment targeting perennial crops, particularly palm oil and those crops associated with biofuels (OECD 2012: 224–229). The main reason for this was the structure of Indonesia's foreign investment regime, which limited the foreign ownership of companies involved in staple food plantations. It was only in 2010 that the government allowed foreign investors to take a 49% holding in individual companies (Ishmar 2010). Thus with the growth of Sino–Indonesian relations – especially in economically-related areas – as well as the under-utilised nature of Indonesia's agricultural sector, there is a policy synergy between China's food supply needs and Indonesia's agricultural development demands.

Indonesia has – in many respects – a similar backstory to the Philippines with a history of wary engagement with China; indeed, it was only in 1990 that diplomatic relations between the two states were finally restored. However, in the contemporary period, this troubled history has been superseded (although not eliminated) through increased bilateral engagements; particularly since the 1997–1998 Asian Financial Crisis (AFC). Politically both countries have become closer since the AFC, supporting new forms of multilateral cooperation in ASEAN+1, +3 and the East Asian Summit. Bilateral cooperation now extends to almost every aspect of social and public policy of interest between the two states. However, economic ties are at the heart of the new relationship. Here the relationship has grown significantly in the past decade; particularly since 2006. However, the balance in the relationship has also changed, even as the volume of trade has grown. In 2006, Indonesia had a trade surplus with China of US$1.1 billion (Mishkin 2012). By 2012, this had shifted to a trade deficit in excess of US$3.8 billion (see Table 1: Indonesia–China trade balance).

Despite the positive developments in the bilateral relationship, Indonesia only attracted US$1.2 billion in Chinese investments in 2011 (Antara News 2012), which represents less than a tenth of the total US$18 billion

Table 1 2007–2012 Indonesia–China trade balance (value: thousand US$)

| Description | 2007 | 2008 | 2009 | 2010 | 2011 | Jan–Sep | |
						2011	2012
Total trade	18.233.389,8	26.883.672,6	25.501.497,8	36.116.829,3	49.153.192,3	35.070.211,2	37.248.533,3
Oil & gas	3.612.035,6	4.148.600,9	3.090.052,2	2.347.861,2	2.101.182,8	1.600.932,8	815.717,4
Non oil & gas	14.621.354,3	22.735.071,7	22.411.445,5	33.768.968,1	47.052.009,5	33.469.278,5	36.432.815,9
Export	9.675.512,7	11.636.503,7	11.499.327,3	15.692.611,1	22.941.004,9	15.818.175,6	15.489.258,7
Oil & gas	3.011.412,8	3.849.335,3	2.579.242,8	1.611.661,3	1.345.420,4	923.454,6	489.325,1
Non oil & gas	6.664.099,9	7.787.168,4	8.920.084,4	14.080.949,9	21.595.584,5	14.894.721,0	14.999.933,6
Import	8.557.877,1	15.247.168,9	14.002.170,5	20.424.218,2	26.212.187,4	19.252.035,6	21.759.274,6
Oil & gas	600.622,7	299.265,6	510.809,4	736.200,0	755.762,3	677.478,2	326.392,4
Non oil & gas	7.957.254,4	14.947.903,3	13.491.361,1	19.688.018,3	25.456.425,0	18.574.557,5	21.432.882,2
Balance of trade	1.117.635,6	−3.610.665,2	−2.502.843,2	−4.731.607,1	−3.271.182,4	−3.433.860,0	−6.270.015,9
Oil & gas	2.410.790,1	3.550.069,7	2.068.433,4	875.461,3	589.658,1	245.976,4	162.932,7
Non oil & gas	−1.293.154,5	−7.160.734,9	−4.571.276,6	−5.607.068,4	−3.860.840,5	−3.679.836,5	−6.432.948,6

Source: Ministry of Trade (2012).

dollars Indonesia attracted that year (Xinhua 2012a); most of which was directed towards the mining sector. This places China below Japan, Singapore, the United States, South Korea and the Netherlands for investments in Indonesia, even though it means that Indonesia is ranked second (behind Singapore) for total Chinese investments in ASEAN. The relatively new phase of opening up the local economy to agricultural investments means that the developed nature of agreements, MoUs, and operations that were seen in the Philippines case are still emerging in the Indonesian context. In a similar structure to the Jilin–Philippines relationship, Henan province is a coordinating investor in parts of Indonesia. In 2010 and 2011, Henan signed investment agreements and MoUs with the Indonesian province of Maluku. 'The investors from Henan, China, will invest in nine fields among others in agriculture, fisheries, science and technology, culture and tourism, but the main target is in agriculture, fisheries, and tourism' (Hitipeuw 2011). Other Chinese provinces – such as Guangxi – are leading the agricultural investments in other parts of Indonesia. In 2010, a Guangxi delegation visited West Java to secure the supply of rattan and bamboo. 'Meanwhile, for agriculture, is being explored investment in seaweed cultivation and processing. As for the marine sector, the company will see the potential of China's fishery product processing' (Adhani 2010).

Other Indonesian cash crops that Chinese AODI is targeting also include rubber plantations and processing sites. Between 2000–2009, Indonesian exports of rubber to China increased significantly; from just under 3% in 2000 to nearly 25% in 2009 (IMF 2012: 27). Interestingly Chinese company Sinochem International claims to be the largest supplier of Indonesian rubber in China, which would mean that it is the major actor behind this significant rise in trade; although independent data to verify this claim is not available (Sinochem 2012). However, different reports to refer to the development of a rubber land-bank by Sinochem International and some of its subsidiaries (*Newsbsb168.com* 2012). Other Chinese companies, such as Mazhongdu International and Hainan Baisha Industrial, are also actively investing in rubber plantations in Kalimantan for export to China (Kong 2011).

Taken together, these case studies reflect the beginnings of a deeper investment in Southeast Asian agricultural enterprises by Chinese companies and state agencies. These supply-side investments fit with the demands for agricultural produce emerging in China as a result of its food insecurity. The Philippines case also clearly shows that Chinese companies need to be more adroit in dealing with local social and political interests and norms if they are not to foster new anti-China tensions within the host state. Although companies have not experienced the same level of difficulties in Indonesia, the relative newness of this aspect in the bilateral relationship would suggest that a similar level of engagement with affected stakeholders is also required. The key issue overarching both cases is that investment requires a longer-term commitment – by both sides – in contrast to trading relationships that, by their nature, are more short-term and less locally engaged.

Biofuels: security beyond food

A sub-theme of the preceding analysis on the Philippines and Indonesia is the use by Chinese companies of offshore arable land for the production of crops for biofuels. Biofuels feed into the debate over China's food security for a number of important reasons. First, China's own supply of fossil fuels is rapidly diminishing. Without a renewable type of energy under the control of the Chinese state, China will become heavily energy dependent on external sources of energy – not only an economic vulnerability but also a strategic one as well. The development of biofuels offers a possible option for China's energy needs. However, production requires arable land. Although China has already begun to convert some of its own arable land for biofuel production it cannot do so to any large degree without compromising its already precarious domestic food security situation. Hence, the purchase of arable land in Southeast Asia allows China to resource its future biofuel needs without creating domestic food insecurities. As with the purchase of arable land for food production, however, this is purely a China-centric perspective; one that does not take into equal account the impact on the recipient state.

In addition to the Jilin Fuhua agreement detailed earlier, the 2007 tranche of agreements signed between the Philippines and China contained another five relating to biofuels. One of them, an agreement between the Department of Agriculture, Department of Agrarian Reform, and Department of Environment and Natural Resources for the Philippines and the Chinese Agricultural Department of Guangxi Zhuang Autonomous Region, was for land for growing cassava and sugar for ethanol production. This covered a land concession of 40,000 hectares for an investment of US$6.2 million. Another agreement between Palawan Bio-Energy Development Corporation and a Chinese POE, the China National Constructional and Agricultural Machinery Import and Export Corporation, was for the construction of facilities in Palawan to produce 150,000 litres of bioethanol a day. This also involved a land concession of 10,000 hectares. The Nanning Yongkai Industry Group (NYIG) was a signatory to two further agreements with BM SB Integrated Biofuels and Negros Southern Integrated Biofuels Company for the joint establishment of a biofuel plant as well as the provision of the equipment to build and run the plant. The fifth agreement was the development of bioethanol plants (each with a 150,000 litre per day capacity) between NYIG and China CAMCE Engineering, on the Chinese side, and One Cagayan Resource Development Center Inc, for the Philippines (san Juan 2007).

It is worth noting that the capacity of just three of the bioethanol generation plants covered in the second and fifth agreements would possibly

Table 2 China's fuel ethanol production 2003–2012

Year	Production quality
2003	25.3 million litres
2004	380.1 million litres
2005	1165.6 million litres
2006	1647.1 million litres
2007	1736 million litres
2008	2002 million litres
2009	2179 million litres
2010	2128 million litres
2011	2225 million litres
2012	2433 million litres

Source: Scott and Jiang (2012).

create in excess of 160 million litres per year,[10] or approximately 6.5% of China's domestic bioethanol production in 2012 (see Table 2). At the same time, the land allocated for two of these deals is larger than the previous local benchmark, further fuelling local concerns as to the new forms of land use of local cash or food crops. This highlights the potential of off-shore bioethanol plants for China's energy security while protecting its own strategic arable land reserve, but the reallocation of arable land away from food crops has consequences for food security in the Philippines.

In Indonesia, Chinese companies have also been active in signing agreements for biofuel production on arable land sites. The largest so far has been the 2007 investment by the China National Offshore Oil Corporation (CNOOC) to invest US$5.5 billion in Kalimantan and Papua to convert one million hectares of forest to palm oil, sugar and cassava plantations (GRAIN 2007). An earlier agreement between CITIC and Sinar Mas in 2005 was at the heart of a 1.8 million hectare palm oil project in Kalimantan (Walker 2006). CITIC's share of this project – 600,000 hectares – is valued in excess of US$2.8 billion. CITIC has further responsibilities for developing the transport and processing infrastructure for the wider project (Klute 2007). However, while such investments – in general – are causing social conflicts to develop as local populations are dispersed and traditional patterns of livelihood disrupted, there are none that generated the types of social and legal backlash examined in the Jilin Fuhua case in the Philippines. Protests against palm oil plantations, for example, do overlap with Chinese interests but are part of a broader set of social conflicts – such as land reclamation and redistribution, low levels of compensation to displaced settlers for loss of land and income, and/or issues relating to centre–province relations – rather than being solely targeted at Chinese operations.

These studies highlight another important facet of China's quest for food security from Southeast Asia, namely the utilisation of arable land for non-agricultural purposes. By off-shoring these activities, Chinese companies are able to further expand their operations without encountering any of the domestic restrictions and problems that are emerging as arable land supply dwindles in China. As is seen from the list of bio-fuel crop investors in the Philippines and Indonesia, both state and privately owned enterprises are active in securing sites. What is perhaps less well-recognised is that provincial government departments are also as active in this sector as commercial entities, further blurring the distinction between 'state-owned' and 'state enterprises' in AODI analysis.

Chinese food security: small state cases

Of course, it is not just the big states in Southeast Asia that are receiving Chinese AODI. The CLMV states are important recipients of Chinese interest in food security and agricultural investments. Of these four states, the Chinese investment footprint is the largest in Cambodia. Between 1994–2011, China's land investments – along with mining, dams and other investments – have reached a total of US$8.8 billion making it the leading overseas investor, more than double South Korea's second ranked investment status of US$4 billion (Xinhua 2012c). In the agricultural sector, Chinese companies have been granted a total of 4,615,745 hectares since 1994. Of these investments '3,374,328 hectares were forest concessions, 973,101 hectares were economic land concessions and 268,316 hectares were mining concessions' (Titthara 2012). This means that 'Chinese companies control about a quarter of the 17 million hectares of agricultural land and forest available in Cambodia' (Titthara 2012). This has resulted in the displacement of local peoples. In 2004, for example, the Chinese company Wuzhishan entered into a joint venture with a local company, Pheapimex. The joint venture then acquired control of 200,000 hectares in Moldulkiri province– despite the legal limit being 10,000 hectares. Local protests against the move were met with force by security personnel (Global Witness 2005).

It is a similar situation in neighbouring Laos where Chinese companies account for half of all foreign investors in agricultural land, with approximately 113,475 hectares (or 42.4% of all agricultural concessions) ceded to their control (Heinimann et al. 2012: 2). However, concerns about overseas investors controlling land led the Lao government in mid-2012 to declare a new moratorium on mining and land concessions until 2015. Despite these concerns the spread of agricultural investments in Laos by foreign investors – and Chinese entities, in particular – is already significant. Two examples of these investments include the rights awarded to Yunnan State Farms 'to develop 166,700 hectares of rubber in four northern provinces' as well as ZTE's acquisition of 50,000 hectares for cassava plantations in the south of the country (Asian Sentinel 2010). A study by Shi (2008) on Chinese investments in the Lao rubber industry found that:

> ... when the China–Lao Ruifeng Rubber Company moved in, the
> frontier village of Changee lost most of its rice fields and grazing land
> and its burial grounds were desecrated. The pleas of villagers got no
> result and some protesters were reportedly held at gunpoint, with the
> Chinese using coercion through local authorities.
> (Gray 2008)

The increasing presence of large-scale agro-businesses displacing traditional food production (and, in some cases, the villagers themselves:

> ... shows no evidence of being primarily designed to reduce poverty
> or food insecurity. Impacts so far suggest many people are qualita-
> tively finding they remain stuck in a state of poverty or food insecu-
> rity, some are even sinking deeper... The net effect is deepening
> vulnerability, if not immediate food insecurity, for a growing number
> of people across the country.
> (Fullbrook 2010)

Although Chinese companies are not solely responsible for the shift towards
plantations in Laos, their (collective) dominant position over foreign and
local investors means that they are increasingly identified as being responsible for the current state of affairs. As one report noted, 'The presence of
foreign, particularly Chinese, investors in Laos, a landlocked communist
country of about six million people, has raised increasing local concern
despite bringing much needed foreign cash' (Myanmar Times 2012).

These concerns are also present in Chinese agricultural investments in
Myanmar, where Chinese companies activities are – by and large –
unregulated by the state, even as the economic presence of China is gen-
erating an increasing resentment. As one monk put it, 'We are China's
kitchen. They take what they like and leave us with the rubbish' (EIU
ViewsWire 2011). This public sentiment has not stopped inbound Chinese AODI. In 2008, Jilin Fuhua and the Union of Myanmar Economic
Holdings signed an agreement to develop the 'Sino–Myanmar green agricultural zone' in Myitkyina, covering 12,000 hectares (Jilin Provincial
Government 2008). This was followed up in 2011 when the two state-
linked companies signed additional memoranda on agricultural cooperation projects (Jilin Provincial Government 2012). There have been other
reports of domestic elites dispossessing local farmers to develop large-
scale agricultural operations for the Chinese market. In one case, the
Yazuna corporation confiscated 200,000 hectares of land in 2006 to plant
sugarcane and cassava crops for the Chinese market (Martov 2012). In
2012, the courts ruled that the owner needed to return 1000 hectares of
land and pay compensation to the farmers (Kya and Htun 2012). These
types of imbalanced decisions only serve to increase local resented
towards the elites and their clients.

Vietnam is a different case from the other three small states. In Vietnam, land grabs and the displacement of rural villagers is just as sensitive a political issue as it is in China, with frequent protests against local and central policy-makers. While the lack of official statistics hampers a detailed understanding of the depth of Chinese agricultural investments, a study by Rutherford et al. (2008) concluded that China is more important as an agricultural export market for Vietnam rather than as a source of agricultural FDI. This study noted that agricultural exports accounted for 35% of all of Vietnam's exports to China. Nonetheless, there is clear evidence that Chinese investors are seeking land opportunities in the country. In Binh Minh district, for example, Chinese investors have been leasing arable land for sweet potatoes at rates between 30–60% higher than local farmers earn (VietNamNet 2011). In a similar manner to the Philippines and Indonesian cases, the Chinese provinces of Guangdong and Guangxi are significant coordinators of AODI into Vietnam. For example, approximately half of Guangxi's investments in ASEAN are directed towards Vietnam, with agriculture and fisheries two of the five strategic sectors for future development (Ngoc 2005). This focus on agricultural trade over investment results in an absence of the types of land grab discourse against Chinese agricultural companies associated with Chinese agricultural activities in other parts of Southeast Asia. Although, as the local debates over other Chinese resource investments (such as mining) in Vietnam demonstrate, there is a reservoir of anti-Chinese investment sentiment that would respond if agriculture moved from a trading to an extractive relationship.

The experiences in these four recipient states highlight different aspects of Chinese AODI in the Philippines and Indonesian cases. However, three of the four (excepting Vietnam) also show a far more aggressive form of AODI by Chinese companies; one where state elites may align themselves with the corporate interests of Chinese investors against the needs of the local population. Regime type is one possible explanation for these examples of more aggressive investment behaviour – with the Philippines and Indonesia both having stronger participatory political systems than Cambodia, Laos and Myanmar. Another explanation might be that the sizes of these three states are all smaller than the two main case studies, with as many competing investment sources, resulting in higher levels of competitive behaviour. A third possible reason could be that the smaller economic sizes of all three states means that Chinese investments have a disproportionate impact on local governance structures than in the Philippines or Indonesia. It is therefore interesting that Vietnam – with its illiberal political structure, competing sources of agricultural partners, and smaller economic size – has not had the same type of experience of Chinese AODI as its three neighbours. Whether it is due to historical or cultural reasons, or whether Vietnam represents a similar – but less developed – case to Indonesia (i.e., with only a recently opened agricultural investment regime of the sort attractive to Chinese investors), it is clear that the predominance of agricultural trade over investment allows for a more harmonious relationship between these two states in this sector.

Food: a new China threat?

As China has increased its geo-political standing in international affairs, there has been a concomitant expansion of the number of Chinese companies now active in overseas markets. Although the official data is far from uniform – even between central government agencies – there has been a dramatic increase in the number of Chinese companies operating overseas. According to Zhang and Yeo, in 2000 MOFTEC data suggested that there were 6298 international operations established by Chinese companies. By the end of 2003, this had increased to 7470 new ventures 'among which a large number are Chinese privately owned enterprises' (2005: 32). Within six years (2009) there were – in total – 'over 12,000 Chinese companies and institutions making overseas direct investments in more than 13,000 foreign companies across 177 countries and regions' (Qu and Sun 2011: 4). By the end of 2011, this figure had increased to '18,000 Chinese-funded companies operating in 178 countries and regions...with total assets reaching approximately $1.6 trillion' (Xinhua 2012b).

In 2011, Chinese companies invested US$68 billion dollars in overseas localities, which was split 44–56 between mergers or acquisitions and greenfield investments. While Europe was the main target of Chinese interests (with over US$10.4 billion invested), Asia was second highest recipient of ODI, with US$8.2 billion invested (ACapital 2011).[11] By the end of the first quarter of 2012, the scope and value of new Chinese overseas investments had increased to '1096 overseas companies in 109 countries and regions around the world... As of the end of March China's non-financial ODI expanded to 338.5 billion US dollars' (Ministry of Commerce 2012).

This rapid increase in Chinese ODI in the last 10 years has fostered a perception that a new China threat is emerging; a threat not based on the size of the Chinese military but on the size – and demands – of the Chinese economy. Alon (2012) captured this perception stating that 'the rise of Chinese multinationals has inflamed global fears about China 'taking over' the world' (Alon 2012: 5). These perceptions become more acute when extractive or acquisitive investments are made; especially in sectors considered important for the source countries own socio-economic future – such as minerals or land. Although most of the debates in this area have focused – post 2002 – on the energy related resources sector, the increasing purchase by Chinese companies of overseas arable land has seen the economic threat debate expand to encompass these types of soft resources as well.

So, do China's efforts to secure its food supply from Southeast Asian states represent a threat to the region? Wang and Tong (2010) conclude that the deeper economic ties forged through the CAFTA will enable

China to shape its neighbourly relations. This can be seen as supporting Friedberg's assertion that China's Going Out strategy enables it to shape the 'general propensity of things'. Given the importance of the agricultural sector to the regional economies in Southeast Asia, shaping this sector would give China strong leverage to direct the economic relationship – and by extension the socio-political and strategic relationships as well. This type of dominant power could well be construed as threatening. However, this article argues that – in the case of China–Southeast Asian relations – it is inaccurate to portray Chinese trade and investment in the agricultural sector as part of a grand strategy. Certainly there are Chinese companies trading and investing in the region. Their activities are able to be supported by the CIC, CDB, Exim Bank as well as other private financial institutions. There are also a large number of small and medium-size Chinese traders and investors who are operating on a more commercial basis. Instead of being representative of a threat, the economic size and operation scope of these investments can instead be seen as an agricultural variant of the security dilemma; where Chinese companies are simply investing as per their own capacity to do so, rather than being due any grand strategy of land grabbing at the intended expense of other states.

The threat thesis is further undermined by the imbalance between China's bilateral trade and its bilateral investment in the agricultural sector. While China is the largest trading partner with the ASEAN economies, and is becoming the largest agricultural trading partner as well, these are short-term activities. Investments are less fluid than trading ties, providing the basis for a longer-term – and, hence, more stable – economic relationship. Although it is difficult to accurately track the sum total of China's agricultural investment portfolio in Southeast Asia, it is clear that it is less well developed than similar investments in Africa and Latin America. Moreover while the activities of these operations may support China's quest for food security, that is an end result of their trading and investment activities rather than a starting point.

In addition, the presence of other major economies (notably Japan and Saudi Arabia) investing in the agricultural sector suggests a high degree of competition for land and produce. This provides the regional economies with additional trade and investment options, rather than being tied to a Chinese-centric marketplace. While China's dominance in other bilateral economic or political areas may provide them with the capacity to diminish the scope of these other linkages, this capacity is tempered by China's programmes in other parts of the world. In other words, any attempt by China to assert its dominance over the production and trade of Southeast Asian agricultural goods would trigger a backlash by other interested states.

A good example of such an attempt (and the backlash) was seen in September 2010 when China restricted the sale of rare earths to Japan, following the arrest of a Chinese fishing captain who rammed a Japanese coast guard vessel near the disputed Senkaku/Diaoyu islands. As China holds the largest supply of rare earth minerals, its actions sparked international concern and calls for 'an end to government "interference with commercial sale of rare earth elements, domestically or internationally, to advance industrial policy or political objectives"' (Richardson 2010). Since then, not only has Japan begun to diversify its supplies of rare-earths but China's actions in this sector are now subject to increased international scrutiny and restrictions.

But there is also the question of the impact of China on domestic socio-economic structures. In the two main cases studies there are few major conglomerates, with the industrial structure dominated by small and medium-size enterprises. However, these larger, national-level companies – especially those headed by Chinese-Filipinos and Chinese-Indonesians – are well-placed to benefit from Chinese investments (US State Department 2005; Gammeltoft and Tarmidi 2011: 8). Hence, with increasing levels of Chinese investments in both countries, it can also be suggested that a two-tier economic structure could emerge with those companies that are commercially and ethnically best placed to meet Chinese objectives performing better at the expense of their less nationally-focused and internationally-oriented competitors. Both countries suffer from large degrees of economic inequality. Thus, any emerging pattern of economic benefits and ethnicity could generate social and political tensions; as both countries have experienced in the past.

Moreover, across all the countries studied there is the problem of elite behaviour. In both the Philippines and Indonesia there is evidence of political–economic elites using their social position or policy strengths to push through land concessions that go against laws, customary practices, or local policies. As Stuart-Fox stated, 'It's simply a matter of greed. Officials are grabbing what they can. Companies need land and are prepared to pay well' (cited in MacKinnon 2008). Although this comment was made in the context of Laos, the examples and sources in this paper would suggest that it is equally applicable across a range of Southeast Asian states. While it has been argued that Chinese companies benefit from targeting countries with low standards of governance, it is a reality that these are the types of political systems that dominate the Southeast Asian landscape.

That said, the threat posed by China in terms of a unilateral ability to direct regional agricultural trade flows and investment patterns is restricted by the fact that (1) the produce lies outside of its sovereign territory, (2) that there are other major economic investors active in this sector providing alternative choices to the Southeast Asian states, and (3) that China's regional actions have international implications. For these reasons, China cannot be seen as a threat to food security in Southeast Asia. The obvious caveat to this conclusion is shaped by the domestic consequences for China should its arable land fall below the 120 million hectares identified as the threshold to ensure domestic food security. Land disputes have already been seen as a significant source of socio-political tension.

However, while this paper earlier concluded that it is likely China's land has already fallen below this critical threshold and will only fall further given the pattern of land usage in China, it also showed that China already produces more than enough foodstuffs to support a significant export market. Further, the growing wealth of China's middle and upper class allows for the importation of overseas produce at market rates. Hence, at least in the medium-term, this domestic source of instability does not present an external threat to the countries entangled in China's agricultural interests.

Conclusion

China cannot support itself unilaterally nor can it feed itself with its own crops. To solve the first challenge, China has – since the late 1970s – been gradually opening up its economy to external actors and forces. In the intervening period, China has transformed itself from a developing state with low levels of integration into global affairs to geo-political and geo-economic superpower, one able to affect the very nature of the global economic system within which it operates. But China still cannot feed itself. To address the second challenge, China adopted the economic structure through which it opened up to the world and grafted it onto an agricultural policy that envisages China's food security being comprised of both domestic and international sources of produce. However, to be reliant on external sources for such an essential public good could expose China to pressures from other states or interests. Given the centrality of food security to China's domestic social and political stability, such exposure needs to be limited. China's food security strategy, therefore, relies on the state as well as state-owned enterprises. Nonetheless, the depth of China's food vulnerability coupled with the scope of the possible markets means that China needs other actors who would, at least, not act against its national interests. Here the emergence of an internationally-literate Chinese private sector has been provident in China's attempts to invest in arable lands in other countries.

Southeast Asia has the most substantial economic and trade ties with China, when compared to any other region. Yet Chinese investment in the region, in general, and in the agricultural sector, in particular, is far lower than elsewhere. Instead China's main agricultural investment sites lie outside Asia, in Africa and Latin America. Southeast Asian sites are secondary for Chinese corporate AODI; important in their own right but smaller and without the scope for expansion in contrast to Chinese agricultural investments elsewhere. The one exception to this conclusion is in the biofuel crop sector, where Chinese companies are active across many regional countries but particularly in the Philippines and Indonesia. However, the increased competition with other countries for the same lands only reduces the available supply at a faster rate; suggesting that even in the biofuels sector the release of future land stocks for Chinese companies will be limited.

When comparing both countries, this study observed that the Philippines was an early destination for Chinese AODI. Even though the initial expectations from the agreements has not materialised, there is evidence that the relationship has not stalled; rather it is focused on more modest investment levels and outcomes. Moreover, the Chinese interest in the Philippines as an offshore base for both food and cash crops is mirrored by high levels of interest from countries and corporations elsewhere around the region and beyond. Indonesia has only recently opened its economy to foreign direct investments in the agricultural sector. From the available data, China's investments in this country appear to be dominated by rubber and biofuel-related crops. Even in these areas, the relative newness of the investment regimes makes micro-level analysis problematic. If, however, the AODI pattern in Indonesia only broadly follows the Philippines model, then the next 5–10 years should show a wider set of agricultural investments developing – as is indeed suggested by the subnational agreements reviewed.

In considering the data from the CLMV states, it can be concluded that – taken together with the Philippines and Indonesian examples – they form a spectrum of Chinese investment behaviour in the agricultural sector. At one end (such as Cambodia), Chinese AODI can lead to highly determined behaviour – driven by commercial and policy imperatives. At the other end of the spectrum (such as Vietnam), there is little AODI, with most of the commercial interactions being trade-based. This difference seems to act as a behavioural modifier on the Chinese companies involved. When the Philippines and Indonesia are added to this sample, new patterns of investment behaviour emerge – most tellingly in the engagement of local stakeholders. Nonetheless, as these cases equally demonstrated, Chinese companies still prefer to deal with national political and economic elites. Larger scales of geographic and economic opportunity may account for this somewhat more inclusive approach, as could the differences in the political systems; although as the case of Jilin Fuhua's investment in the Philippines showed, this does not equate with a secured operation.

Looking to the future, China is only going to become more food insecure. Technology and a greater environmental awareness may slow the pace of this insecurity but so long as population and modernisation pressures increase Chinese policy-makers are unlikely to be able to balance food and national security interests from domestic sources alone. This means that China must continue to look overseas to meet its domestic demands. Indeed, as these twinned pressure rise, China will need to support increased overseas investments in arable land supplies (Zha and Zhang 2013). In doing so, the primary focus of China's agricultural interests in Africa and Latin America is unlikely to change unless the investment climate in these regions becomes commercially unfavourable to

Chinese interests. Nonetheless, the agricultural investments explored in this article are important in their own right and, more broadly, in terms of China's relations with Southeast Asia. On the one hand, they provide economic development opportunities where none previously existed, while allowing China enhanced political capacity to shape 'the general propensity of things' in the region of its greatest diplomatic attention.

Notes

1 In comparison, China's total meat production in 2010 was estimated at 77.5 mln tonnes (Dairy Site.com 2010).
2 Had China already reached its target, this success would have been explicitly highlighted, as can be seen for other areas in Minister Xu's statement.
3 In turn, this disjuncture between domestic demand and overseas acquisitions could reinforce the argument that China's AODI is being driven by longer-term strategic concerns rather than by commercial interests.
4 For reasons of space, this article will only explore land-based cases of food security and Chinese AODI. Aqua-culture related examples, although numerous, will be a topic for future research.
5 An exception to this observation is the banana and pineapple sectors in the Philippines, where large scale vertical integration has brought the type of financial returns discussed previously (Briones 2008: 3).
6 Chinese tourists accounted for 6.21% of tourists to the Philippines in 2011, while half of the Philippines' banana crop and other produce goes to China.
7 Of these, six were mainly focused on aqua-culture related interests, six were related to bio-fuels, three to agri-business, with the remaining three agreements focused on irrigation, technical and policy concerns.
8 An agro-business, Dole, was – until the Fuhua agreement – the largest recipient of land concessions from the Philippines government, with 9000 hectares granted (Bagayaua 2007).
9 In late September 2012, Itochu also took over Dole (Philippines) gaining control of all its farming operations throughout the country (Sarimento 2012).
10 (1) Assuming a production capacity of 356 days per year; (2) as the exact number of bioethanol plants covered in the fifth agreement are unknown (other than that there is more than one), a conservative estimate of only two plants has been used in this part of the calculation.
11 This was split 53–47 between SOE and POE investments.

References

ACapital. (2011) 'How fast is China globalizing: tracking Chinese outbound investments', *ACapital Dragon Index: 2011 Full Year*, accessed at http://www.acapital.hk/dragonindex/A%20CAPITAL%20DRAGON%20INDEX%20Full%20Year%202011%20ENG.pdf, 12 June 2012.
Adhani, R. (2010) 'Provincial government set to receive relocated Chinese industries', *The Global Review*, 28 May, accessed at http://www.theglobal-review.com/content_detail.php?lang=en&id=2078&type=7>, 13 December 2012.
Alon, I. (2012) 'The globalisation of Chinese capital', *East Asia Forum Quarterly* April–June: 4–6.
Antara News. (2012) 'RI is China's second biggest investment destination', 11 October.

Asia Pulse. (2011) 'China's meat output to reach 85mln tonnes by 2015', 23 September.

Asia Times. (2007) 'Food security fears as China's farmland shrinks', 17 May, accessed at http://www.atimes.com/atimes/China_Business/IE17Cb02.html, 31 October 2013.

Asian Sentinel. (2010) 'Laos and the resource curse', 21 October, accessed at http://farmlandgrab.org/17039, 31 October 2013.

Bagayaua, G. (2007) 'Gov't leases 1/10th of RP agricultural lands to China firm', *Newsbreak*, 17 October, accessed at http://www.gmanetwork.com/news/story/64800/newsbreak-gov-t-leases-1-10th-of-rp-agricultural-lands-to-china-firm, 8 December 2012.

Barboza, D. (2011) 'Inflation pressures grow in China as consumer prices increase 4.9%', *New York Times*, 11 March, accessed at http://www.nytimes.com/2011/03/12/business/global/12yuan.html?_r=0, 31 October 2013.

BAS. (2012) *Updates on Agricultural Trade Performance*, 4(2), January–June, accessed at http://www.bas.gov.ph/situationer/Trade1/TradePerJan-Jun2012.pdf, 9 December 2012.

Briones, R. (2008) 'Addressing policy issues and constraints in agricultural diversification: the potential contribution of the fruits and vegetables subsector', *Policy Notes*. Manila: Philippines Institute of Development Studies, December.

Chang, B. (2012) 'ASEAN, China to become top trade partners', *China Daily*, 20 April, accessed at http://www.chinadaily.com.cn/business/2012-04/20/content_15097076.htm, 31 October 2013.

Chang, C., Lee, H. and Hsu, S. (2013) 'Food security: global trends and regional perspective with reference to East Asia', *Pacific Review* 26(5) (in press).

Chen, J. (2011) 'The strategic choice of realising the balance between China's supply and demand of grain', *Farmers' Daily*, 21 May, accessed at http://szb.farmer.com.cn/nmrb/html/2011-05/21/nw.D110000nmrb_20110521_5-03.htm?div=-1, 29 May 2012.

Chi-agri.com. (2012) 'China became a net importer of three major grains in 2011', 2 May, accessed at http://www.guojixumu.com/en/news/newshow.aspx?id=18557, 29 May 2012.

'China: country resources', *Food Security Portal*, accessed at http://www.foodsecurityportal.org/china/resources, 29 May 2012.

China Daily. (2011a) 'Hu stresses arable land protection', 24 August, accessed at http://english.peopledaily.com.cn/90785/7578226.html, 31 October 2013.

China Daily. (2011b) 'China–ASEAN Cooperation: 1991–2011', 16 November, accessed at http://www.chinadaily.com.cn/cndy/2011-11/16/content_14101968.htm, 31 October 2013.

China Daily. (2012) 'Protection of farmland enhanced, minister says', 12 March, accessed at http://english.peopledaily.com.cn/90785/7755082.html, 31 October 2013.

'Chinese commerce minister calls for expanding economic co-op between China, ASEAN', 12 August 2011, accessed at http://english.gov.cn/2011-08/12/content_1924539.htm, 5 July 2012.

Christiansen, F. (2009) 'Food security, urbanization and social stability in China', *Journal of Agrarian Change*, 9(4), October: 548–575.

Dairy Site.com. (2010) 'China – livestock and products semi-annual report 2010', accessed at http://www.thedairysite.com/articles/2330/china-livestock-and-products-semiannual-report-2010, 8 April 2012.

David, C. (1995) *Economic Policies and Agricultural Incentives: The Philippine Case*. Manila: Philippine Institute for Development Studies, DP No. 95–15.

David, C., Ponce, E. and Intal, P. (1992) *Organizing for Results: The Philippine Agricultural Sector*. Manila: Philippine Institute for Development Studies, August.

dela Cruz, R. (2010) *National Agricultural Research Systems in the Philippines*. country report presented at the 'Workshop on Rural Development for High-Level Officers of AFACI member countries, South Korea, Suwon, 7–14 August.

dela Cruz, R. (2011) 'The new conquistadores and one very willing colony: a discussion on global land grabbing and the Philippine experience', *International Land Coalition*, January, accessed at http://americalatina.landcoalition.org/sites/default/files/WEB_ARNow_Philippines_final_layout.pdf, 12 December 2012.

Deloitte. (2009) *The Emergence of China: New Frontiers in Outbound M&A*. November, accessed at http://www.deloitte.com/assets/Dcom-China/Local%20Assets/Documents/Services/Global%20Chinese%20Services%20Group/cn_gcsg_EmCnNewFront_011209.pdf, 13 June 2012.

Department of Agriculture. (2011) 'DA, Jilin China firm up Agri cooperation, trade', 23 September, accessed at http://www.da.gov.ph/index.php/2012-03-27-12-04-15/2012-04-17-09-30-59/1171-da-jilin-china-firm-up-agri-cooperation-trade, 12 December 2012.

Department of Primary Industries. (2010) *Philippines: Market Development and Access Strategy 2011/2012*. 17 September, accessed at http://www.dpi.vic.gov.au/agriculture/investment-trade/market-access-and-competitiveness/?a=2968, 9 December 2012.

EIU ViewsWire. (2011) 'Myanmar politics: Chinese takeaway kitchen', 11 June, accessed at http://www.eiu.com/index.asp?layout=VWArticleVW3, 31 October 2013.

Filipinosocialism. (2007) 'Made for China? A critical look at the RP–China agreements', 5 August, accessed at http://filipinosocialism.wordpress.com/2007/08/05/made-for-china-a-critical-look-at-the-rp-china-agreements/, 2 December 2012.

Freedman, A. (2013) 'Rice security in Southeast Asia: beggar thy neighbour or cooperation', *Pacific Review* 26(5) (in press).

Fullbrook, D. (2010) *Development in Lao PDR: The Food Security Paradox*. Working Paper series – Mekong Region, Swiss Agency for Development and Cooperation, February, accessed at http://vietnam.resiliencesystem.org/sites/default/files/Food_Security_Lao.pdf, 19 December 2012.

Gammeltoft, P. and Tarmidi, L. (2011) 'Chinese foreign direct investment in Indonesia', *CIBEM Working Paper Series*, November, 8, accessed at http://openarchive.cbs.dk/bitstream/handle/10398/8397/Peter_Gammeltoft_2011.pdf?sequence=1, 13 December 2012.

GIEWS. (2012) 'Country brief: China (Mainland)', 13 February, accessed at http://www.fao.org/giews/countrybrief/country/CHN/pdf/CHN.pdf, 29 May 2012.

Global Witness. (2005) 'Natural resource governance – a test of political will for the Cambodian government and the international donor community', *Global Witness*, 29 June, accessed at http://www.globalwitness.org/library/natural-resource-governance-%E2%80%93-test-political-will-cambodian-government-and-international, 19 November 2012.

GRAIN. (2007) 'Hybrid rice and China's expanding empire (Part 1)', 6 February, accessed at http://www.grain.org/es/article/entries/1626-hybrid-rice-and-china-s-expanding-empire-part-1, 11 December 2012.

Gray, D. (2008) 'China now trying to destroy Laos', *GlobalAffairs Forum*, 4 May, accessed http://globalaffairs.lefora.com/2008/05/04/china-now-trying-to-destory-laos/, 19 December 2012.

Habito, C. and Briones, R. (2005) 'Philippine agriculture over the years: performance, policies and pitfalls', a paper presented at *Policies to Strengthen Productivity in the Philippines*, Philippines, Makati City, June 27, accessed at http://siteresources.worldbank.org/INTPHILIPPINES/Resources/Habitoword.pdf, 9 December 2012.

Heinimann, A., Epprecht, M., Von Behaim, D., Messerli, P., Duiven, R. and Palikone, T. (2012) 'Beyond anecdotal evidence: providing systemic and national-level evidence on dimensions and impacts of land concessions in Lao PDR', paper presented at Annual World Bank Conference on Poverty, 23–26 April, accessed at http://www.landandpoverty.com/agenda/pdfs/paper/heinimann_paper.pdf, 8 December 2012.

Hitipeuw, J. (2011) 'Recent rioting in Maluku doesn't deter Chinese investors', *Kompass.com*, 28 September, accessed at http://english.kompas.com/read/2011/09/28/16303296/Recent.Rioting.in.Maluku.Doesnt.Deter.Chinese.Investors, 13 December 2012.

Hodal, K. (2012) 'China invests in south-east Asia for trade, food, energy and resources', *The Guardian*, 22 March, accessed at http://www.theguardian.com/world/2012/mar/22/china-south-east-asia-influence, 31 October 2013.

Hong Kong Trade and Development Council. (2010) *China–ASEAN Free Trade Area (CAFTA): Implications for Hong Kong Merchandise Exports*, 8 March, accessed at http://www.hktdc.com/info/mi/a/ef/en/1×06OJ4B/1/Economic-Forum/China-ASEAN-Free-Trade-Area-CAFTA-Implications-For-Hong-Kong-S-Merchandise-Exports.htm, 20 November 2012.

Hovhannisyan, V. and Gould, B. (2011) 'Quantifying the structure of food demand in China: an econometric approach', *Agricultural Economics* (42, November): 1–18.

IMF (2012) 'Indonesia: selected issues', *IMF Country Report No. 12/278*. September, accessed at http://www.imf.org/external/pubs/ft/scr/2012/cr12278.pdf, 14 December 2012.

Ishmar, A. (2010) 'Indonesia lifts cap on foreign owners', *Wall Street Journal*, 10 June, accessed at http://online.wsj.com/article/SB20001424052748704575304575296124174067194.html, 31 October 2013.

Jiang, Y. (2012) 'Agriculture sector goes out: three main focus sectors defined by central enterprises', *Economic Observer*, 11 February. (In Chinese.)

Jilin Daily. (2011) 'Jilin–Philippines Economic and Trade Cooperation Symposium was held in Manila', 27 September.

Jilin Provincial Government. (2008) 'Our Province's Delegation Concludes the Visit to Myanmar, Singapore and South Korea', 10 June, <http://test3.jljiaxin.com/english/jilin/201006/t20100608_729110.html>, Accessed 17 December 2012.

Jilin Provincial Government. (2012) 'U Thein Oo, Tin Aye and Periodical Myanmar political leaders met with Sun Zhengcai', 4 July, accessed at http://english.jl.gov.cn/News/GeneralNews/201207/t20120704_1237684.html, 17 December 2012.

Klute, M. (2007) 'Green gold biodiesel: players in Indonesia', *BiofuelWatch*, 24 January, accessed at http://www.biofuelwatch.org.uk/2007/green-gold-biodiesel-players-in-indonesia, 12 December 2012.

Kong, L. (2011) 'China, Malaysia team up in rubber deal', *The China Post*, 14 September, accessed at http://www.chinapost.com.tw/business/asia/malaysia/2011/09/14/316550/China-Malaysia.htm, 31 October 2013.

Kya, H. and Htun, A. (2012) 'Yuzana Company says it will compensate the confiscate land in Hugawng valley', 31 August, accessed at http://kdng.org/news/34-news/271-yuzana-company-says-it-will-compensate-the-confiscate-land-in-hugawng-valley.html, 17 December 2012.

Li, J. (2012) 'Trade warning to Philippines', *China Daily*, 14 May, accessed at http://english.peopledaily.com.cn/90778/7815967.html, 31 October 2013.

Lohmar, B. (2004) 'China's wheat economy: current trends and prospects for imports', *WHS 04D-01* May, United States Department of Agriculture, accessed at http://usda.mannlib.cornell.edu/usda/ers/WHS/2000s/2004/WHS-05-18-2004_Special_Report.pdf, 28 May 2012.

Lohmar, B. and Gale, F. (2008) 'Who Will China Feed?', *Amber Waves* (Vol. 6 No. 3, June): 10–15.

Lu, L. (2006) 'The analysis on the similarity of China and ASEAN's agricultural products', World Agricultural Economy 1: 36–40. (In Chinese.)

Ma, H., Huang, J., Fuller, F. and Rozelle, S. (2006) 'Getting rich and eating out: consumption of food away from home in urban China', *Canadian Journal of Agricultural Economics* 54(1): 101–119.

MacKinnon, I. (2008) 'The resentment rises as villagers are stripped of holdings and livelihood', *The Guardian*, 22 November, accessed at http://www.theguardian.com/environment/2008/nov/22/food-biofuels-laos, 31 October 2013.

Mah, F. (1971) 'Why China imports wheat', *The China Quarterly* 45(January/March): 116–128.

Manila Bulletin. (2011) 'Bio-ethanol plant secures local support', 13 December, accessed at http://www.mb.com.ph/articles/344622/bioethanol-plant-secures-local-support, 31 October 2013.

Martov, S. (2012) 'Report urges govt to address land grabbing issue', *The Irrawaddy*, 26 October, accessed at http://www.irrawaddy.org/burma/report-urges-govt-to-address-land-grabbing-issue.html, 31 October 2013.

Ministry of Commerce. (2012) 'China's Q1 overseas investment surges 95%', press release, 26 April, accessed at http://english.mofcom.gov.cn/aarticle/newsrelease/counselorsoffice/westernasiaandafricareport/201204/20120408091637.html, 5 June 2012.

Ministry of Trade. (undated) *Balance of Trade with Partner Country (China)*. accessed at http://www.kemendag.go.id/statistik_neraca_perdagangan_dengan_negara_mitra_dagang/, 11 December 2012.

Mishkin, S. (2012) 'Indonesia–China: trade grows despite commercial tensions', *Financial Times*, 23 March, accessed at http://blogs.ft.com/beyond-brics/2012/03/23/indonesia-china-trade-grows-despite-commercial-tensions/?#axzz2jOizc4c2, 31 October 2013.

MOFCOM. (2010) *Foreign Market Access Report 2010: The Philippines*. accessed at http://gpj.mofcom.gov.cn/accessory/201004/1271301985402.pdf, 8 December 2012.

Mold, A. (2011) 'Shifting wealth and the consequences of rising food prices on social cohesion: a diagnosis and policy responses', *OECD*, January, accessed at http://www.oecd.org/dataoecd/41/58/46921010.pdf, 28 May 2012.

Mongabay.com. (2007) 'China invests in $5.5B biofuels project in Borneo, New Guinea', 18 January, accessed at http://news.mongabay.com/2007/0118-borneo.html, 11 December 2012.

Myanmar Times. (2012) 'Laos "halts new investment, land concessions"', 32(633), 2–8 July, accessed at http://www.mmtimes.com/2012/business/633/biz63306.html, 31 October 2013.

Newsbsb168.com. (2012) 'Sinochem International to accelerate the natural rubber global layout', 28 March, accessed at http://nws.en.b2b168.com/detail/c33-i12728989.html, 14 December 2012.

Ngoc, M. (2005) 'Chinese delegation sign the dotted line en masse', *Vietnam Investment Review*, 18 May.

OECD. (2012) *OECD Review of Agricultural Policies: Indonesia 2012.* accessed at http://www.keepeek.com/oecd/media/agriculture-and-food/oecd-review-of-agricultural-policies-indonesia-2012_9789264179011-en, 9 December 2012.

Philippine Revolution Web Central. (2012) 'Bioethanol project in Isabela: slave-like conditions of farm workers', 21 July, accessed at http://www.philippinerevolution.net/publications/ang_bayan/20120721/slave-like-conditions-of-farm-workers, 12 December 2012.

Qiu, H., Yang, J., Huang, J. and Chen, R. (2007) 'Impact of China–ASEAN Free Trade Area on China's international agricultural trade and its regional development', *China and World Economy* 15(4): 77–90.

Qu, H. and Sun, J. (2011) 'China inside out', *HSBC Global Research*, 29 April, p. 4, accessed at http://www.research.hsbc.com/midas/Res/RDV?ao=20&key=Tjjxi3k2AH&n=297205.PDF, 12 June 2012.

Rae, A. (2008) 'China's agriculture, smallholders and trade: driven by the livestock revolution?', *The Australian Journal of Agricultural and Resource Economics* 52(3): 283–302.

Richardson, M. (2010) 'China's big stick: trade reprisals', *The Japan Times Online*, 18 November, accessed at http://search.japantimes.co.jp/cgi-bin/eo20101118mr.html, 5 July 2012.

Rong, J. and Yang, C. (2006) 'Empirical study on competitiveness and complementarity of China and ASEAN's agricultural products', International Trade Problems 8: 45–50. [In Chinese.]

Rutherford, J., Lazarus, K. and Kelley, S. (2008) *Rethinking Investments in Natural Resources: China's Emerging Role in the Mekong Region.* accessed at http://www.iisd.org/pdf/2008/trade_china_study.pdf, 17 December 2012.

san Juan, R. (2007) 'Summary of RP–China deals relating to fisheries and agriculture', 18 October, accessed at http://rolandsanjuan.blogspot.hk/2009/02/summary-of-rp-china-deals-relating-to.html, 8 December 2012.

Sarimento, B. (2012) 'Dole-Philippines workers welcome takeover of Japan's firm', *Sun Star*, 21 September, accessed at http://www.sunstar.com.ph/davao/local-news/2012/09/21/dole-philippines-workers-welcome-takeover-japans-firm-244018, 31 October 2013.

Scott, R. and Jiang, J. (2012) 'People's Republic of China: biofuels annual', *Global Agricultural Information Network*, No. 12044, 7 September, accessed at <http://gain.fas.usda.gov/Recent%20GAIN%20Publications/Biofuels%20Annual_Beijing_China%20-%20Peoples%20Republic%20of_7-9-2012.pdf, 9 December 2012.

Sinochem. (undated) 'Natural rubber', accessed at http://www.sinochem.com/g736.aspx, 14 December 2012.

Sisante, J. (2010) 'Aquino brings home $2.85-B in investments from Japan', *GMA News*, 15 November, accessed at http://www.gmanetwork.com/news/story/206008/nation/aquino-brings-home-2-85-b-in-investments-from-japan, 31 October 2013.

Songwanich, S. (2012) 'China's drive to modern agriculture', *The Nation*, 28 May, accessed at http://www.nationmultimedia.com/opinion/Chinas-drive-to-modern-agriculture-30182925.html, 31 October 2013.

State Council. (1996) *Quanguo nongchanpin chengben shouyi ziliao huibian* [National Agricultural Production Cost and Revenue Information Summary].

China Price Bureau Press: Beijing, China, 1988–97 as cited in Food and Agricultural Organization. "Annex 3: Agricultural Policy and Food Security in China," *Poverty Alleviation and Food Security in the Asia-Pacific: Lessons and Challenges*, accessed at http://www.fao.org/docrep/004/ab981e/ab981e0c.htm, 31 October 2013.

Supreme Court. (2008) 'Certiorari and prohibition: with application for a temporary restraining order and/or preliminary injunction', 19 February, accessed at http://jaefever.files.wordpress.com/2008/03/rp-china-supreme-court-petition.pdf, 13 December 2012.

Tang, Y. and Wang, W. (2006) 'An analysis of the trade potential between China and ASEAN within China–ASEAN FTA', accessed at http://faculty.washington.edu/karyiu/confer/beijing06/papers/tang.pdf, 20 November 2012.

The Economist. (2010) 'China's rising prices: Hunting down the hoarders', 18 November, accessed at http://www.economist.com/node/17528136, 31 October 2013.

The SunStar Manila. (2012) 'Foreign Affairs chief cites Philippines' high investment in China', 17 May, accessed at http://www.sunstar.com.ph/manila/local-news/2012/05/17/foreign-affairs-chief-cites-philippines-high-investment-china-221828, 31 October 2013.

Thompson, P. (2012) 'Arable land shortage and the case for agricultural and farm-land investing', *Technorati.com*, 28 February, accessed at http://technorati.com/business/finance/article/arable-land-shortage-and-the-case/, 19 March 2012.

Tiongco, M. and Francisco, K. (2011) *Philippines: Food Security versus Agricultural Exports?*. Manila: Philippine Institute for Development Studies, DP No. 2011–35.

Titthara, M. (2012) 'China's reaps concession windfalls', *The Phnom Penh Post*, 2 April, accessed at http://www.phnompenhpost.com/national/china-reaps-concession-windfalls, 31 October 2013.

Tong, S. and Chong, C. (2010) China–ASEAN Free Trade Area in 2010: a regional perspective', *EAI Background Brief No. 519*, 12 April, accessed at http://www.eai.nus.edu.sg/BB519.pdf, 20 November 2012.

Tubeza, P. (2011) 'Philippine president back from China with $13b deals', *Philippine Daily Inquirer*. 4 September, accessed at http://www.island.lk/index.php?page_cat=article-details&page=article-details&code_title=33931, 31 October 2013.

US State Department. (2005) 'Embracing the dragon: The Philippines deepens', 2 May, accessed at http://wikileaks.org/cable/2005/05/05MANILA1987.html, 13 December 2012.

US State Department. (2008) 'Limits of Chinese soft power in the Philippines', *Wikileaks Cable 08MANILA998*, 28 April, accessed at http://wikileaks.org/cable/2008/04/08MANILA998.html, 13 December 2012.

VietNamNet. (2011) 'Chinese lease Vietnamese land to grow sweet potatoes', 11 July, accessed at http://farmlandgrab.org/post/view/18927, 31 October 2013.

Walker, E. (2006) 'The Kalimantan border oil palm mega-project', *AIDEnvironment*. April, accessed at http://www.foe.co.uk/resource/reports/palm_oil_mega_project.pdf, 12 December 2012.

Wang, Y. and Tong, S. (2010) 'China–ASEAN FTA changes ASEAN's perspective on China', *East Asian Policy* 2(2) (April/June): 47–54.

World Bank. (2012) 'Food prices rise again on higher oil prices and adverse weather', 25 April, accessed at http://web.worldbank.org/WBSITE/EXTERNAL/

NEWS/0,,contentMDK:23180612~pagePK:34370~piPK:34424~theSitePK: 4607,00.html, 29 May 2012.

World Bank Data, *World Development Indicators and Global Development Finance*, accessed at http://data.worldbank.org/country/philippines#cp_wdi, 10 December 2012.

Xinhua. (2011) 'China's food prices rise over past week', 26 January.

Xinhua. (2012) 'Indonesia emerges as attractive playground for Chinese investors'. 23 April, accessed at http://news.xinhuanet.com/english/world/2012-04/23/ c_131545052.htm, 31 October 2013.

Xinhua. (2012b) '490 out of world top 500 companies invest in China', 22 June, accessed at http://news.xinhuanet.com/english/china/2012-06/22/c_131670389. htm, 31 October 2013.

Xinhua. (2012c) 'China's investment in Cambodia reaches $8.8b', 6 September, accessed at http://en.ce.cn/Business/Macro-economic/201109/06/t20110906_ 22677188.shtml, 31 October 2013.

Yang, J., Qiu, H., Huang, J. and Rozelle, S. (2008) 'Fighting global food price rises in the developing world: the response of China and its effect on domestic and world markets', *Agricultural Economics* 39 (Supplement): 453–464.

Zakendoen in China. (undated) 'The 12th Five Year Plan-agriculture related parts', accessed at http://china.nlambassade.org/Zakendoen_in/kansen-en-sectoren/ tuinbouw/rapporten-over-tuinbouw/the-12th-five-year-plan-agriculture- related-parts.html, 29 May 2012.

Zha, D. and Zhang, H. (2013) 'Food in China's international relations', *Pacific Review* 26(5) (in press).

Zhang, X. and Yeo, T. (2005) 'On the overseas direct investment of Chinese privately-owned enterprises', *Journal of Korea Trade* 9(1): 31–58.

Zhu, L. (2011) 'Food security and agricultural changes in the course of China's urbanization', *China & World Economy* 19(2): 40–59.

'Land grabbing' or harnessing of development potential in agriculture? East Asia's land-based investments in Africa

Franklyn Lisk

Abstract Large-scale foreign investment in Africa's abundant but largely underutilized arable land has been criticised by international NGOs and social movements as 'land grabbing', which limits access of smallholder farmers to land, deprives local people of their livelihoods and threatens local and national food security across the continent. By way of contrast, many host governments and some leading international development agencies regard land-based investments as beneficial for development in terms of providing the necessary capital and technological know-how for modernising the region's neglected agriculture including take-off in agribusiness and agro-industrialisation, which is vital to much needed economic diversification in many African countries. East Asia's participation in the global land rush on Africa is examined from the standpoint of these two different perspectives: while China's growing presence and involvement in trade and investment in mining, energy and infrastructure in Africa is well known, less recognised is its involvement and those of other East Asian countries such as South Korea, Malaysia, Singapore and Vietnam in agriculture through large-scale land acquisitions. The development consequences and policy implications of these foreign land-based investments are analysed from a political economy perspective, which identifies motives, interests and benefits of the different actors and addresses the question of governance in terms of transparency and appropriate institutional arrangements to safeguard land rights and food security. In the bigger picture, the paper argues that the negative consequences of land grab has to be seen alongside the benefits flowing to Africa from growing economic relations with China and other dynamic East Asian economies and learning from the development experiences of those countries. African countries however need to re-assess the current approach and relationship with foreign land-based investors and decide how best this trend can be used to forward their economic and social agendas.

Introduction

Rising global demand for food stocks and bio-fuels together with weather-related supply disruptions of agricultural production worldwide in recent years have prompted considerable price volatility in international markets and put the global food system under extreme pressure. This situation has induced large and rapid increases in some food prices, particularly basic cereals, resulting in the worst food crisis since the 1970s which seriously threatens food security in developing countries. The sharp increase in international food prices during the years 2006 through 2008 also triggered a spate of cross-border land transactions involving wealthier nations seeking to acquire farmlands in mostly poor developing countries in order to grow food and non-food agricultural commodities for their own needs. In addition, fragility and consequent mistrust in global stock and equity markets have led to increase in speculative investments in land in developing countries by fund managers in developed countries. Escalation of international land deals for investment in agriculture in developing countries is contributing to unsustainable pressure on available land resources and increasing food security concerns worldwide (Anseeuw et al. 2012; Arezki et al. 2011; De Schutter 2011a; Oxfam 2011).

Almost half of the total number of recorded large-scale international land deals since 2008 has taken place in Africa – the region where available or 'uncultivated' arable land is perceived to be more abundant.[1] Growing interest in the global land rush in Africa has triggered a vibrant global debate and an increasing body of literature, although much of the data and evidence so far come from press reports, internet blogs and specific investigations by international NGOs on land acquisition, rather than academic research on case studies. The absence of accurate data on large-scale land acquisitions in Africa is because many of these land deals are concluded in secret including those within broader government-to-government arrangements and actual contracts are unreported.

The trend of foreigners acquiring large tracts of arable land in Africa and other developing regions has been strongly criticised by international advocacy groups and NGOs such as GRAIN and Oxfam and global social movements like Via Compensina, a pressure group working in partnerships with small farmers worldwide. They have denounced such transactions as 'land grabbing'[2] – a practice which, they claim, alienates smallholder farmers in from available land, displaces local populations and advances the marginalisation of the rural poor. Furthermore, several poor countries engaged in large-scale foreign land deals are also net importers of food and, therefore, increases in world food prices can be harmful to them.[3] At the same time, and from a different perspective, some other stakeholders and development analysts – including host-country governments and some international development agencies – have argued that large-scale foreign land-based investment could be an opportunity to develop and modernise the continent's agriculture with potential gains in terms of additional revenues and new employment opportunities (Collier 2008; Deinenger et al. 2011; FAO 2012). This view is linked to concern about the decades of neglect of investment in agriculture in many African countries and disillusionment with low levels of productivity and output of smallholder agriculture in the region.

This paper presents and analyses data and information on large-scale investments in arable land in Africa countries by East Asian nations. Most of the data and information used in the analysis come from country-level records and reports produced by GRAIN (2012) which systematically collates information on large-scale land acquisitions worldwide, and from qualitative country case studies by international advocacy organisations like Oxfam and the Oakland Institute, a California based think tank that specialises in management of land and natural resources in developing countries. The analysis of data and information is undertaken with the aim of assessing the impact of land-based foreign direct investments from the standpoint of the two different views concerning land acquisitions mentioned above – i.e., land grab or development opportunity (Cotula et al. 2009). In this regard, the paper examines key trends and drivers in large-scale land acquisitions within the wider context of national development and the expanding economic relations between Africa and East Asia, particularly China.

The total size of land leased or purchased by East Asian investors is at most no more than 3–5% of the estimated total amount of land that has been transferred to foreigners in Africa.[4] However, it is significant to note that the East Asian countries involved are affected by land scarcity and water depletion or have a very large population to feed (Brahmbhatt and Christiaensen 2008). It can therefore be inferred that the main motive for East Asian land-based investments in Africa has more to do with securing supplies of agricultural commodities to ensure food security and meeting needs for bio-fuels and manufacturing. In line with its growing presence in Africa, the number of Chinese land-based investment projects in African countries is greater than the total of all the other East Asian countries involved in land deals in the continent, notably from South Korea, Singapore, Malaysia and Vietnam. However, in terms of land area acquired, China is not the largest East Asian land-based investor in Africa: according to latest available data, China ranks below South Korea, Singapore and Malaysia.[5]

The paper begins with an overview of the global food system, highlighting the connection between uncertainties in global supply and food insecurity which serves as a background for a review of the underlying factors driving the global land rush on Africa. Next, it presents data and information specifically on East Asian land-based investments in Africa and, more generally, examines the implications and development consequences of the upsurge in large-scale land acquisition in Africa. The analysis seeks to provide greater clarity on the two opposite perceptions: (1) large-scale land acquisition, or 'land grabbing', is impacting negatively on food production, disrupting livelihoods of local people and threatening food security in Africa; and (2) land-based foreign investment for agricultural production can facilitate the modernisation of Africa's neglected agriculture and enhance the continent's role in the global food system.

Making use of a political economy approach, the analysis looks at vested interests of the different actors involved in international land transactions, including not only broader economic benefits such as employment generation and agriculture and rural infrastructure development but also traditional and cultural attributes of land, current aim and action of actors in relation to land access and use, the institutional arrangements they face and the room for manoeuvre in bringing about desirable changes and convergence of interests.[6] From the same perspective, the analysis addresses the important question of whether there is sufficient governance in large-scale land acquisitions by foreign investors – in terms of transparency and fair price and appropriate institutional arrangements to safeguard land rights – and looks at the catalytic role of international institutions, like the UN Food and Agriculture Organisation (FAO) and the World Bank, and regional groupings such as the G-8 and the African Union as framers of regulations, codes of conduct and voluntary guidelines for improved governance. In its conclusion, the paper advocates a need to look at the 'bigger picture' scenario in which possible adverse consequences of foreign land-based investments in Africa are minimised and balanced with potential gains in employment, growth and development from the 'take-off' in agriculture and agribusiness in Africa which can also resolve more long-standing concerns about food security.

Managing the global food system: the land-food security nexus

Managing the global food system, which is critical to the goal of sustainable food security for all, entails addressing concerns relating to both the global demand for food and world supply. The key factors pushing up global food demand are population growth mostly in the developing regions, changing diet patterns in large emerging and transition economies, and the bio-fuel boom which is linked to the quest for clean energy in industrialised countries. On the supply side, world food production is known to be affected by adverse weather conditions and environmental risks perceived to be linked to climate change which limit output of food stocks. Not only is world population increasing in terms of the number of people who have to be fed, but the switch to protein-intensive foods (meat and dairy products) by an increasing proportion of the population in large emerging economies such as China and India, as incomes rise, has led to declining world food stocks because cereals and grains are being diverted from human consumption to cattle feed. In addition, efforts to combat climate change in the industrialised economies through the use of low-carbon energy sources have sharply increased the demand for maize and diverted a sizeable proportion of the crop from food supply to biofuel production. Some developed countries have adopted specific agricultural and other policies, including payment of subsidies and offer of inducements, have led to increased support for the production of energy crops.[7] Other energy crops that grow in the tropics, such as oil palm, sugar cane and cassava, are now competing with food crops for arable land and water in developing countries.

In contrast to much of the twentieth century when the price of food fell in real terms, the first decade of the twenty-first century witnessed a sharp increase in international food and commodity prices during 2007–2008 in response to increasing demand and supply shortfall in global markets (Chang 2009). Distortionary agricultural policies are causing some rich countries to direct agricultural production to their own domestic markets, while import demand for food and bio-fuels is also rising. Price volatility has led large advanced developing countries like China, India and Brazil and net food sellers like Thailand and Vietnam to use trade restrictions to insulate themselves from the global food crisis, which in turn lead to further increase in prices and volatility. It is the poorer developing countries that are net food importers – mostly in Africa and parts of Asia and Latin America – that are hardest hit by the food price hikes which threaten food security.

Producing more food requires more arable land, and developing countries are attractive for foreign investment in land. Even after global food prices returned to moderate levels following the 2007–2008 price hikes the upward trend in the demand for agricultural land in developing countries did not subside, which indicates that there is still concern that the combined effects of demographic pressure, economic transformation and climate change that could again drive up international food prices – as indeed happened in 2010–2011 when grain prices rose steeply in international markets. Then, there is evidence of a surge in investments in agricultural land and commodities for speculative motive by investors who view farmland as an asset that is poised to produce significant returns. It is reported that an increasing number of Western investors, including Wall Street banks, have turned their attention to agricultural acquisitions in developing countries over the past few years (Daniel and Mittal 2009). GRAIN (2012) reported that about US$100 billion of the assets of pension funds in the US, Europe and Japan are invested in commodities, with some $5–15 billion of this money reportedly going to farmland acquisitions.[8] Speculation in farmland in Africa appears to be driven by a perception that large tracts of land in the continent can be acquired from governments at bargain price in anticipation of future price increases. According to numerous surveys and reports, annual returns of 10–20% are being obtained from investments in agricultural commodities and farmlands by private equity funds (Cochet and Merlet 2011). It is also possible that emerging carbon markets, which could be relevant for bio-fuel projects, may be fostering land acquisitions in the expectation of long-term increases in land values.

East Asia's participation in the global land rush on Africa

The dramatic changes that are taking place in the global food system – more so in the context of globalisation and an increasingly interconnected global marketplace for trade and finance – are attracting unprecedented commercial interest in land acquisition from the global investment community. Africa's vast untapped potential in agriculture – in terms of abundant land and investment opportunity in agriculture – makes it particularly attractive in the search for land to grow more food and energy crops to augment global supply. With an estimated 600 million hectares of 'uncultivated' arable land, which corresponds to about two-thirds of the global total and twice as much as Latin America, Africa is perceived as 'the world's last great unexploited agricultural frontier' with abundant arable land, and is presented to the global investment community as 'available and ready for business'.[9]

East Asia's participation in the global land rush on Africa in terms of land size is relatively small – less than 3 million hectares out of an estimated total of between 80 and 130 million hectares. The East Asian countries involved in land deals in Africa in general are not food self-sufficient but depend on imports to supplement their domestic needs. Driven mainly by volatility of food prices and uncertain agricultural commodity markets, these food-deficit nations seek to acquire land in Africa and other poorer developing countries in order to secure steady food and commodity supplies for the future. As shown in Table 1 below, the main East Asian countries investing in land in Africa are China, with its very large population and growing middle class; richer countries in the region with sizeable populations like Japan and South Korea; and smaller emerging economies such as Singapore, Malaysia and Vietnam. East Asian investors in Africa's farmlands include government agencies and their subsidiaries, state-sponsored enterprises and private corporations and individuals involved in agribusiness, manufacturing and construction.

A significant proportion of *China*'s land-based investments in Africa is channelled through state-sponsored commercial enterprises and development agencies. One of the most prominent investors is the China National Complete Import and Export Corporation Group (COMPLANT), which functioned as a foreign aid office for China until 1993 and now trades on the

Table 1 Land grabbing or harnessing agricultural development potential

		East Asian land-based investments in Africa					
Host country	Investor	Investor's home country	Sector	Hectares	Production	Projected investment	Deal status
Angola	CAMC Engineering Co. Ltd	China	Construction	1500	Rice	US$77 million	Done
Benin	'Chinese investment group'	China		10,000	Oil palm		In process
Benin	COMPLANT	China	Agribusiness, construction	4800	Cassava, sugar cane		In process
Cameroon	IKO	China	Agribusiness	10,000	Cassava, maize, rice	US$120 million	Done
Congo-Brazzaville	Atama Plantation	Malaysia	Agribusiness	470,000	Oil palm	US$300 million	Done
Côte d'Ivoire	Wilmar International/Olam	Singapore	Agribusiness	47,000	Oil palm, sugar cane		Done
Democratic Republic of the Congo	ZTE	China	Telecommunications	100,000	Oil palm		Done
Ethiopia	Hunan Dafengyuan	China	Agribusiness	25,000	Sugar cane		Done
Gabon	Olam International	Singapore	Agribusiness	300,000	Palm oil	US$250 million	Done
Ghana	Wilmar International	Singapore	Agribusiness	6157	Oil palm		Done
Liberia	Sime Darby	Malaysia	Agribusiness	220,000	Oil palm	US$3.1 billion	Done
Liberia	Golden Agri Resources	Singapore	Agribusiness	220,000	Oil palm	US$1.6 billion	Done
Madagascar	COMPLANT	China	Agribusiness, construction	10,000	Sugar cane		Done
Mali	China Light Industrial Corporation for Foreign Economic and Technical Cooperation	China	Industrial	20,000	Sugar cane	US$41 million	Done
Mauritius	Intrasia Capital	Singapore	Finance	2500	Rice		Done

(*continued*)

Table 1 (Continued)

Host country	Investor	Investor's home country	Sector	Hectares	Production	Projected investment	Deal status
			East Asian land-based investments in Africa				
Mozambique	Hubei SFAC	China	Agribusiness	1000			Done
Mozambique	Olam International	Singapore	Agribusiness	227		US$35 million	Done
Nigeria	Chinese investors	China		6000	Cassava		Done
Nigeria	Vietnam Africa Agricultural Development Company	Vietnam	Agribusiness	10,000	Rice		Done
Nigeria	Vietnamese investors	Vietnam		4000	Rice		Done
Senegal	China	China	Government	100,000	Peanuts		In process
Senegal	Datong Trading Enterprise	China	Agribusiness	60,000	Sesame		Done
Sierra Leone	COMPLANT	China	Agribusiness, construction	8100	Cassava, sugar cane		Done
Sierra Leone	Shanghai Construction Investment	China	Construction	30,000	Rice	US$1.3 billion	Done
Sierra Leone	FELDA	Malaysia	Government	2500	Palm oil		Done
Sierra Leone	Long Van 28 Company	Vietnam	Agribusiness	200,000	Rice	US$15 million	In process
Sudan	ZTE	China	Telecommunications	10,000	Oil seeds		Done
Sudan	'A joint Arab-foreign company'	Philippines	Agribusiness	25,000	Cereals and other crops		Done
Sudan	South Korea	South Korea	Government	690,000	Wheat		Done
Tanzania	Chongqing Seed Corp	China	Agribusiness	300	Rice seeds		Done
Tanzania	Export Trading Group	Singapore	Agribusiness	8000	Rice		Done
Tanzania	Intrasia Capital	Singapore	Finance	30,000	Rice		Done

(*continued*)

Table 1 (Continued)

		East Asian land-based investments in Africa				
Host country	Investor	Investor's home country	Sector	Hectares	Production	Projected investment	Deal status
Tanzania	Korea Rural Community Corporation	South Korea	Government	100,000	Rice	US$50 million	Done
Uganda	Hebei Company	China	Agribusiness	540	Fruit, livestock, maize, rice, vegetables, wheat		In process
Uganda	Liu Jianjun	China	Finance	4000			Done
Uganda	Wilmar International	Singapore	Agribusiness	40,000	Oil palm		Done
Zambia	Export Trading Group	Singapore	Agribusiness	57,000	Food crops, jatropha		Done

Source: GRAIN (2012); accessed at http://www.grain.org/article/entries/4479-grain-releases-data-set-with-over-400-global-land-grabs, 5 July 2012.

Shenzhen Stock Exchange. COMPLANT's controlling shareholder is the State Development and Investment Corporation, the largest investment holding company in China, and is in a joint venture relationship with US$5 billion China–Africa Development Fund for ethanol and palm oil production projects. The corporation is directly or through one of its subsidiaries and joint ventures involved in ethanol projects in various African countries, such as Benin, Madagascar and Sierra Leone, through land-based investment for sugar cane and cassava production. Subsidiaries of China's national and provincial governmental structures and state-sponsored business groups, such as ZTE Corporation which is China's largest telecommunications company and Shanghai Construction Investment, state farms, have also concluded land deals for agribusiness, construction and infrastructure projects in more than 20 countries including Democratic Republic of the Congo (DRC), Ethiopia, Mali, Mozambique, Nigeria, Senegal, Sudan, Tanzania and Uganda.

South Korea accounts for the largest East Asian land-based investment in Africa in terms of land size (790,000 ha.), according to the latest data collated by GRAIN (2012). Korean investment is split between two countries, the Sudan and Tanzania. In the case of the former, the investment is based on a cooperation agreement on agriculture signed in 2009 between the Sudanese and Korean Presidents, which gives the Korean government access to two large tracts of Sudanese land – 420,000 hectares in the north and 270,000 in the central region – for the production of wheat, which apparently will be shipped to Korea for its own domestic consumption. The involvement of the South Korean government in a 100,000 hectares commercial rice production in Tanzania is part of a larger US$121 million bilateral assistance and loan concluded in 2010 between the two governments. Significantly, the execution of the rice project is based on a separate Memorandum of Understanding (MoU) signed between the Korea Rural Community Corporation and a local-level Tanzanian development agency, the Rufji Basin Development Authority. While details of the MoU are not known, it would appear that the arrangement for dealing directly with a local level authority in the land transaction and the execution of the project may have been adopted in order to avoid the problems encountered by the large South Korean industrial conglomerate Daewoo in a failed land acquisition process in 2008–2009 in Madagascar which revealed a governance disconnect between the central government and local level authorities.

The main aim of the failed Daewoo deal was to procure food and bio-fuels for South Korea based on agricultural production in Madagascar. After an initial public announcement of the negotiation between Daewoo and the Malagasy government, media and governmental reports on the deal including financial transactions were limited and vague. There was hardly any information about payments or compensation to local people for the land, although it should be pointed out that at the time the system of land ownership rights in Madagascar had been in a state of flux and ownership deeds by farmers were largely not filed with governmental authorities. Eventual exposure of the details of the agreement between Daewoo and the national government, in conjunction with revelation of a jet plane offered to the state President as part of the deal and rumours that a significant proportion of the better paid employment positions will be filled by skilled South Africans workers, were strong contributors to series of violent protests in early 2009 in which an estimated 100-plus people died in the unrests, and which led eventually to the resignation of the President in a military-backed *coup d'etat*. The Daewoo deal, which reportedly had been signed in July 2008, was cancelled by the new Malagasy Government.

Singapore with scarce land resources but plenty of investment money has been active in land-based deals in Africa (and elsewhere) over the past decade. Private commodity traders based in Singapore, such as Wilmar International one of the world's largest commodity traders and palm oil producers, Olam an Indian non-resident company, and Vita Grain a Singaporean company interested in hybrid rice have all invested in farming operations and contract farming schemes for palm oil production in Cote d'Ivoire, Gabon, Ghana, Liberia and Zambia, and rice production in Mauritius, Mozambique and Tanzania. In the agreements signed with both Mauritius and Mozambique, it was stipulated that some of the rice produced will be destined for the local markets. Singapore's operation in Tanzania is through ETG Holdings, one of the largest farmland owners in Africa with extensive holdings also in Kenya, Mozambique, Zambia and the DRC and a company that is committed to the development of corporate farms in sub-Saharan Africa. In Uganda, the government was able to get the support of the UN International Fund for Agricultural Development (IFAD) and the World Bank for its joint venture with Wilmar's subsidiary Oil palm Uganda Ltd., under which Wilmar was allocated 40,000 hectares of land for nucleus oil palm plantations in three different areas of Uganda. It can be inferred that the presence of Singaporean land-based investors in Africa is not entirely without immediate benefit for the local economies, both from the standpoints of food security and enhancement of agricultural production.

Malaysia's three land-based investment projects in Africa are in relation to oil palm plantations – two large investments in Congo–Brazzaville and Liberia and a much smaller one in Sierra Leone. The two large investments are by private Malaysian companies: Atama Plantations reportedly signed a deal with the Government of Congo–Brazzaville, which gave the company land concessions totalling 470,000 hectares in two different locations; and Sime Darby, the world's largest agribusiness in palm oil production, which was granted a 63-year lease by the government in 2009 for a 220,000 hectares concession for palm oil production spanning four of Liberia's fifteen counties. The Sime Darby deal in Liberia sparked off protest from local residents who with the support of the international NGO Green

Advocates filed an appeal to the Roundtable on Sustainable Palm Oil. Sime Darby was forced to freeze its operations and, consequently, indicated its willingness to deal directly with local villagers. However, the Liberian President, Mrs Johnson-Sirlief, intervened to end this attempt by Sime Darby at direct negotiation with local residents and, according to GRAIN (2012), remonstrated with the local land owners that their protests, and effectively attempts to defend their land rights could in fact be undermine the development agenda of the government. The continuation of local protest has recently forced the government to renegotiate the contract with Sime Darby to secure increased revenues and enforceable commitments on employment and business opportunities for local communities. Malaysian land-based investment in Sierra Leone has been pursued through an agreement between the two governments with the financial support of the Islamic Development Bank. Interestingly, rather than buy or lease land for its own use, the Malaysian government agency involved in the deal, the Federal Land Development Authority (FELDA), seeks to replicate its smallholder cooperative model in Sierra Leone by providing improved seeds and planting materials and technical expertise to local farmers in exchange for secured long-term supplies.

Investors from *Vietnam* have secured farmlands in Sierra Leone (200,000 hectares) and Nigeria (14,000 hectares) to grow rice. In both countries, the investment is centred on the activities of the Vietnam Africa Agricultural Development Company (VAADCO), which is a Vietnamese and British joint venture seeking to develop intensive-irrigated rice production in Africa. In Nigeria, VAADCO has signed an MoU with two state governments, Anambra and Edo, to cultivate improved varieties of rice that it is developing for local consumption. In the case of Sierra Leone where Vietnamese investment covers a much larger land area, the objective is to grow rice that will meet both local needs and export. VAADCO is also involved in experimental rice production in farm projects in Sudan, Mozambique, Rwanda, Burundi, Liberia, Ghana and Mauritania with various public and private sector partners and technical support from the Government of Vietnam.

This brief review of East Asia's land-based investments in Africa indicates that the pattern is mixed, ranging from investors securing land to produce food wholly for export to their own countries and with hardly any benefits to the local population, to arrangements which provide for some of the food produced by foreign investors to be marketed locally in the host country, to joint ventures between investors and host countries' governments with mutual benefits to both parties including employment gains and transfer of knowledge and modern technique to African farmers. Concerns about the damaging effects of land-based investments by some East Asian (and other) investors on national and local food security and overall development in Africa, has been documented by international NGOs like Oxfam and GRAIN, and expressed in various reports of the

United Nations Special Rapporteur on the Right to Food, Olivier De Schutter (2010, 2011a, 2011b).

The damaging effects of foreign land-based investments have been exacerbated by rising food prices since 2008 and the resulting crisis faced by poor consumers in Africa, which in a way revealed the under-investment in food production and underdevelopment of food markets in Africa. There is no question that Africa needs investment in agriculture to benefit from higher prices in global markets. However, in the absence of domestic funds for large investments in agriculture, Africa could continue to rely on foreign investors for capital and, hence, will be faced with the challenge of ensuring that such investments are properly managed so as to yield revenues for the state and provide employment and incomes benefits for local people, as well as provide access to technology, knowhow and markets.

Development consequences and policy implications

Large-scale land acquisition in Africa in the last five years is in sharp contrast to the situation in the preceding half a century. From 1961 to 2005, an average 4.1 million hectares of land changed ownerships annually for agricultural production, of which 1.8 million were in Africa. Preliminary research by the Land Matrix Partnership, as reported in a recent Oxfam briefing paper on foreign investments in land,[10] indicated that nearly 230 million hectares of land have been sold, leased, licensed, or are under negotiation in large scale land deals globally since 2005. Estimates of foreign land-based investments in Africa, as documented from plausible sources by GRAIN, Oxfam and others vary between 80 and 140 million hectares, with most of the acquisitions taking place in the last five years.[11] A recent extensively researched analysis puts the number of reported deals concluded worldwide between 2000 and 2011 at around 2000, covering 203 million hectares with Africa accounting for 948 acquisitions covering 134 million hectares – an area larger than, France, Germany and the United Kingdom combined (Anseeuw et al. 2012).

Objection to large-scale foreign land deals in Africa is grounded mainly on questionable land acquisition on the basis of lack of consultation and compensation of local people, with risks of land alienation and foods insecurity. Examination of a number of land acquisition contracts as reported by Oxfam revealed that leases were typically offered at extremely low levels of rent and extensive tax exemptions; investors were seldom required to provide employment opportunities for local communities or to contract smallholder farmers; contracts were usually drawn up and negotiated behind closed doors and often without any consultations with affected communities; and, more often than not, there were no social and environmental assessments of the investments or provision for monitoring and auditing of the implementation phase (Oxfam 2011). However, it is the effect of such investments on national and local food security that has attracted much attention and criticisms in various quarters. In most cases, there are usually no food security safeguards requiring foreign leasehold-ers to sell food products grown locally in local markets if necessary. A recent report by Oxfam (2012) claimed that two-thirds of foreign land-based investors intend to export 'everything they produce on the land', even though 60% of land investment deals are concluded in 'developing countries with serious hunger problems'. As Africa continues to be a mag-net for 'land grabs', there is the incongruity of large exports of food from food-deficit countries in the region which themselves end up depending on international food aid.

Food security

Until about 30 years ago most African countries were entirely self-suffi-cient in food production. Today, Africa is the only continent which fails to grow or purchase enough food to feed its people. Population in the region has increased considerably since then, and still increasing but, according to the FAO (2009), staple food yields (e.g., grains and cereals) in sub-Saharan Africa (SSA) have barely increased in the past three decades and are esti-mated at about a quarter of those in the other major developing. Increasing urbanisation rates in many African countries have also expanded the share of the continent's population that depends on food purchases. SSA is the region most affected by food insecurity, and several countries in the region cannot produce enough food locally and have fragile economic structures which render them ill equipped to respond to global price surges. While involvement in international land deals by such food deficit countries could be a possible strategic choice to address the decades of neglect of agricul-ture, this also raises serious and significant food security concerns in times of price volatility. Large net importers of food staples in the region, such as Ethiopia, Guinea, Sierra Leone, Madagascar, Mozambique, Niger, Mali, Senegal and Mauritania, were quick to feel the impact of higher import pri-ces in 2007–2008 which in some cases developed into a food crisis with incendiary effect. Typical is the situation of Senegal, a country that imports up to 80 per cent of its rice, the main food staple, making it particularly vul-nerable to global price instability. According to the FAO, recent develop-ments in terms of price volatility in global markets and resulting export restrictions have increased the magnitude and incidence of food insecurity, hunger and malnutrition more generally in Africa.

Land rights and access to land

Nowhere is land more crucial to livelihood than in Africa where small-holder production is the mainstay of the region's agriculture. Access of households and communities to adequate food for a healthy and productive life in Africa depends on secure access to, and control over, land resources.[12] Furthermore, for most communities across Africa land is not just a productive or economic asset; it is a source of life and well-being of a community and an essential part of local people's social and cultural identity. The perception that there is plenty of unused arable land in Africa waiting to be exploited has to be re-examined against the reality of land use patterns and land tenure systems in the region. It is unclear just what is meant by terms such as 'available', 'unused', 'idle' or 'under-utilized' land, and also whether a country's 'cultivatable' land is in fact, used or unused. In many African countries 'available' land is already being used or claimed –yet existing uses and claims go unrecognised because land users are not associated with formal land rights and access under the written law. Across Africa, the World Bank estimates that only between 2% and 10% of land is held under formal land tenure and this mainly concerns urban land (Deinenger 2003). The key question of land rights and access to land in Africa is rather complex and usually defies Western interpretation of ownership. In Sierra Leone, for example, access to most of the land relates to issues of tutelage, and land transactions could entail the relevance of formal property rights versus informal systems establishing ownership; international versus national versus local government claims to land; and competing uses for land from agriculture to industrial use (Unruh and Turay 2006; The Oakland Institute 2011).

There is ample evidence that the growing demand of foreign investors for agricultural land in Africa is affecting land ownership, access and use for local populations. While increased investment in agriculture seems desirable after decades of neglect and underinvestment in the sector, there is equally a need, from a governance standpoint, for both investors host governments to develop, implement and monitor appropriate regulations to protect land-use rights, improve food security of local communities and populations, and ensure sustainable management of land and other natural resources. This is consistent with various commitments made at the intergovernmental level, such as the 'Rome Principles' endorsed by the UN World Summit on Food Security in 2009; the G-8 leaders New Alliance for Food Security and Nutrition (2012) and the L'Aquila Food Security Initiative (2009); the Tirana Declaration of the International Land Coalition (ILC);[13] and the African Union (AU) Comprehensive Africa Agriculture Development Programme (CAADP) adopted in 2003 – all of which recognised the importance of access to arable land and the crucial role of smallholder farmers in Africa.

Development opportunity

A combination of rapid population growth, lack of knowledge and technological know-how, and low level of investment in rural infrastructure and agriculture has kept per capita food production and agricultural labour productivity in sub-Saharan Africa at exceedingly low levels, when compared with other developing regions. In the absence of irrigation, the effect of adverse climate and more frequently occurring droughts and land degradation is seriously affecting agricultural production in Africa which relies mainly on rain-fed farming. It is, therefore, not difficult to see why it is felt that Africa's vast endowment of arable lands is 'under-productive' in relation to ensuring the continent's food security, and to understand why foreign investments in land could potentially hold out promise for transforming Africa's agriculture for the better (Deineger and Byerlee, 2011).

After decades of neglect of agriculture in many African countries, more governments in the region are embracing investments in land by foreigners as an opportunity to overcome chronic underinvestment in agriculture and to harness financial resources and know-how needed to modernise rural infrastructure and boost production in the sector, create jobs and generate additional public revenue for economic development. This amounts to a supply-driven process in which the host governments play an active role in attracting foreign investments for national development. If managed responsibly, land-based foreign investment can link smallholders to regional and global markets and provide capital, technologies, infrastructure and knowledge needed to raise yields, generate revenue for the state and generate employment and incomes for the local population (FAO 2009). However, when badly managed, international land transactions can give rise to serious development challenges and problems including violation and lack of recognition of land rights and violation of human rights of poor people (Zoomers 2010; De Schutter 2011a). International acquisition of agricultural land in Africa therefore poses a challenge to host governments in the region to protect local land rights and domestic food security, while at the same time seeing large-scale land-based investments as opportunity for modernising agriculture and promoting economic development. The trade-off faced by African governments is thus between promoting foreign investment in agriculture which has long been neglected for economic growth and sustainable development and maintaining some degree of national sovereignty and local control over land as necessary for satisfying the needs of the population for access to and benefit from land.

It would appear that in general African governments are more interested in the direct impact on agriculture and rural development of international land deals, rather than making money in terms of public revenue from land transactions. On the whole, payments for land and land rents in Africa are rather low, particularly for agricultural land in rural areas. In many cases, official fees for land leased by foreign investors are charged at nominal rates (e.g., in the range of US$ 1–5 per hectares), and justifications for transferring land to foreigners are based on expected benefits in terms of stimulating local economic development, creating employment and diversifying their economies away from, for example, too much reliance on extractive industries and in favour of agriculture. But the low opportunity costs of land transferred to foreigners for agricultural production could also reflect the underdevelopment of formal land markets in rural Africa as well as the limited internal capacity or inability of governments to negotiate effectively in international land deals. For example, some governments in Africa have granted land leases to foreigners for 49 or even 99 years with no provision for periodic renegotiation of rents over the entire period of the lease.

Land governance challenges

Unsustainable pressure on land resources in many African countries is putting enormous strain on the fragile and inadequate legal and institutional arrangements that are in place in African countries to handle large-scale land transactions involving foreign investors. Some foreign investors have in turn exploited lack of clarity and confusion created by weaknesses in legal and institutional systems and inconsistencies in local land policies to evade their economic and social responsibilities on land acquisition – sometimes in collusion with national political leaders, ministers of host governments and even local community leaders and traditional chiefs. Enthusiasm for investment in large plantations by African governments has in some cases led them to quickly make land available for foreign acquisition, against local interests and even contrary to national legislation (Havnevik et al. 2011; The Oakland Institute 2011). The multiplicity of land-based projects occurring in a majority of Africa countries raises the question of whether Africa is developing into no more than an extended resource outlet for industrialized food and bio-fuel production systems with, in many instances, minimal considerations paid to fairness and equity issues for their populations and the environment where the acquisitions are occurring. While it is not the business of a foreign investor to determine and resolve issues of local governance, there is a moral obligation to make efforts specifically to act socially responsibly, and in the case of a foreign government to act in accordance with its role as a development partner of the host government.

The lack of transparency around land deals, absence of up-to-date land mapping and registration and limited internal legal and technical capacity to scrutinise the details of contracts serve as catalysts for inequitable agreements and represent problem areas in land governance in Africa. The failed land acquisition deal in Madagascar for food and biofuels production by a subsidiary of South Korean conglomerate Daewoo Corporation revealed that governance disconnects occurred between the state and regional levels, on the one hand, and the village/local community level, on the other, driven largely by a lack of transparency in the negotiation process. It also revealed the common land tenure problem across Africa of unclear land ownership rights and titles. After an initial announcement of negotiations between Daewoo and the national government in the local press in early 2008, nothing more was heard by the public about the negotiations until late 2008 when the deal was reported in a UK-based newspaper, the Financial Time, as a 99-year lease of 1.3 million hectares of Malagasy land but with no information on payments for the land (Olivier 2008). Apparently, the contract had been signed several months earlier in mid 2008 but kept secret. Subsequent exposure of the details of the deal, in conjunction with revelations of personal gains by the head of state, led to violent protests and political unrests locally and the eventual fall of the government in March 2009. It is significant to note that because of lack of transparency internally, the initial discontent with the deal originated from international land rights advocacy groups operating outside Madagascar who provided information on the deal that fomented actual resistance within Madagascar and violent protests by local people.

The importance of land governance in Africa is vividly illustrated by the case of Mozambique which has become one of the prime targets of large-scale investments in agriculture, mainly because of the availability of well-watered land for growing energy crops for bio-fuels. Land-use rights and local communities' access to benefits from land transactions and for the use of their forests and fauna (carbon trading) are among the biggest challenges to poverty reduction and sustainable development in Mozambique. As the percentage of cultivated land allocated to agribusiness and large-scale land-based investments in agriculture (state/private joint ventures and cooperatives) increases in the country, the rights and livelihoods of smallholder farmers are increasingly difficult to protect. This is particularly true when most of the available land is unregistered and untitled: in 2009 only 26 communities in Mozambique – less than 1% of the communities in the country – had their land formally registered. In such circumstance, there is great potential for future conflicts, because land previously demarcated for or informally allocated to local communities can later be formally allocated by the state to investors. In the absence of formal demarcation and registration, local communities find it increasingly difficult to protect their interests concerning land and other natural resources.

Taking into account the sort of problems associated with large-scale land transactions in Africa, responsible land governance in the region should revolve around three basic requirements. First, policies should be put in place to ensure some form of regulation of land deals based on principles embedded in the constructs of good governance at both national and international levels, and aimed at protecting land owners rights in both a free market system and under customary law and traditional system in land transactions (Lipton, 2009). These policies should be guided by core principles on land rights recognised by UN human rights bodies and voluntary guidelines for responsible land-based investments, such as those proposed by the World Bank (2008) and FAO (2012). Second, measures should be introduced to integrate standards of good governance in land transactions at both global and national levels – based on transparency, fairness, accountability and justice in land acquisition process, and aiming at a 'win–win' situation for all concerned (i.e., investors, land owners and host governments).[14] Third, and in the wider context of national development, the issue of large-scale foreign land-based investment should be considered in as a strategic option for moving African agriculture into the twenty-first century and enhancing Africa's role in the global food security system, but ensuring that it is done right and consistent with local and national interests. These three requirements reflect the multi-level nature and complexity of and governance relationships implicit in global, regional and national development strategies and goals, such as the UN MDG's, Global Compact and Right to Food initiatives, the African Union/NEPAD Comprehensive African Agriculture Development Programme (CAADP), the G-8 L'Aquila Food Security Initiative, global civil society campaigns in support of local protest groups against land grabs, etc.

The role of global institutions

Antipathy towards land grabbing has sparked a global debate and attracted international attention and action. The UN Special Rapporteur on the Right to Food, Olivier De Schutter, had argued before various UN sessions that agricultural investments in Africa and other poorer developing regions should benefit those countries in terms of reducing hunger and malnutrition, rather than lead to a transfer of land resources to richer countries (De Schutter 2009, 2010, 2011b). Even the EU which set targets for bio-fuel use, and by implication encourage its member states to invest in energy crops, has begun to take the criticism of land grabbing seriously; it no longer identifies agro-investment as the silver bullet that will simultaneously resolve the global energy, food and climate crises. The subject was on the agenda of the UN climate change summit in Durban in December 2011. The World Bank released a report in 2010 with a set of voluntary guidelines for land-based investments in poor countries. In a recent working paper, the IMF saw the need to increase transparency and improve land governance at country level and endorsed a global effort to document and monitor large-scale cross-national investments in land (Arezki et al. 2011). The International Labour Organisation (ILO) addressed the problem in 2011 at its annual conference in a report on labour rights and land rights with respect to foreign investments in commercial plantations in developing countries. There is also recognition by the FAO of the need for responsible governance environment in foreign land acquisitions which could ensure a 'win–win' situation for all parties (FAO 2012). The African Union, in conjunction with the UN Economic Commission for Africa and the African Development Bank, is now developing a 'framework and guidelines for land policies in Africa'. Principles of corporate social responsibility have been evoked by international NGOs such as Oxfam to advise foreign investors on their accountability in contract negotiations with regard to food security, social and environmental issues.

Conclusions

This paper has examined how the quest for national food and energy security in East Asian countries is impacting on food security and development in Africa through large-scale land acquisitions. There is no evidence to suggest that East Asian nations are primarily engaged in land investment in Africa with a view to profiting from rising land values per se. Their interests are more to do with securing supplies of food and non-food agricultural commodities and, in the case of some Chinese companies, to access regional markets. While the role of investors is critical to the outcomes of land deals in Africa, the paper also looked at the position of host governments in attracting and encouraging investment as a source of employment and growth.

Land-based investment in Africa is regarded by host governments and some international development institutions and policy analysts as the pathway for accessing capital, technology and knowledge needed to transform agriculture from its historic low productive and income levels and for commercialisation for smallholder agriculture. Commercial agriculture is perceived as a powerful driver of economic growth and international competitiveness (e.g., World Bank 2009) and a catalyst for enhancing the role of African agriculture in the international food system. In this regard, it provides an opportunity for poor countries with ample endowment of under-utilized arable land to realise the potential of their agriculture sector, including promoting export and ensuring food security. It can also contribute to economic diversification of national economies and make agriculture a central part of growth strategies in the region. At the same time, there is little doubt, according to available evidence, that so far land-based foreign investments have left African smallholder farmers particularly vulnerable to dispossession and local communities to the risk of increasing marginalisation and threat of food insecurity.

There is a need for balancing food security needs and concerns of both host countries and home countries of foreign investors in the context of managing the global food system. The Declaration adopted by the High Level Conference on World Food Security in Rome in June 2008 proposed a two-prong approach toward this objective: (1) boost global food production by investment in agriculture and rural development in land abundant developing countries for local consumption and export; and (2) improve and increase access to food for the poor and vulnerable. As discussed, this approach invariably involves both the risks and opportunities of large-scale land acquisitions by foreign investors which need to be addressed. Host governments need to understand and clarify what kinds of investment they want to attract. A new national land acquisition policy in which land rights, food security and sustainable development are major objectives should entail in most cases options for legal recognition of customary tenure and the ability of African governments to negotiate land transfer contracts not only in terms of 'fair price', but also from the perspectives of livelihood gains in employment and income, rural development, and social and environmental impacts. Beyond this, there is also a need for African countries to implement regional approaches on food security centred on the Comprehensive Africa Agriculture Development Programme (CAADP) (Seters van et al. 2012).

Some African governments have now taken steps to address land rights and governance problems associated with large-scale land deals. Following the failed Daewoo land deal, Madagascar cancelled several land projects involving foreign investors and declared a moratorium on new large-scale land concessions at the end of 2009. Last year, the government introduced a new agricultural policy which incorporated a process of community land registration to protect smallholder rights. The government of Liberia, spurred on by local protest, recently renegotiated the contract for a large-scale commercial plantation with the Malaysian company, Sime Darby, to secure increased revenues and enforceable commitments on employment and business opportunities for local communities. Growing concern about international land deals is leading to a reconsideration of the 'market-based' option ('let the market prevail') by global multilateral institutions such as the World Bank, FAO, IFAD and UNCTAD, in favour of a more managed approach which calls for development of specific markets in land with recommendations to recognise titles linked to communal system of land ownership and for investors to consult and deal directly with local communities in land deals (World Bank 2008; UNCTAD 2008; FAO 2009, 2012; De Schutter 2009).

Above all, there is the need for African governments to look at the 'bigger picture' in relation to sustainable development: how to minimise the negative consequences of foreign land deals alongside policies for increasing the potential benefits form positive structural changes in the domestic economy and fuller integration in the global system. Through large-scale land-based investments, Africa could benefit from the development experiences of China, South Korea and Malaysia, particularly with respect to agribusiness and industrialisation strategies (Lisk 2011). Both China and South Korea have established continent-wide cooperative partnerships with Africa through institutional links with the African Union (i.e., the Forum for China – Africa Cooperation (FOCAC) and the Republic of Korea – Africa Forum), which can be useful for coordinating and providing technical assistance. Finally, in the light of current global economic

and social transformations which have profound implications for the livelihoods and food security in Africa, it is essential for African countries to
approach international land transactions as strategic market opportunities
for long-term development rather than short-term opportunistic deals.

Notes

1 As inventoried by the Spanish-based international non-governmental organization GRAIN, which provides information on all press reports of transnational
large-scale land acquisitions worldwide on its website *Food Crisis and Global
Land Grab*.
2 GRAIN first drew attention to this issue in its October 2008 brief, 'Seized! The
2008 land grabbers for food and financial security'. Since then, the term 'land
grab' has gained international recognition to describe investments in large tracts
of land for food production and speculation by rich nations, private companies
and individuals.
3 According to the UN Food and Agricultural Organization (FAO), high food
prices in 2008 pushed an additional 40 million people in developing countries
into hunger and increased the food import bill for developing countries by
nearly 75% (FAO, *Crop Prospects and Food Situation*, 2008; www.fao.org/
giews/). During the six months from October 2007 to April 2008 the world price
of rice trebled from US$335 to over $1000 per ton, and the consequent sharp
rise in local prices of this staple led to violent food riots in a number of African
countries – Burkina Faso, Cameroon, Mozambique and Senegal.
4 Major foreign investors in farmlands in Africa for food production include
wealthier food-insecure Gulf states with scarce water and arable land resources,
such as Saudi Arabia, Qatar, Kuwait and UAE, In addition, European investors
are acquiring large tracts of fertile land in Africa mainly for production of sugar
cane for ethanol, in response to the EU's renewable energy directive to increase
the proportion of biofuels in its total energy consumption.
5 Total Chinese land acquisition in Africa is recorded at just over 400,000 hectares, as compared to about 790,000 by South Korea, 733,000 by Singapore and
992,500 by Malaysia.
6 It is important to note the wide heterogeneity of actors even from the same
group, such as those in the host country – central government ministries with
different interests, the private sector which includes both national and international firms, local government authorities and civil society organisations, all facing different incentives and motivated by different interests.
7 The United States has been directing subsidies of several billion dollars to its
farmers for the production of corn-based ethanol. The European Union's
Renewable Energy Roadmap, which includes policies to promote the use of
bio-fuels for transport against time and quantity-based targets, is believed to be
contributing to the increasing demand for agricultural land in Africa and other
developing regions by European-based investment enterprises.
8 GRAIN, 'Pension funds: key players in the global farmland grab', *Against The
Grain*, 20 June; accessed at http://www.grain.org/article/entries/4287, 1 October
2012.
9 A report prepared by the McKinsey Global Institute in 2010, 'Lions on the
move: the progress and potential of African economies', which is directed at
global investors, announced that Africa was home to 600 million of uncultivated
arable land – 60% of the world total.

10 Oxfam (2011), 'Land and power: the growing scandal surrounding the new wave of investments in land', Briefing Paper No.151, 22 September 2011.
11 'Growing Africa's land', by Adam Robert Green in *This is Africa*, News, 2 July 2012, www.thisisafricaonline.com/News/Growing-Africa-s-landtm_capampaign = July.
12 The crucial link between access to land and food security is recognized in the post-apartheid constitution of South Africa identifies land reform (Section 25) as necessary to guarantee food security for all citizens (Section 27). See Republic of South Africa, *Constitution of the Republic of South Africa*, 1996.
13 The ILC, which consists of about 120 organisations, from community groups, to Oxfam, to the World Bank, adopted the Declaration on securing land access for the poor which denounced land grabbing at its Assembly in Tirana, Albania, in May 2011.
14 This implies benefit for all and gives rise to notions of 'codes of conducts' for land deals (e.g., voluntary guidelines by FAO, OECD and IFPRI, G8 L'Aquila Food Security Initiative).

References

Anseeuw, W. Alden Wily, Cotula, L. and Taylor, M. (2012) *Land Rights and the Rush for Land: Findings of the Global Commercial Pressures on Land Research Project*, Rome: The International Land Coalition.

Arezki, R., Deininger, K. and Selod, H. (2011) 'What drives the global land rush?', *International Monetary Fund*, Working Paper, WP/11/251, November, Washington, DC, International Monetary Fund.

Baumgart, J. (2011) *Assessing the Contractual Arrangements for Large Scale Land Acquisition in Mali with Special Attention to Water Rights*, Berlin: GIZ.

Brahmbhatt, M. and Christiaensen, L. (2008) *Rising Food Prices in East Asia: Challenges and Policy Options*, Washington, DC: World Bank.

Chang, J. H. (2009) 'Rethinking public policy in agriculture: lessons from history, distant and recent', *Journal of Peasant Studies* 36(3): 477–515.

Cochet, H. and M. Merlet (2011) 'Land grabbing and share of the value added in agricultural processes: a new look at the distribution of land revenues', paper presented at the *International Conference on Global Land Grabbing*, Institute of Development Studies, University of Sussex, 6–8 April.

Collier, P. (2008) 'The politics of hunger: how illusion and greed fan the food crisis', *Foreign Affairs* 87(6): 67–79.

Cotula, L., Vermeulen, S., Leonard, R. and Keeley, J. (2009) *Land Grab or Development Opportunity? Agricultural Investment and Land Deals in Africa*, Rome: FAO, IFAD and IIED.

Daniel, S. and Mittal, A. (2009) *The Great Land Grab: Rush for World's Farmland Threatens Food Security for the Poor*, Oakland CA: The Oakland Institute.

De Schutter, O. (2009) 'Large-scale land acquisitions and leases: a set of core principles and measures to address human rights challenges', *Special Rapporteur on the Right to Food*; accessed at http://www2.ohchr.org/english/issues/food/docs/BriefingNotelandgrab.pdf, 5 July 2012.

De Schutter, O. (2010) 'The right to food', interim report of the *United Nations Special Rapporteur on the Right to Food*, submitted to the 65th Session of the United Nations General Assembly, August, New York.

De Schutter, O. (2011a) 'The green rush: The global race for farmland and the rights of land users', *Harvard International Law Journal* 52(2): 503–559.

De Schutter, O. (2011b) 'Agro-ecology and the right to food', report presented at the 16th Session of the UN Human Rights Council (A/HRC/16/49), Geneva, 8 March.

Deinenger, K. (2003) *Land Policies for Growth and Poverty Reduction. A World Bank Policy Research Report*, Oxford: World Bank and Oxford University Press.

Deinenger, K. and Byerlee, D. (2011) 'The rise of large farms in land abundant countries: do they have a future?', *World Development* 40(4): 701–714.

Deinenger, K., Byerlee, D., Lindsay, J., Norton, A., Selod, H. and Stickler, M. (2011) *Rising Global Interest in Farmland: Can it Yield Sustainable and Equitable Benefits?*, Washington, DC: World Bank.

Fitzpatrick, D. (2005) '"Best practice", options for the legal recognition of customary land tenure', *Development and Change* 36(3): 449–475.

Food and Agriculture Organization (2009) 'From land grab to win–win: seizing the opportunities of international investments in agriculture'; accessed at ftp://ftp.fao.org/docrep/fao/011/ak357e/ak357e00.pdf, 5 July 2012.

Food and Agriculture Organisation (2012) *Voluntary Guidelines for Responsible Agricultural Investment*; accessed at http://www.fao.org/nr/tenure/voluntary-guidelines/en/, 5 July 2012.

GRAIN (2008) *Seized! The 2008 Land Grab or Food and Financial Security*; accessed at www.grain.org/go/landgrab, 5 July 2012.

GRAIN (2012) Accessed at http://www.grain.org/article/entries/4479-grain-releases-data-set-with-over-400-global-land-grabs, 5 July 2012.

Havnevik, K., Matondi, P. and Beyene, A. (ed.) (2011) *Biofuels, Land Grabbing and Food Security in Africa*, Zed: London.

L'Aquila Food Security Initiative (2009) 'L'Aquila joint statement on global food security', *G8 Summit*; accessed at http://www.g8italia2009.it/static/G8_Allegato/LAquila_Joint_Statement_on_Global_Food_Security%5b1%5d%2c0.pdf, 5 July 2012.

Lisk, F. (2011) 'Stimulating private participation', in K. K. Yumkella, P. M. Kormawa, T. M. Roepstorff and A. M. K. Hawkins (eds) *Agribusiness for Africa's Development*, Vienna: UNIDO, pp. 228–246.

Lipton, M. (2009) *Land Reform in Developing Countries: Property Rights and Property Wrongs*, New York: Routeldge.

NEPAD (2012) *Comprehensive Africa Agriculture Development Programme (CAADP)*; accessed at http://www.nepad-caadp.net, 5 July 2012.

Olivier, C. (2008) 'Daewoo unsure of Madagascar deal', *Financial Times*, December 5, [online] accessed at http://www.ft.com/cms/s/0/38cf416a-c26e-11dd-a350-000077b07658.html#axzz2DSX8BYa1, 5 July 2012.

Oxfam (2011) 'Land and power: the growing scandal surrounding the new wave of investment in land', *Oxfam Briefing Paper 151*, September, Oxford: Oxfam International.

Oxfam (2012) Accessed at http://www.oxfam.org.uk/media-centre/press-releases/2012/10/land-sold-off-in-last-decade-could-grow-enough-food-to-feed-a-billion-people, 15 October 2012.

Roxburgh, C., Doerr, N., Leke, A., Tazi-Riffi, A., van Wamelen, A., Lund, S., Chironga, M., Alatovik, T., Atkins, C., Terfous, N. and Zeino-Mahmalat, T. (2010) *Lions on the Move: The Progress and Potential of African Economies,*: Mckinsey Global Institute. New York.

Seters van, J., Afun-Ogida, D. and Rampa, F. (2012) 'Regional approaches to food security in Africa: the CAADP and other relevant policies and programmes in ECOWAS', *Discussion Paper No. 128d*, February, Brussels: European Centre for Development Policy Management (ECDPM).

The Oakland Institute (2011) *Understanding Land Investment Deals in Africa – Country Report: Sierra Leone*, Oakland, CA: The Oakland Institute.

UNCTAD (2008) *World Investment Directory 2008 – Volume X: Africa*, Geneva: UNCTAD; accessed at http://www.unctad.org/, 5 July 2012.

Unruh, J. and Turay, H. (2006) *Land Tenure, Food Security and Investment in Post-war Sierra Leone*, FAO Livelihood Support Programme (LSP), Rome: FAO.

World Bank (2008) *World Development Report 2008 – Agriculture for Development*, Oxford: Oxford University Press.

World Bank (2009) *Awakening Africa's Sleeping Giant: Prospect for Competitive Commercial Agriculture in the Guinea Savannah Zone and Beyond*, Washington, DC: World Bank, 48 (June): 1–4.

Zoomers, A. (2010) 'Globalisation and the Foreignisation of Space: Seven Processes Driving the Current Global Land Grab', *Journal of Peasant Studies* 37(2): 429–447.

Food security: global trends and regional perspective with reference to East Asia

Ching-Cheng Chang, Huey-Lin Lee and Shih-Hsun Hsu

Abstract The sharp increase in global food prices during 2007–2008 has triggered the awareness of food insecurity problems and their impacts on the low-income, food-deficient countries, many of which are located in East Asia. Protein and fat consumption are higher in East Asia than that of other regions, although the percentage of carbohydrates consumed is slightly lower than the world's average. Nevertheless, the food security situation in East Asia was good relative to other countries in the world. The food security in East Asia is largely contributed by domestic production. Despite of a doubled import of foods over the last decade to meet its ever-growing population, Asia remains the least dependent among all regions on food imports. However, the raised energy costs and grain prices due to increasing grain demand for biofuel purposes appeared to exacerbate the undernourishment of poor households in the region. While most of the government interventions focus on short-term measures such as reducing domestic food prices through trade or price control, the risk of facing a long-term food insecurity still exists, which may render national action inadequate and require multilateral cooperation.

Introduction

The sharp increase in global food prices during 2007–2008 has triggered an increased awareness of potential food insecurity and its impact on the living standards of many, particularly the poor. This study attempts to locate growing interest in (and concern with) food security in East Asia within a wider global context, showing how the region fits in to major global trends. It will also provide a snapshot of the key factors that have led to East Asia's problems, and a brief discussion of key policy responses. While Asia does indeed face many of the same challenges that are leading to food insecurity as in other parts of the world, considering the importance of the rice sector in Asia, the paper concludes with a quantitative assessment of the impact of climate change on this key staple.

The definition of what exactly food security entails has evolved over time. Initially, in 1974, the World Food Summit introduced the concept of food security as 'availability at all times of adequate world food supplies of basic foodstuffs to sustain a steady expansion of food consumption and to offset fluctuations in production and prices'. Basically, the essence was to respond to transitory food insecurity, which also included milk supply-demand gaps during the lean season, and temporary food insecurities like production shortfall due to natural disasters (Kuntjoro and Jamil 2008).

Besides this demand and supply side dimension, an increasing focus emerged over distribution of and access to food. Therefore, the World Food Summit in 1996 offered a holistic perspective of food security: 'The food security exists when all people at all times have access to sufficient, safe, nutritious food to maintain a healthy and active life'. This definition implies that food security should include four dimensions: availability, stability, access, and utilization of food. In recent years, rising energy costs, the falling dollar, and increasing demand of grains for bio-fuel production not only induced a sharp increase in grain prices (Mitchell 2008), but also exacerbated the deficiency in food and undernourishment of poorer households that tend to spend a larger share on food in their total expenditures (Brahmbhatt and Christiaensen 2008). It is from this understanding that our analysis of how East Asia fits into these global trends commences.

The global food security perspectives
Global trends of food security

Key changes to food prices in 2008 highlighted the precarious food insecurity of many low-income countries (Shapouri et al. 2009). By March 2008, grain prices were more than two and a half times higher than in early 2002. More significantly, almost three quarters of this increase occurred since the start of 2007, and about half of it since the beginning of 2008. According to the forecasts of major international organizations (e.g., FAO, UNDP, and OECD), the prediction of high grain prices in the medium term is expected to continue as policies aimed at achieving energy security and carbon dioxide emission reductions present a strong trade-off against food security goals (Brahmbhatt and Christiaensen 2008).

Figure 1 shows that the grain prices rose sharply in the early part of 2008, which caused a major concern for policy-makers, but afterwards fell later in

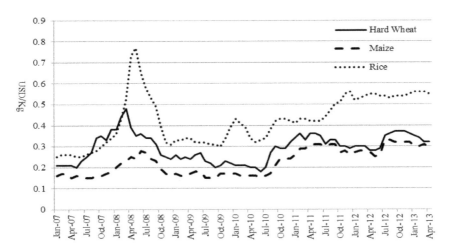

Figure 1 Grain prices from January 2007 to April 2013. *Source:* IFPRI (2013).

the same year. Particularly, from July to December 2008, international prices for food and fuel declined sharply (with oil prices being down nearly 70% and food prices by 33%). But despite these subsequent fallbacks, the price rise shock of 2008 had entered into policy consciousness. And indeed, at the time of writing in April 2013, prices of food and fuel still remain much higher than they were for much of the decade. Energy prices and the competition in crop uses for biofuel purposes also remain a key driver for high food prices. The increase in food prices would be a negative development for low income, food-deficit countries, many of which are becoming more dependent on imported foods and food ingredients.

Figure 2 shows that most net exporters of food crops are located in North America and Australia. The critical problem of inadequate food occurs in Asia and African countries, where the stability of food supply system is often severely impeded. Compared with the prevalence of undernourished[1] population in other regions as shown in Figure 3 and Figure 4, most net exporters have a relatively less undernourished population. Actually, the FAO (2009a) reports that even before the consecutive food and economic crises, the number of undernourished people in the world had been increasing at a steady (though slow) rate for a decade.

Figure 5 shows that the number of undernourished people increased between 1995–1997 and 2004–2006 in all regions except America. In late 2008, as global food and oil prices continued to fall, the global financial crisis was another blow to food-insecure and vulnerable people. Particularly for developing countries, the FAO states that the ongoing economic turmoil is different in three important aspects. First, the crisis is affecting large parts of the world simultaneously, and thus traditional coping mechanisms

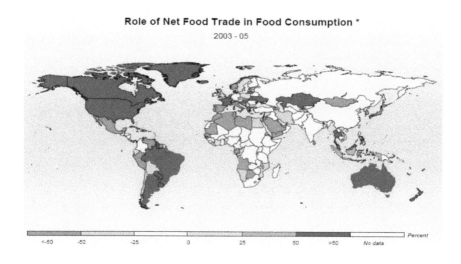

Figure 2 Global net trade position in food. *Source:* FAO (2012a).

used to focus on several countries in particular regions are likely to be less effective than they were in the past.

Second, the economic crisis emerged immediately following the food and fuel crises of 2006 to 2008. While food commodity prices in the world market declined, they remained high by recent historical standards. Also,

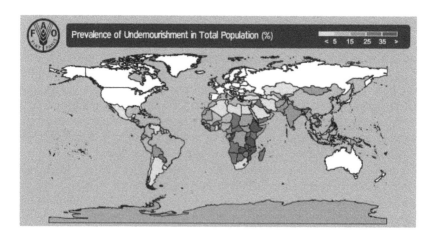

Figure 3 Prevalence of undernourishment in total population (%). *Source:* FAO (2012b).

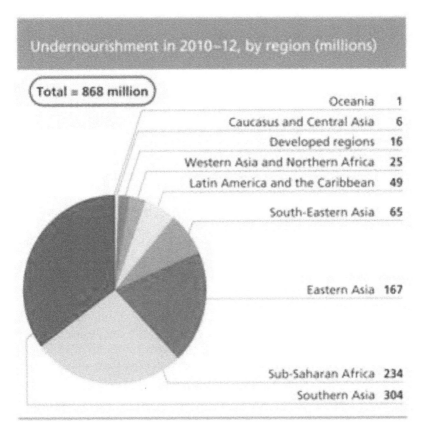

Undernourishment in 2010–12, by region (millions)

Total = 868 million

Region	Millions
Oceania	1
Caucasus and Central Asia	6
Developed regions	16
Western Asia and Northern Africa	25
Latin America and the Caribbean	49
South-Eastern Asia	65
Eastern Asia	167
Sub-Saharan Africa	234
Southern Asia	304

Figure 4 Undernourishment in 2010–2012, by region (millions). *Source:* FAO (2012c).

food prices in domestic markets came down more slowly, partly because of the weakened US dollars, in terms of which most imports are priced. At the end of 2008, domestic prices for staple foods remained an average of 17% higher in real terms than two years earlier.

Finally, developing countries have become more integrated, both financially and commercially, into the world economy than they were 20 years ago. As a consequence, they are more exposed to changes in international markets. Rising income and urbanization are also changing the nature of diets.

Global Food Security Index

Recently, the Economist Intelligence Unit (2013) published a Global Food Security Index (GFSI) across 105 countries using definitions from the 1996

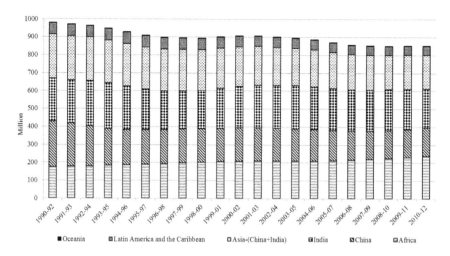

Figure 5 Undernourishment on the rise: number of undernourished in selected regions from 1990–1992 to 2010–2012. *Source:* FAO (2012f).

World Food Summit. This index is constructed from 25 unique indicators that measure the drivers of food security through the categories of affordability, availability, quality and safety. The scores can be used to identify which countries are more vulnerable to food insecurity than others.

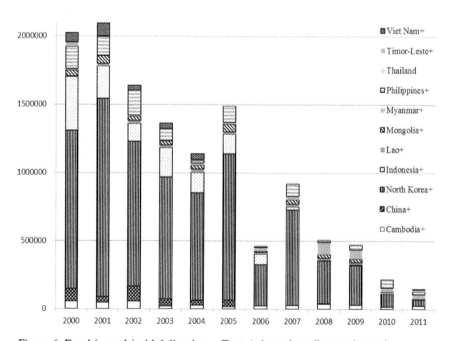

Figure 6 Food (cereals) aid deliveries to East Asia regions (in metric tons).

Table 1 The overall global food security scores and rankings in 17+1 APEC economies, 2013

	Overall scores	Ranking in 105+1 world economies	Ranking of 17+1 APEC economies
United States	89.6	1	1
Canada	83.4	8	2
New Zealand	82.7	11	3
Japan	81.3	13	4
Australia	81.1	14	5
South Korea	77.7	21	6
Taiwan*	75.75	In-between 22 and 23	
Chile	69.1	= 26	7
Mexico	67.5	= 29	8
Russia	67.5	= 29	9
Malaysia	64.2	32	10
China	62.8	37	11
Thailand	58.1	43	12
Peru	54.0	48	13
Viet Nam	50.1	56	14
Philippines	47.1	63	15
Indonesia	46.5	64	16
Papua New Guinea	31.0	86	17

Notes: (1) The overall scores are the weighted averages of all category scores where 100 = most favorable. (2) The index is not available for 4 APEC economies (Brunei, Hong Kong, Singapore, and Chinese Taipei). *Own calculation.
Source: The Economist Intelligence Unit (2013).

Table 1 illustrates the scores and rankings of 17 APEC economies, indicating a wide gap across the region. In addition, we also conducted the GFSI calculation for Taiwan using the Taiwanese statistics. Among the East Asian economies, the net food importing countries of Japan, South Korea, and Taiwan fare quite well in their food security based on the EIU's criterion.

The index reveals a number of interesting findings that suggest areas where interventions and improvements are most needed. For example, the most food secure economies score less well owing to limited availability of vegetal iron in food supplies. Landlocked countries are no worse than coastline economies despite their lack of access to port facilities. Economic opportunity for women shows a very high and positive correlation (0.93) with food security, and thus becomes critical to expand agricultural output in the developing world.

Among the 25 indicators of GFSI, 'extreme weather' is viewed as a major threat from nature through measuring the volatility of agricultural production. In spite of rising economic losses and population affected by natural disasters, global food aid has declined over the past decade. The global financial crisis in 2008 was another blow to the food-insecure and vulnerable people.

Food security in East Asia
East Asia and global situation compared

For a number of years, many Asian countries have been striving for grain self-sufficiency driven by the concerns of agrarian stability, foreign currency conservation, and independence from potential political influences from exporting countries (Corke and Cai 2004). Although food imports doubled over the last decade, Asia appears to be the least dependent among all regions on food imports, and the region as a whole imports less than 10% of its grain supply (Rosen et al. 2012). However, the food-insecure population in Asia increased by 4% for the period of 2007–2008, primarily as a result of population growth. Even then, Asia's food-security status was good relative to the other concerned countries (Shapouri et al. 2009). The 2008 Asian food-insecure population accounted for an estimated 46% among 70 countries as studied in Shapouri et al. (2009), while its total population is nearly two-thirds of the 70-country aggregate. Less than 20% of the Asian population was estimated to consume below the nutritional target in 2008.

Table 2 shows the share in dietary energy consumption and the average nutrient including carbohydrates, proteins, and fats. Comparing the composition and consumption level of the nutrients across the world regions, the percentage of carbohydrates in Northeast Asia is slightly lower than in other regions and the world average. Proteins and fats account for 12% and 27%, respectively, which are higher than that of other regions.

Table 3 lists the food balance sheets of Southeast and Northeast Asia. We take rice, the most important staple crop for Asia population, as an example to illustrate the differences in the food status between these two regions. Southeast Asia has a population nearly three times of Northeast Asia's, yet the rice production in Southeast Asia is only 12% more than in Northeast Asia. Counting in imported rice, a merely 32% extra of rice is supplied to Southeast Asia than to Northeast Asia. Regarding food supply measured in kcal per capita per day, Northeast Asia derived a level of 1531 kcal/capita/day in 2007 from the listed food crops, while Southeast Asia secured a lower level of 1416 kcal/capita/day.

Regional reviews

Based on the FAO (2009b), cyclones, floods, and droughts, in addition to the continuing conflicts and civil strife, affected the food security in most regions of East Asia. The food aid situation of East Asia is listed in Table 4. Between 2000 to 2006, only Cambodia, Indonesia, North Korea, Laos, Mongolia, the Philippines, and Timor-Leste constantly received food aid. Thailand received food aid only in 2000 and 2002. North Korea and Cambodia had a sharp decline in its volume of assistance. However, Cambodia's food aid rebounded from 2007 onwards, at a reduced

Table 2 Share in total dietary energy consumption and average nutrients

Country groups	Macronutrients	g/person/day*	Per cent
WORLD TOTAL	Carbohydrates	2700	64
	Proteins	74	11
	Fats	71	25
Asia and the Pacific	Carbohydrates	2560	67
	Proteins	67	11
	Fats	56	23
Northeast Asia	Carbohydrates	2830	61
	Proteins	81	12
	Fats	71	27
Southeast Asia	Carbohydrates	2410	72
	Proteins	56	10
	Fats	45	18
South Asia	Carbohydrates	2330	71
	Proteins	56	10
	Fats	45	20
Central Asia	Carbohydrates	2750	64
	Proteins	83	12
	Fats	70	24
Western Asia	Carbohydrates	2180	69
	Proteins	65	12
	Fats	40	19
Americas	Carbohydrates	2750	62
	Proteins	74	11
	Fats	78	27
Near East and North Africa	Carbohydrates	2980	68
	Proteins	81	11
	Fats	70	21
Sub-Saharan Africa	Carbohydrates	2080	72
	Proteins	50	10
	Fats	41	19

Source: FAO (2012d). *Carbohydrates are measured in kcal per person per day, while proteins and fats are in grams per person per day.

magnitude. Most of the listed East Asian countries continued to receive food aid, but to a lesser degree.

The FAO (2009b) report also classified several East Asian regions which are requiring external assistance – as shown in Table 5. North Korea is something of an outlier here – both by regional and global comparison. An FAO (2012g) report noted that North Korea continued to be identified as the only country in the East Asian region that needs external assistance, due to climate-induced bad harvest and agricultural infrastructure damage caused by flooding.

Table 3 Food balance sheets of Southeast and Northeast Asia

Item	Total population (1000)	Production (1000 tons)	Import quantity (1000 tons)	Stock variation (1000 tons)	Export quantity (1000 tons)	Domestic supply quantity (1000 tons)	Feed (1000 tons)	Seed (1000 tons)	Food (1000 tons)	Food supply quantity (kg/capita/yr)	Food supply (kcal/capita/day)	Protein supply quantity (g/capita/day)	Fat supply quantity (g/capita/day)
Southeast Asia Population	1,538,250												
Wheat		110,520	11,543	−1,202	4199	116,662	8046	4155	98,993	64.4	563	18	3
Rice		137,534	2698	9	1333	138,908	10,366	4500	115,363	75	782	14.4	2.9
Barley		3893	3351	−211	598	6436	1311	119	433	0.3	2	0.1	0
Maize		154,090	30,078	−5,201	5698	173,269	118,913	1325	12,206	7.9	61	1.2	0.2
Millet		1571	48	0	25	1594	832	30	661	0.4	3	0.1	0
Sorghum		2468	1307	99	238	3636	2648	21	844	0.5	4	0.1	0
Cereals, Other		567	155	100	182	641	206	104	304	0.2	1	0	0
Northeast Asia Population	564,025												
Wheat		159	13,091	−300	698	12,252	959	6	10,873	19.3	140	3.8	0.4
Rice		123,237	4633	−8,440	14,317	105,113	8832	2550	73,863	131	1270	24.3	3.9
Barley		18	1129	−78	26	1043	2	0	35	0.1	0	0	0
Maize		30,401	4,516	−1,230	778	32,909	18,409	276	9162	16.2	116	2.9	1.1
Millet		168	18	1	6	181	22	5	144	0.3	2	0.1	0
Sorghum		57	19	0	3	73	70	0	0	0	0	0	0
Cereals, Other		140	234	100	219	254	23	4	304	0.5	3	0.1	0

Source: FAOSTAT 2007 (FAO 2012e).

Table 4 Food (cereals) aid deliveries to East Asia regions (in metric tons)

	2000	2001	2002	2003	2004	2005	2006	2007	2008	2009	2010	2011
Cambodia+	56,929	46,589	55,699	20,545	28,069	18,212	24,142	26,535	38,717	29,887	18,631	24,882
China+	90,500	42,000	109,157	53,494	35,131	49,046	0	0	1061	0	50	0
North Korea+	116,1103	1,452,172	1,064,212	894,432	790,066	1,071,019	302,348	701,568	315,046	290,121	92,618	45,927
Lao+	4669	18,708	23,728	19,068	25,048	18,747	12,213	18,674	14,494	17,125	14,660	2851
Mongolia+	45,773	59,638	27,611	28,150	28,385	54,785	9316	33,421	27,189	25,000	45	24
Myanmar+	9634	3815	9157	6172	17,088	15,601	26,947	24,728	88,671	68,346	31,278	33,278
Philippines+	164,363	137,743	183,432	86,500	19,600	117,590	6791	90,083	14,056	34,989	59,983	19,313
Sri Lanka+	52,599	116,100	83,664	24,812	33,689	97,719	52,401	57,947	59,208	64,274	57,390	30,217
Thailand	757	0	1223	1140	0	680	0	0	0	0	0	71
Timor-Leste+	28,422	2830	0	250	6901	888	8201	10,384	7103	6086	764	15,400
Vietnam+	69,091	93,730	35,000	40,000	38,880	0	0	0	0	0	0	8

Source: WFP (2013).

Table 5 Countries in crisis requiring external assistance

Nature of food insecurity	Main reasons	Changes from previous report
Widespread lack of access		
North Korea	Economic constraints	No change from FAO (2009b) report
North Korea	A dry spell in May–June 2012 affected early season harvest of wheat, barley and potatoes and main season soybeans. Localized floods in July–August have damaged agricultural infrastructure, including fish ponds. Chronic food insecurity exists, despite improved cereal harvest of 2012 main season, with 2.8 million severely vulnerable people requiring food assistance during the 2012–2013 marketing year (November/ October).	Improving from FAO (2012g) report
Severe localized food insecurity		
Myanmar	Past cyclone	Improving from FAO (2009b) report
Philippines	Tropical storm	New entry in the FAO (2009b) report
Timor-Leste	Internally Displaced Persons (IDPs)	No change from FAO (2009b) report

Source: FAO (2009b) and FAO (2012g).

In recent years, the food self-sufficiency rate (SSR) has become an important indicator to show the extent to which a country relies on its own production resources. According to the FAO report, the food self-sufficiency rate here means the magnitude of production in relation to domestic utilizations. Figure 7 shows the SSR on a calorie basis of Taiwan, Korea and Japan from 2002–2011. These are based on Japan's MAFF (Ministry of Agriculture, Forestry and Fishery report) which are themselves based on FAO 'Food Balance Sheets' showing the calories of each kind of food from 2002 to 2011.

Selected national issues and policy responses

Taiwan

In Taiwan, the SSR on a calorie basis was only 32% in 2010. Total agricultural imports and cereals have increased significantly due to the expansion of livestock and fishery sectors as a result of dietary change following

Food self-sufficiency rate (%)

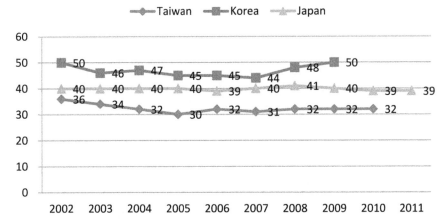

Figure 7 Taiwan, Korea and Japan's self-sufficiency rate from 2002–2011. *Source:* MAFF (2012).

improved living standards. The agricultural sector of Taiwan is facing a multitude of challenges, such as the low level of food self-sufficiency rate, aging farmers, large acreage of set-aside farmlands, small scale farming, soaring price of fertilizers, natural disasters aggravated by climate change, and rapid changes in the world food economy. To cope with these challenges, current agricultural policies are based on three guidelines: 'Healthfulness, Efficiency, and Sustainability'. A program entitled 'Turning Small Landlords into Large Tenants' was launched to turn idle lands into effective use. Facing globalization and the food crisis, Taiwan aims to secure stable food supply through revitalization of its set-aside farmlands and international markets, and provide technical assistance to developing countries for staple food crops, in particular (Huang et al. 2009).

Japan

As Yamashita (2010) reports, Japanese agriculture is in a free-fall decline. Between 1960 and 2005, the share of agricultural output in GDP dropped from 9% to 1%, the calorie-based SSR from 79% to 41%, and agricultural land from 6.09 million hectares to 4.63 million hectares. Japan's SSR is among the lowest of developed countries compared to roughly 80% for Germany and 65% for Britain in 2007. The ratio of part-time farm households, which derives more than half their income from non-farm employment, increased from 32.1% to 61.7%. The number of farmers over 65 years old rose from 10% to 60% of the farmer population.

Domestically produced rice in Japan is highly protected (Tanaka and Hosoe 2011). According to the Basic Law on Food, Agriculture and Rural Areas of Japan, food importation serves only as a supplementary source to meet Japan's demand for rice in times when domestic production falls short unexpectedly. The Ministry of Agriculture, Forestry, and Fisheries (MAFF) of Japan set up a contingency plan to cope with emergency situations of imbalanced domestic demand and supply. Measures proposed to reduce insecurity include promoting domestic production, keeping large emergency stocks, and controlling food markets so as to warrant a minimum calorie intake of 2000 kcal/person/day (MAFF 2006). For rice, the most important staple crop for Japanese diet, the self-sufficiency rate is as high as 98% thanks to a prohibitive tariff rate of 778%. In addition to the highly protective border measures, producer support offered to the farm sectors in Japan is among the highest in OECD countries (see Figure 8) so as to promote domestic production.

The highly protected Japanese rice sector is constantly exposed to the threat of agricultural trade liberalization, as discussed in the Doha round negotiations and the Trans-Pacific Partnership (TPP). The MAFF has been exploring ways to help boost the productivity of rice farming so as to brace for import competition – for example, to expand, more than tenfold, the average acreage of rice farming to between 20 and 30 hectares per farmer over the next five years. Tanaka and Hosoe (2011) regarded the MAFF's efforts for securing a higher food self-sufficiency rate through border protection policies as nonsensical, based on their welfare impact

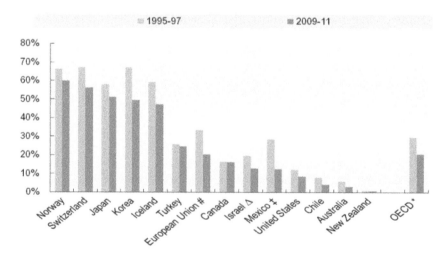

Figure 8 Producer support estimate by country, 1995–1997 and 2009–2011, as per cent of gross farm receipts. *Source:* OECD (2012, Figure 1.5).

analysis with a computable general equilibrium model of global trade. They suggest that national food security would not be a good rationale for agricultural protection and the emergency stocks of staples would be managed more cost-effectively in countries with lower cost of storage.

South Korea

Over the past few decades, much South Korean agricultural land had lost to industrialization and urbanization (Yoo 2003). As such, the agricultural share in South Korean GDP has declined from 29.8% in 1972 to 5.6% in 1999 (Fan and Brzeska 2010). Similar to Japan, South Korea tends to import a rather sizable portion (90%) of its foods from overseas, while highly protecting its rice sector – as indicated by the fact that 73% of farmland and 55% of arable land is used to cultivate rice (Han et al. 2008). The 2008 SSR for grain in South Korea is only 26.2%, among which wheat, maize, and beans are only 0.4%, 0.9%, and 7.1%, respectively. This is in stark contrast to rice (94.4%) and root and tuber crops (98.5%) (Yoo et al. 2012). The Farming population has shrunk rapidly, down to 8% nowadays, in the course of industrialization and urbanization. To secure its food supply, South Korea has been aggressively acquiring farmland overseas; particularly in in Southeast Asia and Africa. A well-known case of such land grabbing is the Daewoo *chaebol*'s (business conglomerate) unsuccessful attempt in 2008 to lease 1.3 million hectares of farmland in Madagascar for 99 years. In 2011, the South Korea government bought an overseas food base of the size as 325,999 hectares of land in Mongolia (Berthelsen 2011). Muller (2011) points out that South Korean companies are investing in farming in 16 countries globally, harvesting around 87,000 metric tons of grain from 24,000 hectares of land. China and Japan are also actively seeking offshore food supply through land grabbing, with Japan's targeting area for Latin America, Central Asia, and Eastern Europe for supply of corn, soybeans and wheat.

To maintain its self-sufficiency, South Korea applies significant government intervention and support, such as high tariff rates, nontariff barriers, and high acquisition prices offered by the government for staple crops (Beghin et al. 2003). Agricultural commodities that are subject to high tariffs include rice, meat, and dairy products. An access-restricted report by the Samsung Research Institute (2011) emphasizes the need of urgent and active measure in tackling the ever dwindling food security of South Korea in the wake of increased global grain price volatility and its intensified concentration of import sources – in particular on United States and European Union. Biofuel development in the US and EU would also spread its impact to South Korea through the trade dependency. The Samsung report advocates for promoting domestic production as a de facto insurance against supply instability in the global markets.

Table 6 Changes (%) in crop area in China from 1980 to 2003

Region	Rice	Wheat (%)	Corn	Grain
Northeast	222.67	−86.13	35.86	21.49
North	−9.27	−5.90	17.48	2.56
Northwest	40.56	−37.59	83.73	−4.15
Central	−19.06	−53.32	17.55	−21.84
Southeast	−30.56	−1.07	68.25	−15.77
Southwest	−5.09	−14.37	0.64	−5.93
South	−31.29	−86.25	23.58	−30.45
China	−16.06	−24.84	25.94	−7.65

Source: You et al. (2011, Table 1).

China

In China, the grain area declined 7.65% during the period from 1980 to 2003 – with rice and wheat areas dropping by 16.06% and 24.84% respectively. At the same time the corn growing area actually rose by 25.94%. With its rapid economic development, China has been seeing water shortage for agriculture and land lost to urbanization and industrialization. Due to increased urbanization in the south, the key production area has shifted towards north and northeast of China, reaping a 2.56% and 21.49% increase, respectively. However, north China and northeast China were not the traditional granary due to constraints of irrigation water supply. Climate change induced water shortage could possibly hit these new granary regions and thus impede the food security of China once more in the future (You et al. 2011). As the super-sized population outgrows the ability to be self-sufficient in food, China's food insecurity is likely to deepen. As such, China has actively sought agricultural cooperation deals with developing countries for overseas farming – particularly for food (rice, soybeans, and maize) and biofuel (sugar cane, cassava, and sorghum) purposes (GRAIN 2008).

North Korea

Of all the regional states, food security remains most precarious in North Korea because of political problems (Shapouri et al. 2009). Because of a series of natural disasters and the dissolution of the Soviet bloc, the number of food-insecure people doubled between 1995–1996 and 2007–2008. North Korea is facing persistent food shortages (FAO 2009c). In 2008, according to the UN World Food Programme, 40% of the country's population was in need of emergency food aid. From 2000–2006, within the recipient countries in East Asia, North Korea receives most types of food (as shown in Table 7).

Table 7 North Korea: food aid deliveries in metric tons

Commodity (tonne)	2000	2001	2002	2003	2004	2005	2006	2007	2008	2009	2010	2011
Common wheat	57,000	0	0	0	0	0	0	0	0	0	0	0
Corn-soya blend	4954	4995	0	5986	7488	0	0	0	5000	0	0	0
Corn-soya milk	0	17,629	12,272	0	0	0	0	0	0	0	0	0
Maize	516,616	526,421	263,014	135,097	95,049	297,386	43,833	57,688	241,392	98,737	25,637	1777
Maize meal	0	18	74	0	10,732	112	0	0	0	0	0	0
Pasta	0	0	0	0	0	0	0	0	0	0	135	0
Rice	327,892	588,158	551,761	569,435	441,002	496,334	107,783	491,581	20,527	35,447	11,206	472
Wheat	170,949	273,450	155,882	135,309	156,695	54,282	12,285	8423	37,270	134,619	49,261	43,131
Wheat flour	83,692	41,502	81,209	48,605	79,100	222,905	138,447	143,876	10,857	21,318	6379	548
Non-cereal	70,330	55,785	113,899	49,972	54,740	26,304	5106	18,958	60,193	7748	2225	647

Source: WFP (2013).

Climate change and rice in Asia: a quantitative assessment

Evidence has shown that agricultural production is rather vulnerable to climate change, temperature and precipitation changes, in particular. As Matthews et al. (1995) indicated, the impact of climate change on rice production in Asia is of particular policy concern, given that rice is the most important component in millions of Asians' diets. Seventeen south, southeast, and east Asian countries produce 92% of the world total rice supply, among which 90% is consumed in these regions as well (Matthews et al. 1995). Rice-growing countries in Asia are located in different latitudes and the terrain conditions of the rice-growing areas vary as well. As such, climate-change impact on rice production of the Asian countries is quite diverse and warrants a detailed assessment at regional level.

Here, we present a summary report from a recent study by Lee and Chang (2010) regarding the impact of climate change on Asia's rice sector. The study employed a multi-region, multi-sector computable general equilibrium (CGE) model – which also considers crop suitability and agro-ecological characteristics – to analyze the climate-change impact on global rice market (supply-side shock through crop yield change), with the consideration of changes in food demand due to population and economic growth. In contrast to Mathews et al. (1995), Lee and Chang (2010) placed more emphasis on the economic side of food security issue regarding rice such as the effect on prices of rice and other competing food crops that is brought about by varied changes in rice yield across countries.

Lee and Chang (2010) took into account changes in both the supply and demand sides to examine the impact of climate change by 2020 on the global rice market and food security for Asian countries should the world develop as plotted in the IPCC SRES scenario A2. Among all these concerns, food price is the key. Thus, in addition to the physical impact of climate change, price-induced adjustments in food production, which would affect significantly the reallocation of agricultural land among uses, are also taken into account. By identifying crop suitability and agro-ecological features of land, the economic model used in Lee and Chang (2010) can model more realistically the production responses of rice-growing countries to climate change, especially when diversity is found for the rice-growing countries in their vulnerability to climate change. Food security of countries located in tropical and sub-tropical zones may be adversely affected by climate change and the fluctuations in global food prices thus induced.

On the demand side, this study considers the fact of fast growing Asian economies, such as China and India, in population and per capita income, which are the key drivers for food demand increase. On the trade front, Lee and Chang (2010) also simulated the production and demand shocks being received by all food exporting and importing countries. Importing countries are more concerned about food security, while exporting countries are concerned about the change in farm income.

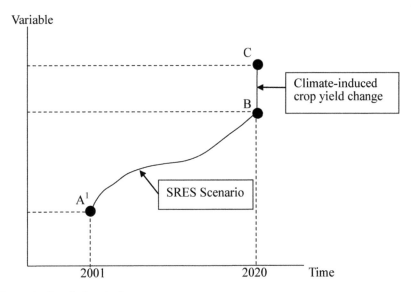

Figure 9 Simulation design.

The simulation design followed that of Lee (2009) and is illustrated in Figure 9. In the first step of the simulation, Lee and Chang (2010) produced line A[1]B, which graphed the growth path of some variable, e.g., supply of a crop, in the GTAP land use model from 2001 to 2020 under the SRES scenario A2. In producing this baseline A[1]B, Lee and Chang (2010) brought in region-specific GDP and population growth forecasts by IIASA (2007a) and IIASA (2007b) to the GTAP land use model and gradually updated the benchmark database of 2001[2] to 2020, i.e., point B. Population and GDP growth forecasts of 19 world regions/countries used in this study draw on those as compiled by Lee et al. (2010).

In the second step, the updated database then served as the benchmark equilibrium for the simulation – that is, to bring in climate-induced crop yield changes (the supply-side shocks). The climate-induced yield changes of three staple crops – i.e., rice, wheat, and coarse grains – by 2020 as estimated by Rosenzweig and Iglesias (2001) are used based on the climate forecasts as projected by the HadCM3 model (Gordon et al. 2000; Pope et al. 2000) under the IPCC emissions scenario IS92a.[3] Japan, Centralized Planning Economies in Asia, Indonesia, and other regions in Pacific Asia[4] gained 6%, 3%, 1%, and 1.58%, respectively, in rice yield. On the other hand, China, India, other South Asian countries received negative impacts of 1%, 8%, and 0.74% on their rice yield.

The results suggest that among Asian countries, India gets the hardest hit of climate change in its rice production, and a huge increase in the unit cost of rice production. Thus, India has to rely heavily on imports from the world market to meet its domestic rice demand. To fill the gap being caused by climate change, China also has to increase rice imports, with a relatively bigger magnitude than the other Asian countries. India and China have been the world's top rice-growing countries, and most of their rice production is consumed domestically. Should negative effects of rice yield occur in these two major rice-consuming countries, their raised demand for rice imports may push up global price of rice, and in turn, affect regions that are very much reliant on foreign supply.

The major finding is that as agricultural trade intensifies, impact of climate change, be it positive or negative, occurring in one region will spill over into other regions, through the channels of trade. As such, policy measures aimed to effectively alleviate food security problem should also take into account the geographically diverse impact of climate change on crop yield along with the agricultural trade development related policies.

Concluding remarks

It is a big challenge for East Asian countries to deal with rising food prices. There may be some speculative procurement in food sectors around the region. According to Brahmbhatt and Christiaensen (2008), it is crucial for setting greater international engagement and collaboration to address the competing demands of energy and food security. Demeke et al. (2009) suggested that the policies include releasing food stock to the market, reducing tariffs, price control, and export restriction. In recent years, the bio-fuel mandates, trade tariffs, and subsidies in the advanced countries have distorted world food markets and have played an important role in rising world food prices. More analysis and international dialogue is needed to decide whether the benefits from the current mix of policies really justify the costs, or whether a new global deal can be struck covering both clean energy and food.

There are numerous examples of policy responses. China eliminated export taxes on some grains, including wheat (3%), rice (3%), and soybeans (5%). The Thailand government set the farmers a guaranteed price for a second-crop paddy at THB 11,800 (USD 332) per ton under a new intervention scheme in 2009. Japan cut the price at which it sells imported wheat to domestic flour millers by an average 23% to 49,820 yen (USD 549) per ton. Indonesia is planning to release 2250 tons of rice through a market operation to avoid price spikes before the harvest of the second season. In the Philippines, the National Food Authority announced that it will allow private-sector traders to import up to 563,000 tons of rice annually. The measure aims at enhancing market participation ahead of liberalization of the sector, including the removal of quantitative restrictions on imports. The Vietnam Food Association (VFA) confirmed the purchase of 400,000 tons of husked rice for state reserves under the first phase of the procurement plan announced by the government in mid June. Under the plan, the VFA is instructed to buy two million tons of summer-autumn rice to prevent a fall in domestic prices at the peak of the harvest, when export demand is low.

But while the examples are numerous, we argue that they are likely to be ineffective. Most of the government interventions tend to focus on short-term measures such as reducing domestic food prices through changes in trade policies or changes in domestic taxes or subsidies. Price control is also implemented in some cases. Despite these efforts, the severity of food insecurity renders national action inadequate and requires multilateral cooperation. The establishment of a regional food reserve (e.g., ASEAN Emergency Rice Reserve or East Asia Emergency Rice Reserve) as a long-term measure would serve to stabilize extreme price fluctuations in the international market.

Notes

1 According to FAO, the undernourishment exists when caloric intake is below the minimum dietary energy requirement (MDER). The MDER is the amount of energy needed for light activity and a minimum acceptable weight for attained height, and it varies by country and from year to year depending on the gender and age structure of the population.
2 Lee et al. (2009) for AEZ land use; Dimaranan (2004) for other economic variables and parameters.
3 In order to simulate for more Asian countries, we tried to use the yield change estimates of as disaggregated regions as possible. Rosenzweig and Iglesias (2001) has, so far, the most disaggregated regions of estimates that fit with the need of our study purposes.
4 Vietnam is included in CPA; Thailand and the Philippines are in PAS.

References

Agriculture and Agri-Food Canada (2013) *Japan Agriculture Policy Review*; accessed at http://www4.agr.gc.ca/AAFC-AAC/display-afficher.do?id=12255 86815566&lang=eng, 9 April 2013.
Beghin, J. C., Jean-Christophe Bureau and Sung Joon Park (2003) 'Food security and agricultural protection in South Korea', *American Journal of Agricultural Economics* 85(3): 618–632. DOI: 10.1111/1467-8276.00460.
Berthelsen, J. (2011) *South Korea's Food Security Alarm. Asia Sentinel*; accessed at http://www.asiasentinel.com/index.php?option=com_content&task=view&id =3159&Itemid=434, 9 April 2013.
Brahmbhatt, M. and Christiaensen, L. (2008) *Rising Food Prices in East Asia: Challenges and Policy Options*, Washington, DC: World Bank.
Corke, H. and Cai, Y. Z. (2004) 'Grain production and consumption – Asia', in H. Corke, C. E. Walker and C.W. Wrigley (eds) *Encyclopedia of Grain Science*, Oxford: Elsevier, pp. 77–86.
Demeke, M., Pangrazio, G. and Maetz, M. (2009) *Country Responses to the Food Security Crisis: Nature and Preliminary Implications of the Policies Pursued, Initiative on Soaring Food Prices*, Rome: Food and Agriculture Organization (FAO), United Nations.

Dimaranan, B. V. (2004) *Global Trade, Assistance, and Production: The GTAP 6 Data Base*, Center for Global Trade Analysis, Purdue University, West Lafayette, IN 47907, USA.

Economist Intelligence Unit (2013) 'Global Food Security Index 2013: an assessment of food affordability, availability and quality', *The Economist*; accessed at http://foodsecurityindex.eiu.com/, 13 April 2013.

Fan, S. and Brzeska, J. (2010) 'Production, productivity, and public investment in East Asian agriculture', in P. Pingali and R. Evenson (eds) *Handbook of Agricultural Economics*, Amsterdam: Elsevier, pp. 3401–3434.

FAO. (2009a) *The State of Food Insecurity in the World – 2009*, Rome: Food and Agriculture Organization (FAO), United Nations.

FAO. (2009b) *Crop Prospects and Food Situation, No. 4*, Rome: Food and Agricultural Organization (FAO), United Nations.

FAO. (2009c) *Crop Prospects and Food Situation, No. 3*, Rome: Food and Agricultural Organization (FAO), United Nations.

FAO. (2012a) *FAOSTAT*, Food and Agriculture Organization (FAO), United Nations; accessed at http://faostat.fao.org/site/291/default.aspx, 1 December 2012.

FAO. (2012b) *FAO Hunger Map*, Food And Agriculture Organization (FAO), United Nations; accessed at http://faostat.fao.org/site/291/default.aspx, 1 December 2012.

FAO. (2012c) *FAO Hunger Portal*, Food and Agriculture Organization (FAO), United Nations 2012; accessed at http://www.fao.org/hunger/en/, 1 December 2012.

FAO. (2012d) *Food Security Statistics*, Food And Agriculture Organization (FAO), United Nations 2012; accessed at http://www.fao.org/economic/ess/food-security-statistics/en/, 1 December 2012.

FAO. (2012e) *FAOSTAT 2007*, Food And Agriculture Organization (FAO), United Nations; accessed at http://faostat.fao.org/, 1 December 2012.

FAO. (2012f) *The State of Food Insecurity in the World 2012*, Rome: Food and Agriculture Organization (FAO), United Nations.

FAO. (2012g) *Crop Prospects and Food Situation, No. 4*, Rome: Food and Agricultural Organization (FAO), United Nations.

FAO. (2013) *FAOSTAT 2013*; accessed at http://faostat.fao.org/site/485/DesktopDefault.aspx?PageID=485#ancor, 20 April 2013.

Gordon, C., Cooper, C., Senior, C. A., Banks, H., Gregory, J. M., Johns, T. C., Mitchell, J. F. B. and Wood, R. A. (2000) 'The simulation of SST, sea ice extents and ocean heat transports in a version of the Hadley Centre coupled model without flux adjustments', *Climate Dynamics* 16(2/3): 147–168.

GRAIN. (2008) Seized: The 2008 landgrab for food and financial security; accessed at http://www.grain.org/article/entries/93-seized-the-2008-landgrab-for-food-and-financial-security, 20 April 2013.

Han, D. B., Keun Shin, J. and Im, J.-B. (2008) 'Assessing impacts of rice import expansion and policy change', in REST (eds.) *2008 International Conference on Agricultural and Resource Economics, Organized by The Rural Economics Society of Taiwan (REST)*, Taipei, Taiwan: REST.

Hertel, T. W. (1997) *Global Trade Analysis: Modeling and Applications*, Cambridge: Cambridge University Press.

Horie, T., Nakagawa, H., Centeno, H. G. and Kropff, M. J. (1995) 'The rice crop simulation model SIMRIW and its testing', in R. B. Matthews, M. J. Kropff, D. Bachelet and H. H. van Laar (eds) *Modeling the Impact of Climate Change on Rice Production in Asia*, Oxon: CAB International, pp. 51–65.

Huang, C. T., Fu, T. Y. and Chang, S. S. (2009) 'Crops and food security-experiences and perspectives from Taiwan', *Asia Pacific Journal of Clinical Nutrition* 18(4): 520–526.

IFPRI (2013) *World Commodity Prices*, International Food Policy Research Institute (IFPRI) 2013; accessed at http://www.foodsecurityportal.org/api/world-commodity-prices.

IIASA (2007a) 'GGI scenario database'; accessed at http://www.iiasa.ac.at/Research/GGI/DB/, 20 April 2013.

IIASA (2007b) '13 IIASA–POP world regions, definition'; accessed at http://www.iiasa.ac.at/Research/POP/edu01/countries.html, 20 April 2013.

Kuntjoro, I. A. and Jamil, S. (2008) *Food Security: Another Case for Human Security in ASEAN*, NTS – Asia 2nd Annual Convention, Beijing.

Lee, H. L. (2009) 'The impact of climate change on global food supply and demand, food prices, and land use', *Paddy and Water Environment* 7(4): 321–331. DOI: 10.1007/s10333-009-0181-y.

Lee, H. L., Hertel, T. W., Rose, S. K. and Avetisyan, M. (2009) 'An integrated global land use data base for CGE analysis of climate policy options', in; T. Hertel, S. Rose and R. Tol (eds) *Economic Analysis of Land Use in Global Climate Change Policy,* Abingdon: Routledge, pp. 72–88.

Lee, H. L., Cheng, M. T. and Chang, C. C. (2010) 'A economy-wide impact analysis of global climate change on food crop production, prices and welfare', paper presented at the 2009 Annual Conference of the Taiwan Economic Association, Taipei, Taiwan, December 19.

Lee, H. L. and Chang, C. C. (2010) 'The potential impact of climate change on global rice market and food security in Asia', paper presented at the Symposium of Climate Change and Food Crisis at Tainan Agricultural Improvement Station, Tainan, Taiwan, July 8.

MAFF. (2006) *Fusokuji-no Shokuryo-anzen-hosho Manyuaru* [Food security manual for contingency situations], Tokyo: Ministry of Agriculture, Forestry, and Fisheries, Japan (MAFF). (In Japanese).

MAFF. (2012) *Taiwan, Korea and Japan's self-sufficiency rate from 2002–2011*, Tokyo: Ministry of Agriculture, Forestry and Fishery (MAFF); accessed at http://www.maff.go.jp/index.html, 10 May 2012.

Matthews, R. B., Horie, T., Kropff, M. J., Bachelet, D., Centeno, H. G. and Shin, J. C. (1995) 'A regional evaluation of the effect of future climate change on rice production in Asia', in R. B. Matthews, M. J. Kropff, D. Bachelet and H. H. van Laar (eds) *Modeling the Impact of Climate Change on Rice Prodcution in Asia*, Oxon: CAB International, pp. 95–139.

Mitchell, D. (2008) *A Note on Rising Food Prices*, Policy Research Working Paper 4682, The World Bank.

Muller, A. R. (2011) 'South Korea's global food ambitions: rural farming and land grabs', *Conducive Magazine*, March 19; accessed at http://www.conducivemag.com/2011/03/south-korea%E2%80%99s-global-food-ambitions-rural-farming-and-land-grabs/, 20 April 2013.

OECD. (2012) *Agricultural Policy Monitoring and Evaluation 2012: OECD Countries*, Paris: OECD.

Pope, V. D., Gallani, M. L., Rowntree, P. R. and Stratton, R. A. (2000) 'The impact of new physical parametrizations in the Hadley Centre climate model – HadAM3', *Climate Dynamics* 16: 123–146.

Rosen, S., Meade, B., Shapouri, S., D'Souza, A. and Rada, N. (2012) *International Food Security Assessment, 2012–22*, Washington, DC: Department of Agriculture, Economic Research Service.

Rosenzweig, C. and Iglesias, A. (2001) 'Potential impacts of climate change on world food supply: data sets from a major crop modeling study'; accessed at http://sedac.ciesin.columbia.edu/giss_crop_study/, 20 April 2013.

Samsung Research Institute. (2011) 'New food strategies in the age of global food crisis'; accessed at http://www.asiasentinel.com/index.php?option=com_content&task=view&id=3159&Itemid=434, 9 April 2013.

Shapouri, S., Rosen, S., Meade, B. and Gale, F. (2009) *Food Security Assessment 2008–09*, Washington, DC: Economic Research Service/USDA.

Tanaka, T. and Hosoe, N. (2011) 'Does agricultural trade liberalization increase risks of supply-side uncertainty? Effects of productivity shocks and export restrictions on welfare and food supply in Japan', *Food Policy* 36(3): 368–377. DOI: http://dx.doi.org/10.1016/j.foodpol.2011.01.002.

WFP (2013) *Food Aid Information System*, World Food Programme (WFP) 2003; accessed at http://www.wfp.org/fais/reports/quantities-delivered-report, 20 April 2013.

Yamashita, K. (2010) *Rice Policy Reforms in Japan: Seek Food Security Through Free Trade*, AJISS-Commentary, No. 83, 15 February 2010, Tokyo: The Association of Japanese Institutes of Strategic Studies (AJISS); accessed at http://www2.jiia.or.jp/en_commentary/201002/15-1.html, 20 April 2013.

Yoo, C. H. (2003) 'Korea's agricultural strategy in the globalization era', in O. Y. Kwon, S. Jwa and K. Lee (eds) *Korea's New Economic Strategy in the Globalization Era*, Northampton, MA: Edward Elgar Publishing, pp. 133–154.

Yoo, S.-H., Kim, T., Im, J.-B. and Choi, J.-Y. (2012) 'Estimation of the international virtual water flow of grain crop products in Korea', *Paddy and Water Environment* 10(2): 83–93. DOI: 10.1007/s10333-011-0267-1.

You, L., Spoor, M., Ulimwengu, J. and Zhang, S. (2011) 'Land use change and environmental stress of wheat, rice and corn production in China', *China Economic Review* 22(4): 461–473. DOI: http://dx.doi.org/10.1016/j.chieco.2010.12.001.

Appendix. Countries in each region

Region	Country
ASIA AND THE PACIFIC	East Asia, Oceania, Southeast Asia, South Asia, Central Asia, Western Asia.
Northeast Asia	China, Korea Dem People's Rep., Republic of Korea, Mongolia.
Oceania	Papua New Guinea.
Southeast Asia	Cambodia, Indonesia, Laos, Malaysia, Myanmar, Philippines, Thailand, Viet Nam.
South Asia	Bangladesh, India, Nepal, Pakistan, Sri Lanka.
Central Asia	Kazakhstan, Kyrgyzstan, Tajikistan, Turkmenistan, Uzbekistan.
Western Asia.	Armenia, Azerbaijan, Georgia
LATIN AMERICA AND THE CARIBBEAN	North and Central America, The Caribbean, South America.

(continued)

Region	Country
North and Central America	Costa Rica, El Salvador, Guatemala, Honduras, Mexico, Nicaragua, Panama
The Caribbean	Cuba, Dominican Republic, Haiti, Jamaica, Trinidad and Tobago
South America	Argentina, Bolivia, Brazil, Chile, Colombia, Ecuador, Guyana, Paraguay, Peru, Suriname, Uruguay, Venezuela.
NEAR EAST AND NORTH AFRICA	Near East, North Africa.
Near East	Afghanistan, Islamic Rep. of Iran, Iraq, Jordan, Kuwait, Lebanon, Saudi Arabia, Syrian Arab Republic, Turkey, United Arab Emirates, Yemen
North Africa	Algeria, Egypt, Libyan Arab Jamahiriya, Morocco, Tunisia.
SUB-SAHARAN AFRICA	Central Africa, East Africa, Southern Africa, West Africa.
Central Africa	Cameroon, Central African Republic, Chad, Dem. Republic of Congo, Republic of Congo, Gabon.
East Africa	Burundi, Eritrea, Ethiopia, Kenya, Rwanda, Somalia, Sudan, Tanzania, Uganda.
Southern Africa	Angola, Botswana, Lesotho, Madagascar, Malawi, Mauritius, Mozambique, Namibia, Swaziland, Zambia, Zimbabwe.
West Africa	Benin, Burkina Faso, Côte d'Ivoire, Gambia, Ghana, Guinea, Liberia, Mali, Mauritania, Niger, Nigeria, Senegal, Sierra Leone, Togo.

Source: FAO (2012d).

Index

INDEX